NO RETURN
The Gerry Irwin Story,
UFO Abduction or Covert Operation?

by David Booher

ANOMALIST BOOKS
*San Antonio * Charlottesville*

An Original Publication of ANOMALIST BOOKS
No Return: The Gerry Irwin Story, UFO Abduction or Covert Operation?
Copyright © 2017 by David Booher
ISBN: 978-1-938398-98-8

Cover art by Yuri Arcurs/iStock
Inuit Haida Salmon image © Connie Kelts, CKDesigns

Book design by Seale Studios

For information about the publisher, go to AnomalistBooks.com, or write to: Anomalist Books, 5150 Broadway #108, San Antonio, TX 78209

Contents

Foreword by Jacques Vallee..vii

Prologue xi

Chapter 1: A Detour on the Road to Bliss... 1

Chapter 2: A Blast from the Past.. 6

Chapter 3: A Salmon Runs Through It... 17

Chapter 4: BREAKING: *UTAH MYSTERY 'VICTIM' AWAKE*..................... 35

Chapter 5: The Crucible of the Unknown... 40

Chapter 6: Atom Bombs and Space Brothers 56

Chapter 7: Alien Abduction and APRO 65

Chapter 8: Two Locations 74

Chapter 9: No Return 96

Chapter 10: The United States v. Gerry Irwin 104

Chapter 11: Amnesia from Space?... 124

Chapter 12: A Saucerful of Spies 135

Chapter 13: The Jung-Lorenzen Letters—Converging Clues............... 149

Chapter 14: Moving On 182

Chapter 15: Abduction Revisited... 188

Epilogue 208

Acknowledgments 212

Bibliography 214

Index 221

To my father,
Arnold D. Booher
1938-2014

Foreword

On February 21, 1959, a man named Gerry Irwin woke up in a hospital in Utah, his mind in a state of profound confusion. He had been unconscious for a full day and night, during which time the nurses had heard him mumble incoherently about a "jacket on bush." When his condition improved his first question was: "Were there any survivors?" All he remembered was that he had stopped his car because an aircraft was falling.

Gerry Irwin was a Nike missile base technician on his way back to his barracks at Fort Bliss, El Paso, Texas. When he saw the glowing object in the oddly brightened landscape, he stopped his car, wrote a note he placed on his steering wheel ("Have gone to investigate possible plane crash. Please call law enforcement officers"), and used shoe polish to scribble "STOP" on the side of the vehicle before starting out on foot.

A search party found him unconscious. He had no jacket. There was no airplane crash.

Over the following six months Gerry Irwin was examined by doctors at various facilities, found in good general health, and reintegrated to his unit, but things got complicated and he reentered the hospital in July. On August 1st he failed to report for duty. One month later he was listed as a deserter.

He was never seen again. Or so I thought.

The case remained an enigma for 55 years. It would still be an enigma if a man with an inquisitive mind, a single-focus dedication to the truth and a bit of an obsession for fishing in the wilderness hadn't picked up the trail.

The man in question is David Booher, whose book tells the fascinating story of his patient follow-up investigation of the case. He'd refused to believe that Private Irwin had disappeared forever as too many researchers, myself included, had hastily concluded. He'd convinced me that enough solid indications remained to restart the chase and that the incident—potentially the first UFO abduction in recent American history—deserved to be an object of serious scrutiny. In the long collaboration that followed, I had the privilege of hearing about the various phases of David's research, the breakthroughs and the discouraging setbacks, occasionally providing a small resource, a useful contact, or a tentative idea.

The author assembled all the indices, re-analyzed the events from the vantage point of the elapsed decades, and was rewarded by a rich series of complex discoveries you will enjoy retracing with him as you read the book.

What does the detailed reconstruction of Private Irwin's ordeal uncover? What are the hard lessons it can teach us, as we drive to improve our ability to analyze the larger mystery of unidentified flying objects and to provide assistance in the psychological crises of which too many witnesses are victims?

I believe two major themes stand out from the insights we can derive from David Booher's work: First, the virtue of a patient, long-term perspective on cases that seemed forever lost in amnesia or hidden in secrecy; and second, the critical need for an intelligent alternative to the shoddy, pop psychology of hypnosis that has come to masquerade for "research" in numerous reports of UFO abduction.

It would have been easy to subject Private Irwin to a mockery of analysis, as we have seen in too many other cases, by subtly suggesting to him that he'd been victimized by Aliens or entertained by super-human creatures, scenes now common on television and cheap movies. David Booher resisted that temptation, steadfast in his deep respect for Gerry Irwin's own memories of the event, fragmentary as they were. Over that many years the recollection of dramatic events becomes blunted, yet repressed insights can emerge by themselves and tentative hypotheses can be reasonably substantiated, even if the ultimate proof remains inaccessible.

We do know there was a jacket purposely left on that bush. We know there was a hurriedly-written note calling for rescuers. There was an object in the sky and an imminent catastrophe.

We know that what took place after that was beyond Irwin's mind to comprehend. It is appropriate, therefore, that the journey to which David Booher invites us begins at Fort Bliss and ends up on the shores of the River of No Return.

Jacques Vallee, June 2017

Prologue

"Take the Salmon of Knowledge and eat it," said Finegas… "And now go hence, for I can teach thee no more."
— the legend of Finn mac Cumhal[1]

The story you are about to read hinges on a slippery faculty that most of us, most of the time, take for granted. However, even under the best of circumstances it can elude us, and there are times when it seems to fail us altogether. This is the wondrous yet erratic gift we call memory.

The river of life carries us downstream from past to present to future, but like a salmon returning home against the current, our memory can ferry us back upstream from whence we came. Of course, we often experience memory as a flashback, as if our minds simply leap across the chasm of time to the moment we want to relive. Likewise, salmon are remarkable leapers; in fact, the very name salmon (Latin *salmo*) means "leaper," deriving from the Latin verb *salire*—"to leap." Furthermore, multitudes of memories are lost to us along the way of our life's journey, just as legions of salmon never make it home to spawn; such is the uncertainty of their, and our, passage.

When it's not leaping, remembering is often an act of retracing, backtracking, following the river of memories upstream, to retrieve that one sought-after moment in time. Similarly, the deep-seated memory of salmon enable them to follow their trail of recollection from their

---

1   Rolleston, T.W. *Myths and Legends of the Celtic Race* (NY: Thomas Y. Crowell Co., 1911), 256.

feeding areas thousands of miles at sea, swimming and smelling their way through open ocean and past the mouths of countless rivers, streams, and tributaries, back to that one little mountain brook where they were hatched. This miraculous ability is reflected in the way that salmon have been revered and celebrated by cultures far and near; for their yearly migrations have delivered the ocean's bounty to humanity's waiting nets—as far as a thousand miles inland—since time immemorial.

There is a wild and famous river that is named for these marvelous fish—the Salmon River of Idaho. This free-flowing jewel of nature is also known as The River of No Return. This foreboding epithet could likewise evoke the fallout of a major trauma, in which a whole storehouse of one's memories is swept away by a flood of experience so strong that the banks of the mind cannot contain it. A void of amnesia lies in its wake.

The man whose story is told here grew up on a fork of the Salmon River, a man whose mind was tossed into its very own river of no return by just such an experiential deluge. In the pages that follow we will attempt to leap back through the rapids and eddies of time to examine these events, including one in particular that literally knocked this man out and proceeded to alter the very course of his existence.

Chapter 1: A Detour on the Road to Bliss

It's a cold, moonlit night in the high desert of southern Utah. On a lonely stretch of highway, a young soldier drives en route from his home in Idaho back to his base at Ft. Bliss, Texas. The road snakes up and down over a long series of high ridges and broad valleys. He steps on the gas as the old sedan labors uphill toward the next summit.

The date is February 20, 1959.

Suddenly there's a brilliant flash in the sky ahead. He stares, spellbound, as it resolves into a strange glowing…*something*…coming down on a slow glide path. Stopping the car and getting out for a better look, he's struck by how close it seems. From where it disappears beneath a nearby ridge, a dazzling light blazes forth and rapidly fades without a sound.

The young man's mind races. *Was it a plane crash?* Its odd appearance and weird silence argue against it, but he can't rule it out. After weighing his options, he decides to go have a look; if it really *is* a crash, he figures, he'd better get moving. Preparing to set out, he leaves a note on the steering wheel, which reads: "Have gone to investigate what looks like a plane crash about one-quarter mile to my right. Notify state police immediately." To draw attention to the note, he writes "STOP" in shoe polish across the side of his car, and flips on the blinkers for good measure. Then, without a moment to spare, he grabs his flashlight, dons his Army overcoat atop his new sports jacket, and trudges off through the snow.

He's hardly gotten anywhere though, when everything goes black.

Thus begins the peculiar odyssey of one Private Bernard G. Irwin, aka Gerry. He saw *something*; nothing more and nothing less than a strange light in the sky. It's a prelude that recalls a host of mysterious legends that echo across the ages—stories of the lone wayfarer encountering a supernatural light in the darkness. And as these tales warn us, those who happen upon such a light will never be quite the same again. The case of Gerry Irwin, PFC, would prove to be no exception.

The young soldier gradually awakens, only to find himself in the safe environs of a hospital room. He looks around in amazement. *How did he get here?* A doctor standing at his bedside sees him stirring and murmurs something to the nurse. Turning to Gerry, he says, "Take it easy Irwin, you're safe now, and you're among friends." With a look of alarm, Gerry blurts out, "Were there any survivors?"[1]

Ignoring the question, the doctor asks Gerry whether he's experiencing any pain. Gerry responds that he has no pain and that he's actually feeling fine. He then anxiously repeats his query about survivors. First the doctor and then the county sheriff (who has just entered the room) reassure Gerry that no sign of a crash could be found.

The sheriff, whose investigation so far has uncovered more questions than answers, seizes his chance to grill Gerry about the incident. Unfortunately, there's not much Gerry can say beyond describing the mysterious object, its oddly silent landing, and his preparations before setting off on foot. Everything else is a blank.

With that out of the way, Gerry gets a full rundown on what happened during his blackout. He discovers that, remarkably, he's been passed out *for a full 24 hours*. The night before, Gerry's shoe polish message was spotted by a fish and game warden about half an hour after Gerry left his vehicle. He read Gerry's note and radioed the sheriff for help. While waiting for his backup, the warden flagged down some passing motorists to form a makeshift rescue team, who followed Gerry's tracks and found him about a quarter-mile from the highway. By the time the ambulance arrived and rushed Gerry to the hospital in Cedar City, it was nearly midnight.

In the hospital, they'd tried repeatedly to awaken Gerry for questioning, but to no avail. His vital functions were normal, but he'd remained unresponsive. In spite of this, however, Gerry had occasionally muttered

---

1   Lorenzen, L. J. "Where Is Private Irwin?" *Flying Saucers* Nov. 1962: 17-19.

the words, "jacket on bush." Mulling this over, Gerry asks what became of the new sports jacket he'd been wearing, only to be told that when he was found—lying face down in the snow—he wasn't wearing it; nor was it seen by the searchers. The only outerwear he had on when he was found was his army overcoat.

The hospital keeps Gerry a few days for observation and testing. Aside from amnesia, they can find nothing wrong with him. Then he's released to Army personnel, who fly him back to Ft. Bliss aboard the Commanding General's plane. Upon arrival, he's immediately checked into the psychiatric ward of William Beaumont Army Hospital for further examination. After a few more days, he's released back to duty with a clean bill of health.

Something is clearly amiss however, because several days later, he unexpectedly faints after work while walking near his barracks. He recovers quickly this time and resumes his duties without medical care. One evening a couple of weeks later however, he collapses again—this time in downtown El Paso[2]—whereupon he's taken to El Paso General Hospital. When he finally awakens in the dark hours of the morning, the first words he utters are, as before, "Were there any survivors?" He's skeptical when he's told the date is really March 16 and not February 20, as he believed![3]

A few hours later, Gerry is picked up by the Army ambulance and taken back to the Army Hospital for further examination and treatment. His doctor duly notes that Gerry, whom he'd attended only a few weeks earlier, no longer recognizes him or any of the other staff members. After a while, Gerry seems to regain some of his recently lost memory, and since they are again unable to find anything else wrong with him, he's released after 32 days.

But if they think Gerry is back to normal, they're in for a surprise.

The next morning Gerry finds himself in a trance, and in this strange condition he's overcome by an urge to return to the scene of his original incident. Abandoning the base without leave, he catches an overnight bus to Utah. He disembarks in Cedar City the following afternoon, walking

---

2 The city adjacent to Ft. Bliss.
3 Lorenzen, L.J., 21.

east out of town along Highway 14 about six miles. When he reaches a certain point, he veers off into the desert scrub without hesitation, walking straight to the spot where his missing jacket is hanging on a bush. Oddly enough, there's a pencil inserted through one of the buttonholes, and around the pencil is wrapped a piece of paper; a note. He removes the pencil, unwraps the note, and *promptly burns it without reading it.* The scent of smoke rising up seems to snap him out of his trance.

Awakening to his strange predicament, it dawns on him that he's AWOL. At the same time, he observes that the sun is dropping fast along with the temperature, and he's poorly dressed for it. His jacket is of no use in this regard, having been badly weathered in the intervening months. Leaving it on the ground, he resolves to hike back to town and turn himself in. Inexplicably though, while he'd navigated here with utter confidence, now he's disoriented and has trouble locating the highway.

Finding the road again with real difficulty, Gerry treks the five or six miles back to Cedar City. As he walks, he's haunted by troubling questions that others would later raise as well. *What could have caused his bizarre trance and the overpowering urge to return here? How did he know, with such certitude, where to find his jacket; and for that matter, what was it doing there? Why did he burn the note, and what was written on it?*

Arriving back in Cedar City, he turns himself in to the sheriff, whom he no longer recognizes. Taking note of Gerry's amnesia, the sheriff fills him in on what happened the last time their paths had crossed. Through the mental fog of his affliction, Gerry begins to recall scattered details, pondering what it could all mean. The sheriff notifies the Army of Gerry's whereabouts, and soon he's picked up by the M.P.s and transported back to Ft. Bliss (though oddly, with a side trip all the way to Ft. Ord, California). Upon his return, Gerry has to go and face his commanding officer whose job it is to determine the appropriate punishment. Gerry is hit with a fine and loss of rank, and sent back to resume his duties.

Gerry is troubled not only by his baffling condition but by the kind of treatment he's getting from the Army. After all, his recent strange behavior—in which his actions seemed beyond his control—followed right on the heels of a month in the hospital psych ward. Thus, whatever it was the doctors were doing, it wasn't helping. And with the onset of these startling new symptoms, just when he needed more help than ever, he'd been punished and hung out to dry.

Gerry decides to take up the matter with the Army Inspector General. The IG is sympathetic to his plight and arranges for Gerry to undergo yet another round of observation and treatment. To that end, he's readmitted to the Army Hospital on July 10, only to be discharged three weeks later, yet again with no finding of disease.

And then, as the story goes, the following morning, on August 1, 1959, "…he failed to report for duty. One month later, he was listed as a deserter. He was never seen again."[4]

---

4   Vallee, Jacques. *Dimensions: A Casebook of Alien Contact*, (Chicago: Contemporary Books, 1988), 115-117.

Chapter 2: A Blast from the Past

It was mid-November 2013 in southern Wisconsin. I was catching up on seasonal chores: splitting firewood, winterizing buildings, and preserving the last of the garden veggies. At the end of one of these long but satisfying days, after settling in for the night, I was browsing through one of those fine old books that one enjoys revisiting on occasion. As I skimmed the pages, one story in particular grabbed my attention.

It's the story of Gerry Irwin, as told by the renowned UFO investigator Jacques Vallee. And though I had read it before, I was struck anew by the strange drama of the soldier who was *never seen again.* For some reason, this time around the story wouldn't let me rest. *How could it end like that? What happened to the poor man? Was he just left to wither away and die alone in the desert? Or did he end up as some crazy homeless guy wandering the streets?* It was 55 years after the fact—didn't *anyone* know what became of him?

Where Did He Go?

After an extensive search on the internet, the answer appeared to be "No." How could that be? Wasn't this the "Information Age"? Over the next few days, I was seized with a determination to find out what happened, inspired and spurred on by Vallee's words:

> It [the Gerry Irwin story] has been mentioned only once in UFO literature, by James Lorenzen, director of the APRO group, and has not, to the best of my knowledge, been the subject of subsequent investigation. Such an investigation, however, would throw light on the sociological context of

UFO reports.[1]

Remarkably, although these words were published in 1988, it appeared that even 26 years later, no further investigation had taken place. Many accounts had been published on the internet to be sure, but they were all essentially rehashing either Lorenzen's original article or Vallee's summary of it.

While I'd always taken a keen interest in mysteries of this kind, I'd never actually attempted an investigation of this sort. But the lure was too strong to resist. What happened to Gerry Irwin on that long-ago night in Utah? And where did he disappear to five and a half months later? Or, for that matter, was I just getting my leg pulled by a moldy old hoax from long ago? With these questions left hovering in the air like some saucer-shaped object, I started down the ice cold trail, the 55 year old trace, of the story of Gerry Irwin.

Take a Number

So I had my mission—now the only question was where to begin? I decided to start by making Freedom of Information Act (FOIA) requests; it seemed as good a starting point as any. I sent requests to the Department of Defense/Army and the National Archives and Records Administration (NARA). Alas, the many long hours spent going back and forth with the labyrinthine array of government departments ultimately proved fruitless.

More productive were my searches for newspaper accounts of the initial event. I discovered that along with a number of independent reports, the story was carried on the AP as well as the UPI news wires, and I located 22 articles from 12 cities in 8 different states. These articles raised many intriguing questions about what actually took place.

A Lucky Break

Then I decided to try a different tack, wondering why it took me so long to get to it. Why not just track down any family members who might still be around and find out what they knew? Surely that would lead to some useful information. For help in this crucial and sensitive intelligence

---

1   Vallee, 1988, 115.

gathering operation I turned to my "secret weapon"—yes, I'm talking about my neighborhood public library! With the librarian's assistance, I got more than I bargained for; suddenly I had the contact info for Gerry Irwin himself! *Could it really be him?*

I called the phone number the next day. Yes, it was Gerry Irwin. Yes, he was the man who saw the strange object in the sky in Utah in 1959. And best of all, yes, he was willing to talk about it. So we set a time that evening for a phone interview.

But my excitement was tempered by serious doubts. I really had no experience with this sort of thing, so I was essentially winging it. For better or worse though, and in spite of my apprehension, foolhardy enthusiasm took the day. At the appointed time, I made the phone call to Gerry's home in Idaho. After our greetings, I asked Gerry if he had ever seen the articles that were written about him.

"I never read or saw anything," he replied in his backcountry drawl.

"Oh, really?" I asked.

"No! And after that one incident, I went to Germany and spent a lot of time over there in the military, and I went to Austria …and I finally came home, you know? I never...got any information—they wouldn't tell me much."

I was about to read one of the stories I had about him, when for the first time he told me the story in his own words.

"I was en route back to my base," he said. "I had been on leave up here in Idaho, and I was on my way back to Ft. Bliss, Texas. And I was driving at night and what I first recall was that I saw something like a falling star, but it was real close and it appeared to, you know, to hit. I stopped the car, and I was going to go over to see what that was. And evidently, I passed out, because somebody found me, and I was unconscious. In other words, somebody...you know, I put my blinkers on and I was just walking over to where I thought whatever it was hit or landed—I had no idea. And then I woke up in a hospital, and I was just told that some people had stopped and had notified local authorities that something was going on—they had no idea. And they found me and I was unconscious. And I ended up back at Ft. Bliss, Texas— they transported me back there, and they run a bunch of tests and stuff, but they never told me results of anything I told them.

They put some sort of drug and put you out and it's like a truth serum, and I couldn't recall what I said or who asked me what, or what. They wouldn't say anything about it. And that was just about the only thing I remember of it. And then later I got transferred over to Ft. Leavenworth, Kansas."

Well, this seemed like a great start. However, at this point a pattern began to emerge, which remained consistent throughout my interviews with him. Gerry kept wanting to skip ahead to his service in Germany (he said they had sent him there from his post at the Ft. Leavenworth Army base). Whether because of wanting to conceal something, or because of difficulty remembering, or simply wanting to avoid thinking about that time period, this pattern kept repeating.

Gerry, Meet Coral. Again.

I then began to read Gerry a story about him published in 1959 that he had never seen nor heard of before (at least that he recalled), written by a woman he no longer even remembered. It just so happened that she was one of the most prominent and well-respected UFO researchers of that era. She had some information to draw upon from the flurry of newspaper articles that had been published and combined this with what she'd learned from interviewing Gerry. Her name was Coral Lorenzen. The headline read "Soldier Sees Flash, Unconscious Twenty-Four Hours."

> A mysterious flash in the sky, which PFC Bernard G. Irwin of Ft. Bliss, Texas, thought was a plane crash and set out to investigate, was possibly the cause of his unconscious state for the next 24 hours. On the evening of the 22nd of February, Irwin, who was en route to Ft. Bliss via a shortcut in Southern Utah, after a furlough to his home in Nampa, Idaho, stopped on a small highway after seeing what he thought was a plane crash. He wrote the word "STOP" on his car with shoe polish to attract other motorists, then wrote a note to explain where he had gone.[2]

"Yeah, I remember that," said Gerry, "because when I saw that flash, I put my blinkers on. And I didn't want anyone to wonder why that car was

2   Lorenzen, Coral E. "Soldier Sees Flash: Unconscious 24 Hours." *APRO Bulletin* Mar. 1959. 1. Reproduced with permission from Larry Lorenzen.

parked there with the blinkers on. And then when I woke up I was in the hospital. But they wouldn't give me any information about what I said or anything."

I continued reading the article to him.

> Later, a Utah Fish and Game Department agent saw the car and the sign and stopped and read the note. He summoned police and a search was begun. Shortly, Irwin was found lying face down in the mud, unconscious. He did not awaken until 24 hours later on Saturday evening. Doctors who treated him and observed him at Cedar City, Utah, where he was taken by the police, said that he had no visible marks or wounds which would account for his state of unconsciousness. According to press reports, Irwin could shed no light on what had happened to him. The note read, 'Have gone to investigate what looks like a plane crash about one quarter mile to my right. Notify state police immediately.'
>
> The press, in their reports, said 'flash in the sky.' Irwin's note said, 'what looks like a plane crash,' and gave its apparent location. Investigation indicates there was no plane crash, none whatsoever, and therefore it must be assumed that Irwin saw something else. A meteor? If remains of such had been found it certainly would have been noted, but it wasn't.
>
> On the 12th of March, I called PFC Irwin at his duty location in Ft. Bliss, and asked him numerous questions about his adventure. Irwin had no explanation of what happened, but a more complete picture of the actual incident was obtained.
>
> Irwin said he saw the light coming toward the ground, and it appeared to land about a quarter mile from where he was. He thought it was a plane crash although he heard no sound to identify it as such. The light was very bright and had a shape, but not definite. When it came to ground, it flared up, and then died out completely.
>
> The soldier, who is a 23 year old volunteer, said he was walking up the hill, and does not know when or where he blacked out. When he came to...[3]

"Well, that's exactly what happened," said Gerry. "I went to see what it was and that's the last I remember, and then I woke up in the hospital."

---

3   Ibid., 1,10.

The Jacket Enigma

I continued reading the Lorenzen article:

> When he came to 24 hours later in the Cedar City Hospital, he was talking about, 'jacket on the bush' but doesn't know why he mentioned it. There is one important point, however, and that is the fact that Irwin was wearing, besides the normal clothing, a sports jacket with an overcoat buttoned over it. He had it on when he left the car, and said that his overcoat was on and buttoned when he got to the hospital, according to hospital attendants, but that his jacket was missing. The jacket was just simply not on him when he was undressed by attendants at the hospital. Nor was it found during the air and ground search, nor was it in the car. It can be theorized that the jacket was stolen, but by whom and when, except during the period that he was lying unconscious near that lonely road?[4]

"I don't recall all the details about me losing the jacket," replied Gerry, "but it's probably fairly accurate...It's been a long time since then."

I returned to the article again:

> My conversation with Irwin also brought out the fact that Irwin was given a complete physical checkup at Cedar City, and was found to be a very normal, healthy young man. He has no history of neurosis or blacking out spells.
>
> Pfc Irwin was flown to William Beaumont Army Hospital by the Army, and underwent a 4-day psychiatric and medical examination and observation by Army doctors, who also found him to be normal, according to Irwin. I asked him if he had any troubles or anxieties which he felt might have caused the "blackout" and Irwin answered that he had none that he could think of. However, several days after he had returned to normal routine at Fort Bliss, Irwin did suffer a fainting spell during his off-duty hours. No evident physical reason for this, either. [5]

You know the French guy in *Close Encounters*?

I then skipped to a different story, which was written many years

---

4   Ibid., 10.
5   Ibid.

later, from the book *Dimensions: A Casebook of Alien Contact* by Jacques Vallee. I asked Gerry if he had seen the movie *Close Encounters of the Third Kind*?

"Not that I remember..." he replied.

I explained that there was actually a character based on Vallee in that movie—the French scientist Claude Lacombe—played by Francois Truffaut. Vallee's source material for Gerry's story was actually written by Jim Lorenzen, Coral's husband. They were the husband and wife team who headed APRO (Aerial Phenomena Research Organization). They worked together, but they each, separately, authored articles about Gerry.

I read for Gerry the portion of Vallee's summary recounting the rest of the story: Gerry's month long stay in the hospital following his blackout in El Paso, his discharge, and his subsequent return to Utah wherein he hiked into the desert and found his missing jacket, burned the note without reading it, etc. I ended the reading with Vallee's closing lines—"One month later, he was listed as a deserter. He was never seen again."[6]

Ironic words under the circumstances! "So it sounds like you *were* seen again," I said, laughing.

"Well, yeah," said Gerry, "because I went to Germany, I was assigned...I think somebody's carried it (laughs)... a little further than I remember."

I replied: "Well, that's why it's good to talk to you because I want to hear what your account of it is."

"The author may have added a few details that weren't accurate," said Gerry. "But, anyway, I went to...I was sent to Germany, to the A company...I was there, and I was sent to Austria..."

Not in Kansas Anymore

I tried to steer Gerry's attention away from the time when he was shipped from Ft. Leavenworth, Kansas to Europe, and back to the time following his sighting. "Okay," I asked, "So, you don't remember anything about the second part of the story where you took a bus back to Cedar City to find your jacket?"

"No," said Gerry. He again derided the inaccuracy of the reporting, and then immediately resumed talking about his overseas military adventures

---

6   Vallee, 1988, 117.

and other aspects of his life.

With that, our first interview came to a close.

I had mixed feelings about our exchange. We had certainly covered some important ground, but I also felt troubled about asking Gerry questions that seemed to make him feel uncomfortable. If the shoe was on the other foot, I don't know if I would have been so gracious. Gerry must have thought he'd left that whole bewildering ordeal far behind him—with 55 years under the bridge—and then suddenly there's this guy on the phone wanting to stir it all up again. Be that as it may however, I couldn't shake the feeling that this story was just too important to let go.

I was certainly left with some interesting puzzles. First, did Gerry desert the Army, or didn't he? And what about his return trip to Utah to find his jacket? Why would a reputable researcher make up details as important as these? A researcher who was a trusted source by no less a personage than Jacques Vallee? Was that likely?

And what about the other details? What was this about a "truth serum?" This was the first time I had come across that piece of information. It would turn up again, some weeks later, when I finally got hold of the original article that Vallee had summarized in his book. In that piece, entitled "Where is Private Irwin?" by Jim Lorenzen, it says that Gerry was questioned under the influence of sodium amytal (commonly referred to as "truth serum") near the end of a 32-day period of confinement in the William Beaumont Army Hospital psychiatric ward.[7] Clearly Mr. Lorenzen was not making *everything* up. What else did he get right?

What *Was* That Thing, Anyway?

I called Gerry the next day to clarify, among other things, what exactly he thought he saw in the night sky all those years ago over Utah.

> Gerry: Well, just…I thought maybe either it was a meteorite or…It was pretty bright. That's why I thought it might've been a meteorite. It was something like that because I didn't think it was particularly an airplane or something on fire…My initial instinct was that it was a meteorite.

---

7   Lorenzen, L. J., 21-22.

Me: But you had a question [that] maybe it was an airplane?

Gerry: Yeah, because it was...to me it was falling a little slow for something that's on a free-fall...That was my initial reaction I think.

Me: Okay, so your initial reaction was, "it looks like a meteor but...it's moving a little too slow for a meteor.

Gerry: Well, I don't know if I actually thought that...I mean it was just, you see something and, it happened so quickly you don't have time to sit around and contemplate what it is...It was something burning, or you know something bright, or something like that coming down, so... There's only just a very few things that do that.

Me: Were you motivated more by curiosity, or...were you trying to help in case there was some kind of emergency?

Gerry: I just wanted to, basically, see what it was. You know, when something like that happens, you don't sit around and contemplate.

Over the weeks and months to follow, I would arrange a visit to Idaho to conduct a series of in-person interviews with Gerry at his home, and then kept in contact with him by phone while I continued my research. During one phone call, Gerry mentioned the fact that he was reduced in rank sometime after his incident occurred. I asked why that had happened, and he replied bluntly, "Because I deserted." When I asked what he did after he deserted, he said with a chuckle, "I was having a good old time up in the hills!" He didn't seem clear on how long he was gone, or when exactly it took place; but he said he did eventually return, at which time he was busted a rank. Why had he done it? He said something to the effect of he didn't know and that it was a long time ago.

The Lorenzens' account was definitely gaining credibility from my perspective. Regarding what happened after the initial events of February 20, 1959, they were the only source I had to go on besides Gerry's testimony. And his testimony was compromised by one quite vexing problem. As time went on it became increasingly clear that Gerry's amnesia, which emerges as a major theme in the Lorenzens' account, did not end in 1959. Much of the period of his life examined here seemed virtually absent from his memory right up to the present—although intriguingly, he seemed to have no problem remembering what happened in his life *after* those fateful events. Gerry's coping strategy for this apparent void seemed to be: if he didn't remember it, it didn't happen.

The Guy Next Door
The big moment finally arrived; it was time to meet this seemingly enigmatic figure in person. On April 3, 2014, I narrowly escaped a late winter blizzard by catching my flight to Idaho, where I met Gerry at his home on what was a bright, warm, sunny afternoon in that corner of the world. The weather was a welcome relief after spending many long months in Wisconsin's icy death-grip. Here it was already green and fruit trees were bursting into bloom. As I pulled up in the driveway of his ranch-style home I noticed a large RV parked beside the house. Gerry welcomed me at the door amidst the shrill barking of his tiny canine companion, Fifi.

Before me was an elderly man, rather spare and diminutive in stature, wearing blue jeans, a button-down shirt, an old ball cap and over-sized glasses. At the age of 78, he seemed spry and light on his feet, and his eyes never seemed to be far from a wink, reflecting his ever-ready sense of humor. Gerry made me feel right at home in his modest, well-maintained and comfortable home, giving me a tour of the place and showing me all the improvements he had built himself, including a large and inviting sun-room on the back of the house (now piled up with antique radios in various stages of assembly or dis-assembly) and the wheelchair ramps he had built for his recently departed wife (who had passed away at home about two years earlier).

It was a far cry from the sensational image I had formed in my mind's eye from reading the published stories about Gerry—that of a desperate fugitive on the verge of insanity, possibly surviving in a remote wilderness or in some foreign land. Gerry was here just enjoying a very ordinary retirement in the comfort of the suburbs, in his own home. He was alone now, but his daughters and grandchildren came to visit from neighboring states when time allowed. In short, it appeared that Gerry was just a regular guy living a regular life—the "guy next door" so to speak.

Over the course of the next several days, Gerry and I talked about the various aspects of his incident and the larger context of his life. He was quite congenial and forthcoming the whole time. However, he did have his doubts about the whole enterprise and he would let me know it from time to time.

"The fact that I had that incident happen," said Gerry, "I can't see anybody's interest in that! Honest to goodness! I saw some light, and I was gonna go over and take a look and see what it was, and I fell and I was unconscious for a while, and I was okay and that's all I know about it! And all these people write these articles about this or that...it amazes me that... Who gives a damn! I mean, give me a break! Who really does? There's nothing... I don't know anything other than that... I woke up, I was in a hospital. And the doctors, they, they had no answers for it. *I* don't have an answer."

One day, he was even more blunt. After answering my questions for a couple of hours he turned to me as we were wrapping up and said, "Now *I* have a question for *you*. Why the hell are you interested in this story?!?"

It was a fair question. Indeed, what *was* I doing here, half a continent away from home, chasing after this ghost of a tale and pestering this unfortunate elderly gentleman about something that happened 55 years ago that he'd just as soon forget about? Well, as I explained at the beginning of the chapter, it all started innocently enough. And as time passed, I found myself being drawn further and further into this bizarre case by a rapidly growing list of unanswered questions. The project, it seemed, was taking on a life of its own.

But this story is not about me. It's about Gerry. And the story of Gerry Irwin begins in a faraway land bathed by the sound of rushing water.

Chapter 3: A Salmon Runs Through It

The South Fork of the Salmon has for time immemorial been a "terra incognita" because of the frozen mountain passes and steep river breaks. The Sheepeater Indians lived in this land of rugged mountains and vibrant rivers until defeated in battle in 1879 and herded onto a reservation. For the most part it has been left to miners, trappers, and homesteaders. — Jerry Dixon[1]

During my stay in Idaho, Gerry and I spoke at length regarding the circumstances of his upbringing, and from this a surprising and fascinating story emerged. I discovered that Gerry's family lived in a time and place where living legends of Idaho's frontier days were literally right next door, in an area that remains to this day famously remote and isolated. There could be no better introduction to Gerry Irwin than to take a look at this lost world of his early years, where the scent of pine needles and the song of whitewater would have seeped into his very marrow; and which called him to return as a young man—as we'll see— when his mind was foundering on invisible shoals.

Gerry Irwin was born in 1935 in the wilds of central Idaho to Catherine and Patrick Irwin, the fifth of eleven children. His family lived on a pair of homesteads straddling the South Fork of the Salmon River, about 12 miles away and over a mountain pass from the little mining town of Warren, Idaho (now mostly a ghost town). The South Fork runs from south to north, emptying into the Main Salmon River some 20 miles downriver

---

1   Dixon, Jerry S. *South Fork of the Salmon River, Wild and Free* (McCall, ID: Dixon, 1979), "Chapter 2: Across the Salmon River Mountains."

from the where the Irwins lived. The boundary of the Frank Church River of No Return Wilderness is a mere four or five miles east of their former home. It's an area with a rich and storied past, and its untamed and rugged spirit was reflected in the lives of those who settled there.

A Big Place

To get an idea of the sheer magnitude of the Irwins' backyard, here are a few dimensions to consider. The great, "block-shaped massif" that is the Salmon River Mountains covers an area of 8,900 square miles,[2] almost the size of New Hampshire. The Salmon River courses through these mountains in a canyon that, for 180 miles, is over a mile deep—deeper than the Grand Canyon.[3] The Salmon River country contains the largest roadless area in the lower 48 states, made up of the Frank Church River of No Return Wilderness, (at 2.3 million acres, larger than Yellowstone National Park), the adjacent Gospel Hump Wilderness, as well as roadless, unprotected Forest Service lands which combine to form a roadless area of 3.3 million acres, or nearly the size of Connecticut.[4] If you add on the 1.3 million acre Selway-Bitterroot wilderness to the north, separated by only a single dirt road from the rest, you're getting an area larger than Connecticut and Long Island together. The combined area of the five main National Forests of central Idaho make up a mostly continuous landmass that could be seen as one giant "super" National Forest approaching the size of West Virginia.

And in all that magnificent, wide-open space, even far outside the designated wilderness and including the tiny hamlets scattered throughout, there are precious few people. A quick look at a population density map of Idaho speaks volumes. Practically the whole midsection of the state of Idaho has a population of less than one person per square mile.

My first experience of the remoteness of the region occurred half a continent away from there, in a cellphone store in Madison, Wisconsin.

---

2 "Salmon River Mountains." *Wikipedia*. Wikimedia Foundation, 13 Jan. 2013. Web.
3 "Salmon River (4 Rivers), ID." *Wilderness Area Details*. Recreation.gov, 2014. Web.
4 "Frank Church—River of No Return Wilderness." *Wikipedia*. Wikimedia Foundation, 10 May 2016. Web.

I was shopping for a plan that would give me good coverage in Idaho, in preparation for my first visit there. What I discovered was quite a reality check. Good coverage? In Idaho? There is no such animal! An enormous swath of central Idaho has no cellphone coverage, no towers, at all. None. While the populated areas of Idaho are well-covered as one would expect, the hinterlands are still basking in microwave-free tranquility, well into the 21st century.

A Salmon by Any Other Name…

The Salmon River was named by the native peoples in the area for the fish that enlivened its waters, providing life-giving food in great abundance. For the white settlers in the 19th century though, it had a different name. They called it "The River of No Return," due to their discovery that, although parts of that fear-inspiring gauntlet could be negotiated downstream, there was no going back.[5] Before the settlers, yet another name was attached to the river—for a while anyway—this one by Captain William Clark of the Corps of Discovery. He named it Lewis' River in honor of his expedition partner who (as far as they knew) was the first non-Indian to see it. But this name never gained currency, "because later inhabitants, like the Lemhis before them, continued to identify the river with its prolific salmon runs."[6]

The Lemhis were a branch of The Mountain Shoshone that had adopted the horse and the mounted buffalo hunt into their culture.[7] These adaptations gradually distinguished them from their close kinfolk who kept more to the mountains and observed the old ways. These more

---

5 The Salmon River Canyon turned out to be forbidding enough to force the indefatigable Lewis and Clark to take a long overland detour to the north—to eventually reach an easier passage on the Clearwater River. Clark wrote: "The river…is almost one continued rapid…the passage…with canoes is entirely impossible." Excerpt from Clark's expedition journal, August 23, 1805.

6 Mann, John W.W. *Sacajawea's People: The Lemhi Shoshones and the Salmon River Country* (Lincoln: U of Nebraska, 2004), 2.

7 The Lemhis aka Lemhi Shoshone, lived in the environs of the Lemhi River—a tributary of the Salmon. When Lewis and Clark chanced upon the Lemhi band led by Cameahwait, they soon learned in amazement that Cameahwait was actually Sacajawea's brother. (Mann, 18.)

traditional people were known as the Tukudika (literally "meat eaters"[8]), or "Sheep Eaters", as the white settlers called them, alluding to their habit of hunting bighorn sheep. The place where Gerry's family lived, farther west in the Salmon River Mountains, had been Sheep Eater country only 40 or 50 years earlier. Although they were officially dispossessed of their homeland, a few family groups of the tribe managed to evade the Indian removals of 1880, and a small but persistent enclave remained in the South Fork area as late as 1941.[9]

On the east side of the South Fork, the Irwins lived on a homestead settled by the illustrious Three-Fingered Smith—a local legend from the Warren gold rush days of the 1860s. Three-Fingered had struck it rich in the mining game twice over—first at Florence, Idaho, and then 20 miles to the south at Warren—and in 1868 he settled down with his family at the confluence of Elk Creek and the South Fork. They dubbed their newly built home Elk Creek Ranch.[10]

Patrick Irwin first came to live at Elk Creek Ranch around 1923, when he was hired by a mining company to help build, and later to operate, a hydroelectric power plant located there. By this time, the ranch had changed hands a few times since Three-Fingered had owned it, and now belonged to Patrick's employer, Unity Gold Mines—which needed the electricity to power their gold dredges near Warren. At first Patrick lived only on the east side of the river in the cabin near the power plant. By 1925 he was married to a woman named Teresa, and they had purchased a property across the river from the plant, the old Flynn homestead.[11] By 1927 or 1928 however, Patrick was either a widower or divorced, because

8   Loendorf, Lawrence L., Nancy Medaris Stone, and David Joaquin. *Mountain Spirit: The Sheep Eater Indians of Yellowstone* (Salt Lake City: U of Utah, 2006), xii. Print.

9   Hull, Valerie. "The History of the South Fork Ranch." *Judy's Idaho Backcountry Cookbook.* Idaho-backcountry-cookbook.com, 2017. Web.

10 Reddy, Sheila D. *Payette's Past - The Story of Sylvester S. "Three-Fingered" Smith,* USDA Forest Service, Payette National Forest, Heritage Program, July 2002. Web. Condensed from Reddy's book *Wilderness Pioneer.*

11 Helmers, Cheryl. *Warren Times: A Collection of News about Warren Idaho* (Odessa, TX: C. Helmers, 1988), 1925 section.

that was the time frame in which he married Catherine,[12] the mother of Gerry and his siblings.

The Irwin/Brewer Ranch hay meadow, now part of Payette National Forest.
(Photo by David Booher)

By the mid 1930s—i.e. around the time when Gerry was born—the Irwins' land holdings along the South Fork expanded considerably with the addition of the Brewer Ranch. This large parcel bordered the old Flynn homestead on the north, and it featured a great sprawling hay meadow high above the river. It was a belated wedding gift for Patrick and Catherine from Patrick's mother, who had purchased it from another famed pioneer of the area, the legendary miner and frontier mail carrier Curly Brewer.[13]

---

12 Obituary of Catherine Veronica Irwin, *The Oregonian* [Portland, OR] 23 Nov. 1999.
13 Curly Brewer's fame extended far beyond the South Fork. An article from 1902 offers a colorful introduction: "Strong of limb and dauntlessly courageous, the man who braves the blizzards of the Saw Tooth range arrived in Boise last night. It is six long years since Curly Brewer came out of the mountains to mingle in the haunts of men..." Excerpt from: "Carries the Mail," *Idaho Statesman* [Boise, ID] 17 Mar. 1902: 5.

The Irwins' Life on the South Fork

Patrick Irwin was a hardworking man who, in addition to running the power plant, labored at his own gold mining claims as well as farming the fields, putting up hay, tending the livestock, hunting, fishing, and cutting firewood. His mining and prospecting would often necessitate leaving home for weeks at a time. He would enlist his eldest son, John, to help work the claims, and occasionally Gerry and his one-year-older brother, Mike, were recruited as well.

Whether working with his father, or more often, being left behind to tend the chores of the homestead, Gerry remembers that his father was "A strict authoritarian type of a man. No backtalk (laughs). What he says— that's what it was." He recalls that when his father was gone for an extended period, working his mining claims, he and Mike would tend to slack off for a while. However, his mother had only to remind them of their father's imminent return to send them into a frenzy, rushing to finish their chores in time to avoid the dreaded punishment. "He'd give you a whack on the butt, but it was hard! He wouldn't hurt you, you know… he'd use a belt. Whip you on the butt!" he exclaimed with a chuckle.

In some ways, the Irwins' rustic lifestyle of that time and place might sound idyllic to modern ears. As John recalls, "We grew almost everything we ate. The only thing we ever bought during that time [on the South Fork] would have been basic staples like flour, sugar, that type of product. Other than that, we raised everything." In Gerry's words, "We didn't have much, but we didn't go hungry."

To preserve the abundance, their mother would can an astounding 4,000 quarts of foodstuffs per year. They had a fruit orchard, a two-acre garden plot, dairy cows, beef cows, pigs, chickens, and turkeys. They had a smokehouse for curing pork shoulders and hams. There were draft horses for farm work, as well as horses for riding. They put up hay to supply the winter feed for their cows and horses. They supplemented the home food production with hunting the plentiful game in the valley. There were herds of hundreds of elk and lots of deer and bear as well. Salmon and trout teemed in the river and the numerous creeks.

The Return of the King

Chinook (or "king") salmon season, in the springtime, was eagerly awaited. Patrick and a few other men in the area would rise at first light and slip away to the prime fishing spots before the crowd from Warren arrived. As a 1914 newspaper article described it, "The town of Warren is entirely deserted now, all the residents having gone to the South Fork for the spring fishing. The salmon are up and the sport good at this season of the year."[14]

Patrick would often come home with one or two Chinooks, which were typically 30-to-35 pounds and three-to-three-and-half feet long.[15] One or two salmon might seem a rather paltry catch. However, in spite of the massive numbers of fish involved, catching salmon by rod and reel is not as easy as one might imagine, as migrating salmon actually eat very little, and thus are rather blasé about taking bait. The location, however, was superb. The South Fork watershed was (and still is to some degree) especially renowned for its Chinook run, ranking right at the top. And consider what a miracle this is.

To get to the spawning grounds of the South Fork watershed, Chinook salmon have to swim upwards of 700 miles once they leave the Pacific, climb over 6000 feet in elevation, negotiate eight mammoth dams as well as waterfalls and Class 5 whitewater, and dodge gill nets, hooks, and pollution, hardly eating the whole way.[16] The dams on the Columbia and Snake rivers (thankfully, the Salmon is still dam-free), more than anything else have taken a terrible toll, despite the tremendous sums of money spent trying to mitigate the situation.[17]

As a result, salmon runs are a tiny fraction of what they once were (as in Gerry's day, before the dams were built), and without the nursery raised and released fish, they would be vanishingly small. The sad truth is that Pacific salmon of today are in grave danger. And yet, in spite of

14 *Idaho County Free Press* [Grangeville, ID] 23 Apr. 1914.
15 Chinook salmon typically range from 10 to 50 lb., with a record of 126 lb.
16 Barker, Rocky. "Returning Home to Die." *The Idaho Statesman* [Boise, ID] 25 May 2000.
17 Those interested in learning more about the effort to restore wild salmon can find loads of information at the Save Our wild Samon (SOS) website: http://www.wildsalmon.org

all the odds against them, there are still small but significant numbers of wild-raised salmon successfully returning home to breed.[18] These guys are *tough!*

This all points to an intriguing irony in the sobriquet "River of No Return"; a name which seems, in an odd and accidental way, to try to deny the living reality of the river's true namesake. Just look at these remarkable creatures that we call salmon, these iconic fish of the Pacific Northwest. Returning is what they *do.* It's their defining characteristic. The Salmon River watershed is home to perhaps the world's *champion* returner; if not in distance, then at least in terms of sheer guts and endurance.

Returning salmon have nourished the people of this region for thousands of years, not to mention a host of species both large and small. It's probably no exaggeration to say that if the rivers of the Columbia River watershed are the arteries of the Northwest, then the salmon are its red blood cells. Thus, their prodigious ability to return enriches an entire ecosystem with the bounty of the sea.[19] Above and beyond all else, returning is what this river is all about. And, as we shall see, when Gerry had nowhere else to go, he returned here as well.

Gerry's Big Brother

Gerry's eldest brother, John, was another one who returned, after a long life of peregrinations to places as far afield as Argentina. I had the opportunity to meet John and his wife Shirley in September of 2014. They

---

18 Hawley, Steven. *Recovering a Lost River: Removing Dams, Rewilding Salmon, Revitalizing Communities* (Boston: Beacon, 2011), 33. "The Columbia and Snake River Basin was once the world's most productive salmon watershed. Today, only about one percent of the historic number of these fish return." Excerpt of a letter (reproduced in Hawley's book) written by a team of whale biologists, urging government officials to remove dams from the Snake River. They explained how this was necessary in order to restore healthy salmon populations—upon which the orcas of Puget Sound depend for survival.

19 Ibid., 22. Hawley notes that a tremendous diversity of species owes its existence in "Pacific ecosystems" to salmon, "from the tiny Trowbridge's shrew to the cumbersome killer whale. Decomposing salmon bodies provide the coniferous forests of the Pacific rim with a baseline of soil-enriching nutrients, nitrogen in particular, that add girth to the region's spruce, cedar, Douglas fir, hemlock and pine trees."

lived only about ten miles from Warren, in a cabin that sat on the edge of a gorgeous alpine meadow with the clear waters of the Secesh River gurgling right through their backyard. As they explained to me, this area is a critical spawning area for the Chinook salmon of the South Fork Salmon watershed.

Gerry had told me a little about his brother, but he didn't have John's phone number, and he didn't have a phone directory for that area, so I had to wait till I was fairly close before I could find a local phone book and give them a call. However, in spite of the surprise of being called out of the blue by a complete stranger, they cordially invited me up to their place.

I arrived at John and Shirley's cabin—an impressive hewn-log structure they had built themselves—shortly before sunset. I felt a bit sheepish about imposing upon them like this, but to my relief I received a warm and friendly welcome anyway. We spoke for a couple of hours about John's memories of growing up on the South Fork, as well as of John and Shirley's adventures and world travels together, and then the subject of Gerry's UFO encounter came up. I had been hoping we could talk about it, but I had already guessed that John didn't know much, since Gerry had told me that John was away in the Navy at the time. As it turned out, all he really knew about the event was from a little article in *The Idaho Statesman* that their mother had mailed to him shortly after the incident.

Recalling the article, John said that Gerry was in Utah, "...and he claimed he got abducted by aliens." Shirley observed, "He was wandering in the desert," and John added, "Yeah, wandering in the desert, and somebody, I don't know if it was law enforcement—or somebody—found him and...they took him to the military."

Soon our talk turned to other matters, and then it was time for me to drive off into the night to find a campsite at a nearby Forest Service campground, which was completely empty when I arrived, and inky dark and cold in the deep woods. I had a quick dinner, gazing up periodically above the treetops at the blazing stars, winking enthusiastically in the clear mountain air. It was cold enough that I wanted nothing more than to slip into my sleeping bag as soon as I finished eating, and catch up on my notes.

It was a bracing twenty degrees when I arose early the next morning. I stopped by at the Irwins after breakfast to ask a few more questions. After asking for more details about various things we had talked about the night before and going through some family photos, I asked John, "You said yesterday that Gerry claimed that he was abducted by aliens...Did he say that to you?"

John replied, "No, I'm going by what was in the little article in the paper. I don't remember exactly [how it was] worded. It was something about possible alien abduction. I think it was probably just an excuse to cover up his being AWOL [laughing], I don't know."

Apparently, John and Gerry had never actually talked about it. I can understand this. There's a lot that doesn't get talked about in families. Gerry had already told me that he had never discussed it with his family. When I expressed some surprise at this, Gerry shrugged it off by saying, without a hint of irony, "There's not much to tell."

Seasons on the South Fork

Floods, wildfires and blizzards all came with the territory in the Salmon River country, part of the seasonal rhythms that gave shape and texture to the lives of the Irwins, who called it home. The South Fork of the Salmon neatly divided their lands, meaning the family farmed and resided on both sides of the river. Thus, one could say the annual salmon runs hurtled right through the middle of their lives; an exuberant, shimmering reflection of those resourceful people who were—by necessity—deeply attuned to the cycles of nature.

For the Irwins, life on the South Fork must have been a rather "no frills" kind of existence, yet there *were* some conveniences. For one, the house next to the hydroelectric power plant was supplied with electricity. And although the Brewer Ranch did not enjoy this luxury, a diversion ditch from Brewer Creek supplied (besides irrigation for crops) running water to the cabin via a gravity-fed pipe for cooking, bathing, and drinking.

Gerry's schooling is one aspect of South Fork life that could inspire feelings of nostalgia for a rural lifestyle of yesteryear. A tiny school was formed on the South Fork around the time when Gerry reached school age. Classes were held for a while at the power plant, but soon were shifted a mile and a half downriver to the Ranger Station (known as the "South

Fork Guard Station"). These classes were taught for a while by the Forest Ranger's wife, among others. Class sizes were very small, mostly the Irwins with a few others, including the ranger's children. Gerry joked, "If one of the Irwins was sick, why, there was a 10 or 15 percent reduction in class size!" John, Gerry's elder by 5 years, and Patricia, the eldest sibling, had to attend Catholic boarding school in Cottonwood (160 miles away) in the years before the South Fork School began. (The two of them would return eventually to finish high school there.)

Education at the South Fork School did not extend to the higher grades. Before long, the family had to relocate to Warren so the older children could get the schooling they needed. Warren, at nearly 6000 feet elevation, was situated roughly 3000 feet higher than their home on the South Fork. The alpine climate brought new challenges but also some fun. The Warren School had its own ski hill behind the school, and the students were given daily ski breaks. Gerry remembers that an older man in the town made a pair of skis for him.

Childhood's End
In 1942, the sun set on this wilderness idyll of the Irwin family. Warren was turning into a ghost town. Of course, it had seen its glory days, enjoying the usual boom preceding the bust of mining towns everywhere. There had been a gold rush in the region in the 1860s, with a consequent surge in population. At its peak, Warren had 2000 residents.[20] By Gerry's time, the easy gold was long gone, and Warren was down to fewer than 200 persistent individuals, some working their claims, large and small, and some working in one or two "hard rock" i.e. underground mines nearby. There was a boom in dredge mining around Warren in the 1930s as well, which also employed some people (these were the dredges that the power plant was built to supply).

But the death knell for what was left of little Warren, Idaho sounded with America's entry into World War II. To increase recruitment for the

---

20 This figure included up to 1500 Chinese immigrants. Between 1870 and 1900, in fact, the Chinese in the Warren Mining District outnumbered the whites by 3 to 1 (according to a U.S. Forest Service Informational Placard outside the Warren Guard Station).

war effort, as well as to channel more resources into military use, the federal government shut down the mines in 1942. With the economic basis of the town yanked out from under underneath it, the village practically became a ghost town. Soon, the school closed, and the Irwins had to move to Cascade, Idaho, 74 miles away.

Patrick Irwin, however, was still busy in the area working on his own mining claims. His work at the power plant ended with the closing of the mining operations in Warren. Although he worked hard at it, the profits from mining were far from reliable. "Well, he never made a lot. Sometimes the money was there, and most of the time it wasn't," Gerry recalls. In order to keep putting food on the table, the multitalented Patrick tried his luck at the poker table. "From what my mother told me—after a while—she said he was a pretty good gambler, he won a lot of money gambling."

Due to Patrick's ongoing mining work in the South Fork area, the Irwins maintained a strong connection to the area and the people who lived there, long after they moved away. Gerry had a good friend named Terry—who was about his same age—who lived not far from the Irwins' old homestead. Gerry greatly enjoyed his horseback outings with Terry in the surrounding wilderness.

In 1949, shortly before Pat's 49th birthday, tragedy struck. While burning brush on the riverbank in preparation for hydraulic placer mining, the fire blazed out of control. Patrick and two others (his son, John, and one of John's friends) worked frantically to control it, but the strain of the exertion seems to have caused Patrick to have a heart attack, and when he collapsed his head struck a rock with great force. He died shortly afterwards. What must have been a devastating blow to the family was compounded by the fact that they did not have much of a nest egg to fall back on. They had already sold the ranch and spent most of that money as well. Without a breadwinner and short on cash, with 8 of the 11 children still at home needing to be fed, it was a time of poverty and desperation for Catherine and her children. Gerry was 14 years old.

With no other alternatives available to her, Catherine's only recourse was to go on government assistance. Gerry recalled, "We were destitute... Mother had to be on welfare and that was probably pretty bad." They were living in Donnelly, Idaho at the time, but they soon relocated to the town of Nampa, near Boise, to take advantage of a new subsidized housing project there. For Gerry it was exciting, because he and his brother Mike had their own separate bedroom for the first time. Gerry went to high school there for a couple of years, adjusting to the much larger student body without much trouble, as he remembers.

When school let out for the summer of 1952, with the Korean War raging, Gerry and a friend decided to join the military. Without his mother's knowledge or consent, he enlisted, underage (he was 16 at the time), in the U.S. Air Force, eager for adventure. When I asked if he thought he might end up in combat, he replied, "Oh I thought, 'Well, yeah!' I was ready, you know? [chuckles] You know how kids are!" His two older brothers had already joined the military, and he was following suit. When it was time for him to leave for basic training, he told his mother he was going up to the South Fork to visit his friend Terry. She believed his ruse, glad that Gerry was getting out of her hair for a while, as he recalled with a laugh. With that, Gerry said goodbye to his Idaho childhood and headed for wartime adventure.

Gerry at 16 in the guise of a fighter pilot, shortly after enlisting in the Air Force.
(Gerry Irwin photo)

You Didn't See That!

After basic training in California, Gerry was sent to the Air Force radio school in Biloxi, Mississippi, according to his preference. There he learned about radio communications and was trained in Morse code. He had actually wanted to go to Korea with his radio school buddies, but when it was discovered that he had enlisted under age, he was barred from serving in a combat zone. That was good news to Gerry's mother.

Instead Gerry was sent to a remote outpost in Alaska to work on the DEW (Distant Early Warning) Line. This was a system of Arctic radar installations built for monitoring the skies of our most northerly reaches for any sign of an airborne attack from Russia. Gerry's post was one of a long line of radar stations, stretching from Alaska to Greenland, that were built for this purpose. Having been trained in radio communications, he worked as a ground radio operator while stationed there, as well as for the duration of his air force career.

Gerry's post was at the Tin City Air Force Station on the Western tip of Cape Prince of Wales in Alaska, the most westerly point of land in North America, and only 48 miles from the Siberian mainland. Gerry joked that if the Russians attacked, he and his fellow airmen would just have to run, because there were only about 120 men stationed there.

Although life in the isolated camp could be tedious, there were moments of intrigue and excitement. "We had occasions," said Gerry, "when we would pick up on radar some air vehicle coming down out of northern Canada going over our site straight into Russia. And we had orders to track it with our radar, but make no mention electronically of seeing anything, and that was a precursor to, remember Gary Powers, and how he got shot down over Russia eventually? Even back then, the U.S. was flying rocket planes out of northern Canada right into Russia."

Otherwise Gerry recalled that life could be a little boring at Tin City because of the lack of facilities or activities to engage in when off duty. To help pass the time, Gerry worked as a bartender at the tavern on base in his off hours. He described the different standards that applied in their special circumstances.

"You had good food," he recalled. "You didn't have to wear a uniform…you had to say 'yes sir' to the officers, military stuff like that, but you could grow a beard if you wanted to, and they would slack off on [formalities]…Of course you had to take a shower every day and that kind of stuff. And they would fly you down to Nome for a weekend [of R&R]."

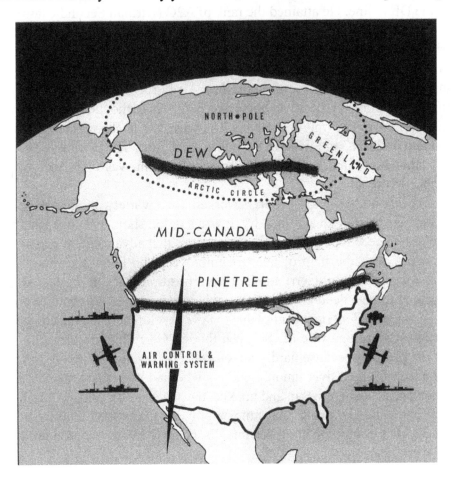

Image of DEW (Distant Early Warning) Line and the other two lines that comprised the "Air Control & Warning System." (U.S. Government, 1960)

According to his service records, Gerry was given high marks for his service as an airman. During his enlistment, his evaluations for both character and efficiency were "excellent" in his first two years and in his last two years he was rated "excellent" in character and "superior" in efficiency. He received a National Defense Silver Medal as well as a Good Conduct Medal. Starting in 1953, he carried a "Secret" security clearance as well, for his work of transmitting secret coded messages while working on the DEW line. He attained the rank of A2C (Airman Second Class).

When his tour in Alaska was over, the Air Force granted Gerry the privilege of choosing his next duty location because they considered working on the DEW line to be hardship duty (owing to the remoteness and lack of amenities). Gerry chose Hill Air Force Base in Ogden, Utah, on account of its proximity to home and family in Idaho. During this time, he met the woman who became his first wife, Linda. They settled down, had two children, and lived in a residence off base. The marriage did not last long, however. Soon after Gerry's enlistment was over, the young couple divorced.

For about two years, Gerry worked in a variety of occupations, including a year or so at a foundry. It was a union shop, and consequently stable with decent pay. The disadvantage was that advancement was slow. However, with the help of another employee who knew the ropes and took a liking to him, Gerry applied for a position that, on the face of it, appeared to be a dead-end. In reality this job prospect was about to open up into an excellent opportunity due to new developments in the company that most were unaware of. So even though Gerry had no seniority, he got the position because hardly anyone else bothered to apply. As he put it, he leap-frogged over union members who had been there many years. When he, a rookie, quickly and unexpectedly rose to the rank of foreman, he was resented by many long-time employees. Gerry took it all in stride, but decided to quit when he became disenchanted with the monotony of the work.

A Monumental Opportunity

Then Gerry took a job as an employee of the U.S. Forest Service. Over the summer of 1957, Gerry worked with a small Forest Service crew out of Big Creek, Idaho, (a tiny hamlet with an airstrip above Big Creek, a tributary of the Middle Fork of the Salmon River.) The actual area they worked in was along Monumental Creek, which feeds into Big Creek. This was well within the current boundaries of the River of No Return

Wilderness, then simply called the Idaho Primitive Area, which itself was tucked deep inside Payette National Forest. That area was only about 20 miles east as the crow flies from where Gerry grew up on the South Fork of the Salmon River. Gerry was practically working in his own backyard!

Gerry's crew was hired to work on the spruce budworm aerial spraying program. They would set up base camp in locations along Monumental Creek, and the three or four of them would each ride out on horseback in a different direction each day to collect insect samples. As Gerry remembers, "... the first thing we would do when we got there, we would go out and clip off twenty branches, and then take the bugs off of that twenty branches, measure them with a caliper—you measure their head width which will determine their larval development stage. And if the majority of them had a certain measurement it was probably time to spray that area. Because there was only one time when the bugs were susceptible to the spray—was when they were in the fourth or the third larval development stage."

This information was used to pinpoint target areas for spraying insecticide to ensure its effectiveness. Here is an excerpt from an official report summarizing the program Gerry was working on:

> Spruce budworms again reached epidemic proportions in 1956 in the Douglas fir and white fir stands in large sections throughout the forest. In that year, a large scale aerial spray project using DDT and oil treated approximately half a million acres on the Hornet, Boulder, and New Meadows Districts. The following year (1957) approximately 500,000 acres were sprayed by aerial tankers. Most of the area treated was on the Big Creek drainage [i.e. where Gerry worked] in the Primitive Area.[21]

Salmon Woes

I couldn't help but wonder what happens ecologically when half a million acres of critical salmon and steelhead trout habitat is sprayed with DDT. As I looked up details about the program, one hit that popped up on my internet search was a passage from Rachel Carson's landmark book on ecology, *A Silent Spring*. The excerpt refers to a similar DDT spraying

---

21 Hockaday, James. *History of Payette National Forest* (USDA Forest Service, 1968), 81. Payette National Forest History and Culture, USDA. Web.

program, also in 1957, this one in neighboring British Columbia to control the black-headed budworm: "Despite these precautions, and despite the fact that a sincere effort was apparently made [to reduce risks to the fish], *in at least four major streams, almost 100 percent of the salmon were killed....*"[22] [emphasis in original]

Putting environmental concerns aside for the moment, this was a job that brought Gerry great pleasure, as it allowed him to enjoy the backcountry of a region he knew and loved. He found working on horseback to be quite agreeable, developing an easy rapport with his steed. As an added benefit, his experience there familiarized him with the Monumental Creek area. As we'll see further along, this familiarity would come to play a decisive role at a key moment in Gerry's unfolding saga.

In the Army Now

When the spruce budworm season came to an end, Gerry's Forest Service employment ended with it, whereupon he decided to return to military duty. In November of 1957, Gerry re-enlisted, this time in the Army. The Army put him through its own version of basic training, and because of his previous service in the Air Force, he was given the temporary rank of corporal during training. Then he was sent to the Nike Missile Training Program at Ft. Bliss, Texas. Graduating from the program, he rose to the rank of SP4 (Specialist, E4- meaning pay grade 4), one rank below sergeant, just 15 months after enlisting as a Private (E2).

His duty, as an "Electronics Mechanic" was repairing and maintaining the launching equipment for the Nike missiles, which were state of the art surface-to-air missiles (or "SAM"), a critical component of national defense at the time. According to Jim Lorenzen, he was also granted a security clearance. Although this is not shown in Gerry's service records so far recovered, it would seem to be consistent with Gerry's knowledge of, and access to, the Army's most advanced missile program. In short, Gerry appeared to be sailing right along in his renewed military career.

Then, just 16 months after re-enlistment, something inexplicable happened that sent him into a downward spiral and derailed his promising Army career.

---

22 Carson, Rachel. *A Silent Spring* (Boston: Houghton Mifflin, 1962), 138.

Chapter 4:
BREAKING: *UTAH MYSTERY 'VICTIM' AWAKE*[1]

*NAMPA SOLDIER FAILS TO RECALL EVENTS FOLLOWING
PLANE CRASH. —Idaho Daily Statesman* [2]

I was curious to see how the Gerry Irwin incident was portrayed in the media, as it would undoubtedly provide a revealing glimpse into public perceptions of that day and age—which was many years before the words "alien abduction" or "close encounter" ever appeared in print. In addition, these reports would likely offer a glimpse into the reactions of the local sheriff as well as hospital personnel, as they tried to make sense of an event that was not only puzzling but also potentially life threatening.

One of the first and most thorough news reports ran in *The Deseret News and Telegram* on Feb. 21, 1959:

Iron Police Puzzled by Unconscious Man

CEDAR CITY- Iron County Officials had a mystery on their hands Saturday after finding an unconscious 23-year-old Idaho man lying face down in the mud Friday night about a quarter mile from his car on U20 near Cedar City.

The young man, identified as Bernard G. Erwin, [sic] 1919 3rd St. North, Nampa, Idaho, was brought in to Iron County Hospital about

1   "Utah Mystery 'Victim' Awake." *The Daily Oklahoman* [Oklahoma City] 23 Feb. 1959: 15.
2   "Nampa Soldier Fails to Recall Events Following Plane Crash." *Idaho Daily Statesman*, [Boise] 23 Feb. 1959: 11.

midnight. An attending physician could find no apparent injuries, but the man could not be revived to talk.

The mystery began about 8 p.m. when Saunders Clark of the State Fish and Game Commission was driving along U20 and saw a parked car with the word "STOP" written on it in shoe polish.

He found a note in the car which read, "Have gone to investigate what looks like a plane crash about one quarter mile to my right. Notify state police immediately." It was signed Bernard G. Erwin.

Using his two-way radio, Mr. Clark called Sheriff Otto Fife in Cedar City for help. After checking and finding that there was a plane reported missing, the sheriff sent deputies and an ambulance to the scene.

Meanwhile, Ernest Cavanaugh, Anaheim Calif., a truck driver, and four men in another car, Vance Underwood, Kanosh; Jerry Underwood, Jones Maxwell, and Bernell Thomas, all of Eureka, came by the parked car and stopped.

While Mr. Clark waited at the scene, they followed footprints in the snow for about a quarter of a mile where they found the unconscious youth lying face down in the dirt.

They started a fire to keep him warm until the ambulance arrived to take him to the hospital.

Sheriff Fife said Saturday that papers found on the ...[two lines of garbled text] ...U.S. Army... and that a paper signed by his commanding officer indicated he was due back at his base on Friday.

The Sheriff also said that a check made with the CAA[3] after the youth was found showed that the plane which had been missing had reported in safely in Arizona. A later check of all air facilities, including those in Salt Lake City, indicated no missing planes over Utah.[4]

Before we move on, it's worth observing here that in Gerry's note the estimate given is "one quarter mile to my right," and Gerry was later found a quarter mile from his vehicle (although reports differ—some say he had walked a mile through foot-deep snow). Intriguingly, this conceivably places the site where Gerry was found unconscious at the very location

---

3 Civil Aeronautics Administration. The CAA was transitioning at that time into the newly formed FAA.

4 "Iron Police Puzzled by Unconscious Man." *The Deseret News and Telegram* [Salt Lake City] 21 Feb. 1959: A7. (Used with permission.)

where he thought he saw the brilliant object land.

More reports filtered out the following day. Some quoted a hospital spokesman who said that Gerry had mumbled some words while still unconscious that sounded like, "jacket on bush."[5] Most reports stated that no cause for his condition could be determined; that in every other respect he was normal and healthy. It seemed as if he was simply in a deep state of sleep from which he could not be awakened. And attempts *were* made— "...the man could not be revived to talk," —not surprisingly, since the sheriff had a possible plane crash to investigate.

A Close Call

It seems that Gerry's adventure also resulted in a close brush with death, according to one source: "Sheriff Fife reported that the Nampan would have died if he hadn't been reached soon."[6] Presumably speaking about the rescue scene and Gerry's appearance, the sheriff stated, "There were no marks of violence or any indication of foul play."[7] Later, examination by medical personnel seemed to confirm this finding: "Doctors there reported they couldn't find any injuries."[8] Most reports also revealed that when Gerry finally came to on Saturday night after being out for nearly 24 hours, he could remember nothing of what had transpired from shortly after the moment he left his car to when he awoke in the hospital. One report stated that an aerial search was conducted the next day, and reports are unanimous in stating that, according to officials, no sign of a wrecked plane could be found.[9]

When Gerry revived, a new flurry of news reports appeared. Typical was the coverage in the *Idaho Daily Statesman* story entitled "Nampa Soldier Fails to Recall Events Following 'Plane Crash,'" which reported that Gerry regained consciousness on Saturday night. It said that Gerry recalled he was taking a shortcut between U.S. highways 89 and 91 when

---

5   "Injured Serviceman Creates Mystery." *Seattle Times* [Seattle] Washington, 22 Feb. 1959: 2.

6   "Mystery of Nampa GI is Unsolved." *Idaho Free Press*, [Nampa, ID] 23 Feb. 1959: 1.

7   "Injured Serviceman Creates Mystery." *Seattle Times* [Seattle] Washington, 22 Feb. 1959: 2.

8   "Mystery of Nampa GI is Unsolved." *Idaho Free Press*, [Nampa, ID] 23 Feb. 1959: 1.

9   Ibid.

he noticed a flash of light, which he thought was possibly an airplane. He remembered writing the note and the word STOP on the side of his vehicle before heading off toward the presumed crash site, but nothing after that.[10] Surprisingly, these few details amounted to the only new information that Gerry could offer upon awakening.

River of Doubt

Although when I initially spoke with Gerry he at least remembered writing the note, in later interviews, he was quite dubious about the possibility that he wrote either the note or the message in shoe polish. "I'd like to see that note!" he said. And as for the shoe polish, "That doesn't sound like something I would do. Where would I get the shoe polish?" As we follow the story, these unremembered details will accumulate like so many rivulets into a raging river of uncertainty. What really did happen?

One thing was becoming clear: Gerry's amnesia dating from 1959 was still in evidence and would become all the more obvious as my research progressed. At times the amnesia was obscured by false memories, which threw me off on occasion. *But what caused the amnesia?* That question sat there like a sphinx in the very center of this mystery, effortlessly brushing aside any attempt to solve it. However, my efforts would uncover some surprises, as we shall see.

First, however, here are the details of the rest of the story as reported by the print media of the day. Some later reports stated that physicians attributed his apparent coma to fatigue. (According to these reports, he had walked a mile through foot-deep snow. While certainly dramatic, this would seem to be a rather weak explanation for causing a 24-hour coma in a young healthy soldier.) Four days after the incident, on Tuesday, April 24, the AP reported that Gerry's condition was "excellent" and that he was going to be turned over to an "Army team" on Monday evening. This *Idaho Evening Statesman* article also states—rather intriguingly—that Gerry's doctor "declined to describe" Gerry's malady.[11] Another article—

10 "Nampa Soldier Fails to Recall Events Following 'Plane Crash'." *Idaho Daily Statesman* [Boise] 23 Feb. 1959: 11.
11 "Nampa Man Recovers, Rejoins His Regiment." *Idaho Evening Statesman* [Boise] 24 Feb. 1959: 3.

of the same date—from the *El Paso Times* stated that Gerry would be flown back to Fort Bliss on Tuesday.[12]

As for the missing plane that later reported in safely, one cannot help but wonder if its temporarily missing status had anything to do with the object Gerry saw. Equipment malfunctions and interference with electronic systems are frequently reported in conjunction with UFO sightings, so I checked into this possibility. However, my search of northern Arizona newspapers for the corresponding dates did not bear fruit, and I learned that neither airports nor the FAA keep flight data for anywhere near that span of time. The same holds true for radar returns—whether military or civilian. So for now, it remains an open question.

In my conversations with Gerry, he did not remember being flown to Ft. Bliss, but he does remember never seeing his car again. He recalls that it was towed and impounded, without release until payment received by the towing company. He says he was unable to come up with the cash at the time but was not overly concerned because it was an old car anyway.

I mention this seemingly unimportant detail because there are so very few details that Gerry *does* recall from the period after his incident. What could be the cause of this amnesia? How are we to pursue this question with no traces of a possible suspect? Well, as it turns out, perhaps we do have a trail of clues to follow after all.

---

12 "Injured GI Due at Bliss." *El Paso Times* [El Paso, TX] 24 Feb. 1959

Chapter 5: The Crucible of the Unknown

*In general, the press has responded to this outpouring of witnesses
with the same dismissive approach as the scientific community and the
government. For the most part, witnesses are ignored or—if they should
dare to make public claims—ridiculed.* — Whitley Strieber [1]

How did Gerry's life change in the aftermath of his encounter
in Utah? This aspect of the story probably contains the most
compelling evidence for the reality of his experience, whatever
it was. If we look at the map of Gerry's existence in the year and a half
following his confrontation with the unknown, we can clearly see the
hoof-prints it left as it rode roughshod through the sanctum sanctorum of
his mind.

Surely, I reasoned, Gerry's military service records would provide some
insight into the changes Gerry experienced. How did Army authorities
respond to these changes? What role might they have had in compounding
his difficulties? Gerry helped me to find out by filing a formal request for
his military records during my first visit to Idaho.

We had to wait four and a half months to get these documents, and it
was quite suspenseful, because there was no guarantee that the National
Personnel Records Center would come up with anything at all. In theory,
they *should* have had Gerry's files, but they had lost a tremendous number
of records in a catastrophic fire at their facility in 1973; in fact, more
than 40 years later, they are still in the process of restoring damaged

---

1   Strieber, Whitley. *Breakthrough: The Next Step* (New York: HarperCollins, 1995),
    104-105.

documents. But the documents finally arrived, and it was well worth the wait. They proved invaluable in providing new information to fill in some of the gaping holes in Gerry's memory, as well as corroborating many important details from the reports written by the Lorenzens.

After Gerry was flown from Cedar City back to his base on Tuesday, February 24th, he was sent immediately to the William Beaumont Army Hospital (WBAH), Ward 30 (the "NP" or neuro-psychiatric ward) for testing and observation. He was kept on the ward for five days and then released on March 1st, with a clean bill of health (according to hospital records).

Jim Lorenzen had written that Gerry's security clearance was revoked and he was reassigned as a file clerk. This detail is not documented in the service records, although the records may be incomplete. If true, then this is the first hint of what was in store for Gerry; even at this early stage he may have been going downhill in the Army's way of reckoning. It does seem understandable however— in light of the strategic importance of the Nike missile program—that any hint of mental or emotional instability would be reason enough to revoke a clearance.

Several days later, "he was walking in the company area near his barracks when he fainted. He had no history of fainting and recovered rapidly with no ill effects."[2] The next recorded event occurred about two weeks after that. On March 15, he was walking in downtown El Paso when he either fainted (Lorenzen) or was found either unconscious or in a wandering condition by El Paso police (WBAH Records). He was taken to El Paso General Hospital, either by ambulance or police officers, (Lorenzen, WBAH Records), then transferred early on the 16th to WBAH, back to Ward 30. His attending physician, Capt. Valentine, reported:

> When questioned at this hospital, he stated that it was the 20th of February, that he was returning from a 30-day leave in Utah, that he saw an airplane crash and since then he can remember nothing. He denied ever having been in this hospital before, or recognizing me or any other members of the hospital staff, although he had intimate contact with all

2   Lorenzen, L.J., 20.

of us less than a month ago.[3]

Valentine goes on to make another interesting observation:

> This interviewer has been in contact with two of his barracks mates who
> know him only casually but state that he has not been unusual or acting
> strangely recently. The patient mentioned to one of these men that a man
> in New Mexico was interested in his seeing a flying saucer, and was
> going to bring a doctor down to hypnotize him.

Here we see an early indication that Gerry was possibly experiencing
confusion about what exactly it was that he saw. Speaking to his doctor
he describes a possible "airplane crash," while to his barracks mates, he
talks about "a flying saucer," adding that a "man in New Mexico" was
interested. This was undoubtedly none other than Jim Lorenzen, who
was in contact with Gerry at that time, along with his wife Coral. The
Lorenzens' residence, which also served as APRO headquarters, was
located in Alamogordo, New Mexico, only about 86 miles north of El Paso.

Alternatively, of course, he may have been censoring himself when
speaking with the doctor, in order to avoid a possible "stain" on his
record. There has always been a stigma attached to those who claim to
have witnessed "flying saucers," which was probably even stronger in the
military where, as we shall see, there was a law banning military personnel
from publicly reporting UFO sightings.[4]

Gerry was evaluated again and this time they kept him under
observation for 32 days. It was a locked ward as well as—paradoxically
sounding—an open ward; meaning patients were locked inside, with the
"open" part meaning they had no privacy, as all the beds were together
in one large, unbroken space. Although Gerry remembers nothing of his
time there (indeed, he remembers very little of what happened for a good
year and a half), I do have the testimony of a woman who was admitted as
a patient to the same ward only three years later (April 1962).

---

3   Hospital records, April 28th, 1959.
4   See Chapter 12.

Testimony from Ward 30

This woman, who as it happens is someone I've known all my life, was admitted to WBAH after a nervous breakdown following severe medical complications that developed during a pregnancy. Like Gerry, they kept her for about a month. Here is some of what Liz (not her real name) recalled about her time on the ward (the women's side that is—men and women had separate facilities):

> Locked ward, you go in, they take everything—no rings, no hairpins, no watch... they take you in a little room, and you strip everything off... They give you a dress to wear that had no buttons, no ties, no belts, so you could not harm yourself. An open bay with your bed and a little nightstand—which had nothing in it, because they kept all your personal belongings locked up, [no] hairbrush, comb. Take a shower— they watched you, put shampoo in your hands...they'd give you liquid soap so you didn't have a bar of soap—they'd put that in your hand. You'd shower and they just watched everything you did. You had no privileges, no privacy. Go to the bathroom—there were no doors on the stalls. You had to ask to go to the bathroom, and they would watch you. It was a big, open ward, no privacy, lights on all night. They [also] had locked, padded rooms... They did the electro-shock [there]... they'd do the shock therapy and bring 'em back to the ward, and they'd be *out of it*...We never watched TV, we never read, your family couldn't come to visit the first two weeks... and the door is locked, and you're not ever getting out of there...until you prove you're well.

It's an interesting coincidence that Ken Kesey's novel, *One Flew over the Cuckoo's Nest,* was published that very year, 1962. It was based on Kesey's own experiences working as a night aide in the Menlo Park, California, V.A. hospital psych ward, in 1960. There are clearly some disturbing parallels here between Kesey's novel and Liz's testimony. However, regarding Gerry's time on Ward 30, we may never know the details, because it is one of the many things that has fallen into the void of his amnesia. There are notes from his doctor in the records we received, but these provide no information at all concerning Gerry's day-to-day activities or treatment (aside from discussing his sodium amytal interview, which we'll take a look at in a later chapter). We know he was kept on the ward for observation, but what if he was given psychoactive drugs, or a course of electro-shock therapy? What effect would that have had on his memory?

Circling the Void

On my first visit to Gerry's home, there was an intriguing moment in our interview on the third day. Gerry was quite skeptical about many of the things that were written about him, even though he couldn't remember much of what really *did* happen. We were talking about what took place after his unidentified object sighting, when he was back at Fort Bliss. He had already dismissed what Jim Lorenzen had written about him spending a month on the psych ward (which is beyond dispute now that we have the hospital records documenting that period). But he was at a complete loss as to what he supposedly *was* doing at Fort Bliss:

> Gerry: I don't think I was doing anything, just, eating and sleeping, getting up and eating and sleeping…I wasn't *doing* anything.
>
> Me: And why is that? Why wouldn't you have your regular duties?
>
> Gerry: Well, I have no idea! They issue their orders I guess (laughs) and, I didn't have, have any duties to do.

I kept pressing him on the subject, as the prospect of not having any duties to perform certainly didn't seem typical for a soldier.

> Gerry: For the life of me, I try to remember what kind of a duty I was *doing* during each day, and I don't know. Like it wasn't significant enough (laughs) to… In the morning when you wake up, you normally go to a place of duty. You get dressed, you go eat breakfast, and you must have some duties required…You just don't go eat, and stand around until it's time to eat again… I have no idea what duties I was supposed to have been doing. That's the only thing that bothers me, I don't, I don't recall!
>
> Me: Hmm.
>
> GI: Maybe they zapped my brain, I have no idea! (laughs) …

Maybe they zapped my brain. In view of the mental health protocols of that time period and the testimony I obtained from Liz, this seemingly offhand joke comes off as a little too close for comfort. But whether it was the shock of his mysterious encounter, or the sodium amytal interview,[5] or some possible electroshock therapy that didn't show up on the records, or even something else altogether, one thing is clear: the gaps in Gerry's memory from that period appear to be far beyond what would naturally slip away with the passage of time.

MKUltra
Aside from the standard mental health treatments of that era, there was a dark agenda stalking the psychiatric profession in those days. The 1950s were at the height of the federal government's secret experimentation with mind control. This subject is far too large to fully explore within the scope of the present work, but there are some relevant points which bear mentioning here.

The secret CIA mind control program codenamed MKUltra was first exposed to public scrutiny by the Church Committee, chaired by Senator Frank Church in 1975, which conducted an in-depth investigation into the activities of the U.S. intelligence agencies. That same year, President Ford initiated a presidential commission (The Rockefeller Commission, headed by V.P. Nelson Rockefeller) to do its own study of intelligence abuses. The ensuing revelations prompted further investigation, culminating in an investigation by the Senate Select Committee on Intelligence in 1977. (The full texts of the Church Committee's report,[6] as well as the Senate Select Committee's report[7] are available online.)

The picture that emerged from these investigations was quite shocking. The CIA (in partnership with the U.S. Army Chemical Corps) had been

---

5   This particular option seems doubtful. A psychiatrist I spoke with about this said that the long-term effect of a dose of sodium amytal on one's memory would be negligible—like drinking a couple shots of bourbon—virtually nothing compared to the effects of even a single alcoholic blackout.

6   United States Senate, Church Committee. *Church Committee Reports*. Washington D.C.: U.S. Gov. Printing Office, 1975.

7   United States Senate, Senate Select Committee on Intelligence. *Project MKULTRA*. 95th Cong., 1st sess. Washington D.C.: U.S. Gov. Printing Office, 1977.

using a combination of voluntary, involuntary, and *completely unwitting* human subjects in experiments aimed at controlling behavior through various means, including hypnosis, psychedelic drugs, ECT (electro-convulsive aka electro-shock therapy), and sensory deprivation.

Psychiatrists were given grants to conduct these experiments, and some of the abuses that occurred were quite horrific. Many thousands of human subjects were involved. Resultant amnesia in subjects was commonplace and quite often *intentional*. The full scale of these atrocities is probably unknowable at this point, thanks to some fancy footwork by CIA Director Richard Helms, who, in 1973, ordered the destruction of all MKUltra documents. [8]

The Magic Bus

As noted, some of the MKUltra subjects came willingly. One of these volunteers was destined to leave an indelible mark on American culture as a direct result of his experience. In 1960, author Ken Kesey signed up for an MKUltra sponsored drug study at the Menlo Park Veteran's Hospital in Palo Alto, California (although it should be noted that he couldn't have known the CIA was involved, let alone something called "MKUltra"). It was in this study that Kesey was first exposed to LSD. As Kesey remarked in the 2011 documentary *Magic Trip*, "I was training for the Olympics Team…as a wrestler. I'd never been drunk on beer, let alone done any drugs! But this was the American government!"[9]

Soon, Kesey began experimenting with LSD among friends. The group that congregated around Kesey, the "Merry Pranksters," organized LSD parties they called "Acid Tests" in the mid-1960s, musically enhanced by Gerry Garcia and his newly formed band, the Grateful Dead. A notable Prankster was famous Beat Generation figure Neal Cassady (thinly disguised as "Dean Moriarty" in Jack Kerouac's novel *On the Road*).

---

8   Lee, Martin A., and Bruce Shlain. *Acid Dreams: The Complete Social History of LSD: The CIA, the Sixties, and Beyond* (New York: Grove/Atlantic, 1992), 27, 285-286. Significantly, the project was Helms' idea to begin with. Although MKUltra was initiated under then CIA Director Allen Dulles in 1953, it was Helms who hatched the concept and gained Dulles' approval.

9   *Magic Trip: Ken Kesey's Search for a Kool Place*. Dir. Alex Gibney and Alison Ellwood. Perf. Ken Keysey and Neal Cassady. Magnolia Pictures, 2011. DVD.

Cassady was the driver of the converted school bus dubbed "Further" in which the Merry Pranksters took their epic psychedelic road trip from San Francisco to New York in 1964.

This remarkable story seems like a perfect example of the law of unintended consequences in action: Cold War spies—hell-bent on enslaving the human mind—sparked the very Promethean fire that ignited the hippy revolution.

The Dark End of the Rainbow

It must be remembered that, unlike Kesey—who was *voluntarily* participating in relatively harmless experiments—a large proportion of MKUltra research subjects were neither volunteers nor cognizant, and thus a great number of them did not enjoy a happy ending. Due to the records purge by CIA Director Helms, we'll probably never know the full scale of the damage done, but we do know it was widespread. According to the U.S. Senate Select Committee on Intelligence, "Eighty-six universities or institutions were involved."[10] This number included "44 colleges or universities, 15 research foundations or chemical or pharmaceutical companies and the like, 12 hospitals or clinics (in addition to those associated with universities), and 3 penal institutions."[11]

In one MKUltra funded study in Montreal (at McGill University's Allan Memorial Institute), unwitting patients who checked themselves in for treatment of routine, minor complaints like anxiety and postpartum depression were subjected to long regimens of physically and mentally devastating "treatments" that were virtually indistinguishable from torture, all under the direction of the notorious Dr. Ewan Cameron. The goal of all this, according to Cameron, was to actually "remake" his patients. This was achieved by first "depatterning" them, which amounted to wiping out the existing personality and returning the mind to a blank slate: "Cameron saw shock therapy as means to blast his patients back into their infancy, to

---

10 United States Senate, Senate Select Committee on Intelligence. *Project MKULTRA.* 95th Cong., 1st sess. Washington D.C.: U.S. Gov. Printing Office, 1977, 3.

11 Ibid., 7. Quote from prepared statement by then CIA Director Stanfield Turner.

regress them completely."[12]

This depatterning regimen included abnormally high voltage ECT, regular doses of a nightmarish cocktail of powerful drugs (including hallucinogens like LSD and PCP, as well as barbiturates, nitrous oxide, sodium amytal,[13] Thorazine, and insulin), complete sensory deprivation in the "Isolation Chamber" for weeks at a time, and drug-induced extended sleep in the "Sleep Room" nearly around the clock, with some being forced to endure uninterrupted slumber for over two months! The ECT Cameron used was by no means typical either. He employed something called a "Page-Russell" device, which allowed him to apply up to six successive shocks in one session. The inventors of the machine recommended a total of 24 separate shocks per patient, but Cameron's patients received up to *360 separate shocks* in the course of their treatment.[14]

Besides the horrifying frequency and number, the shocks were delivered with a much greater force:

> In standard, professional electroshock, doctors gave the subject a single dose of 110 volts, lasting a fraction of a second, once a day or every other day. By contrast, Cameron used a form *20 to 40 times more intense*, two or three times daily, with the power turned up to 150 volts.[15][emphasis added]

Having facilitated the "massive loss of all recollections" and thus achieving the desired "complete depatterning" (i.e. "blank slate"), the next phase could begin, what Cameron called "psychic driving," in which patients were forced to listen to tape-recorded messages. Considering that by this point the patients were virtually incapacitated by their "treatment", they were helpless to resist these messages—which came at them for up to twenty hours per day over a period of weeks, with one unfortunate soul

---

12 Klein, Naomi. *The Shock Doctrine: The Rise of Disaster Capitalism* (New York: Metropolitan /Henry Holt, 2007), 32.

13 Interesting to see sodium amytal on the list—the one drug that we know for sure was used on Gerry.

14 Klein, 32-36.

15 Marks, John. *The Search for the "Manchurian Candidate": The CIA and Mind Control* (New York: Times, 1979), 134-135.

being barraged unceasingly for a hundred and one days straight![16]

The end result, as one might expect, was not a pretty picture. One article notes the tragedy of traumatized patients left to suffer with incontinence and even "total amnesia." In a particularly striking example, a woman "lost all recollection of her first 26 years, including the birth of her five children." The majority of the patients suffered either permanent injury to their brains or were "psychologically shattered."[17]

A Nazi Kindred Spirit
One detail that makes the actions of Dr. Cameron seem all the more sinister is that he surely must have known better. In fact, due to an important role he played in the aftermath of WW II, he should have known painfully well just how wrong he was:

> The CIA violated the Nuremburg Code for medical ethics by sponsoring experiments on unwitting subjects. Ironically, Dr. Cameron was a member of the Nuremburg tribunal that heard the case against Nazi war criminals who committed atrocities during WW II.[18]

Far from being repulsed by the appalling revelations he was hearing in Nuremburg, it appears that Dr. Cameron was—on the contrary—picking up pointers for his own dark experiments in the near future.

So what does any of this have to do with Gerry? Perhaps nothing, but the possibility that Gerry may have been a subject of the program directly, or of practices developed by it, cannot be easily dismissed. For starters, Gerry's confinements in various Army facilities occurred during the height of MKUltra research (which officially lasted from 1953 to 1973, but was scaled back considerably in 1964). We also know that it was a joint program between the CIA and the Army (specifically the Army Chemical Corps) which is to say that Gerry's employer and health care provider was actually a partner in this nefarious business. And as far as motives go; besides the general need for research subjects, there is

---

16 Klein, 32.
17 Turbide, Diane. Television: DR. CAMERON'S CASUALTIES: A series revisits
     Canada's 1950s brainwashing scandal. *Maclean's*, [magazine] 04-21-1997, 60.
18 Lee and Shlain, 24.

evidence that someone in the Army was working to keep a lid on Gerry's memories. (We'll take a look at this evidence in a subsequent chapter.)

Lack of Memory is *Not* Lack of Evidence

Of course, the fact that Gerry remembers nothing of the sort taking place is, under the circumstances, not really a valid argument against the possibility of it having occurred. A case in point is the story of MKUltra experiment survivor Gail Kastner, as reported by investigative journalist Naomi Klein—who interviewed her in person. Kastner, a Montreal resident, had suffered her entire adult life from both constant physical pain and mental dysfunction, as well as a complete lack of memory of anything that happened in her life before age 20.

Her long-estranged identical twin sister Zella had complained to her (before they stopped talking to each other) about a time when Zella had been compelled to care for Gail as a young woman, when Gail was basically helpless. Chastising Gail, Zella described the hardship she'd endured: dealing with Gail's incontinence, and putting up with Gail's strange, infantile behavior— including sucking her thumb and babbling like a baby. Gail had no memory of these terribly disturbing details, and she also had no idea how she had wound up in her current condition.[19]

Then, one day when she was in her late forties, Gail was out walking with her boyfriend (himself a Holocaust survivor), who was very concerned about the question of what had caused her amnesia and other debilitating symptoms. As they passed a newspaper vendor, they spied a banner headline reading, "'Brainwashing Experiments: Victims to Be Compensated.'" As Gail scanned the story, a number of details reminiscent of her symptoms—both past and present—caught her attention, and she asked her boyfriend to buy a copy.[20]

Gail began to put the puzzle pieces together and eventually obtained documentation that confirmed she'd been admitted at age 18 to the Allan Memorial Institute as a patient of Dr. Cameron, for treatment of anxiety. Her nurses initially described her as "'cheerful,' 'sociable,'" and 'neat.'" She was then subjected to "huge doses of insulin, inducing multiple

---

19 Klein, 27-28.
20 Ibid., 28.

comas; strange combinations of uppers and downers;", as well as drugged into prolonged spells of sleep and repeatedly shocked in the course of a brutal ECT regimen. Kastner had a diagnosis of schizophrenia upon release—an appalling tragedy for someone who checked in with such a relatively minor condition.[21]

The Lowdown on Amnesia

Before we get into the general subject of amnesia, it will benefit our inquiry to take a brief look at the general effects of ECT, which as we know, was a technology in use on Gerry's psych ward. Klein noted that amnesia "was by far the most common complaint associated with [ECT]."[22] The important point here is that whether or not MKUltra was involved, if Gerry had merely been subjected to the standard ECT of that time period (which evidently was considerably riskier than the ECT of today), that alone apparently could have been enough to wipe out parts of his memory.

Regarding amnesia generally, there is a lot to consider. It must be remembered that—as far as we know, anyway—Gerry's amnesia and blackouts *preceded* any medical or psychiatric intervention. Having said that however, it seems natural to wonder—whatever the original cause of his symptoms— if the intervention Gerry received from the Army could have made his condition worse.

Fugues Considered

Bearing in mind all the different types of amnesia as defined by the psychiatric establishment, what kind of amnesia did (or does) Gerry have? In investigating possible categories for his condition, I came across the diagnostic term "dissociative amnesia." In general terms, it's a condition wherein people find they are unable to remember important personal information. In rare cases, subjects can even forget who they are. Dissociative (aka psychogenic) amnesia is typically caused by, or associated with, psychological trauma (as opposed to physical damage or injury to the brain). A closely related condition, called dissociative fugue or fugue state, is described in part by one source as:

---

21 Ibid., 29-30.
22 Ibid., 31.

... usually short-lived (ranging from hours to days), but can last months or longer. *Dissociative fugue usually involves unplanned travel or wandering...* [23] [emphasis added]

With this in mind, let us now pick up where we left off in the story of Gerry's ordeal. A day after he was released from his 32-day confinement on Ward 30, Gerry did something highly unusual.[24] Here is the way he described his experience of what transpired that day (Saturday, April 18), which we've touched upon in Chapter 1:

> "I experienced an urge to return to the location of my original experience and I proceeded to follow this urge. Although I can remember everything that happened, it all seems more like a dream than an actual memory. I just seemed to know that I was going back—I didn't know why and I didn't question it."[25]

Jim Lorenzen's narrative resumes here, recounting that Gerry then caught an overnight bus to Utah, disembarking in Cedar City the following day (Sunday afternoon). From there he hiked five or six miles out of town along Highway 14, whereupon he veered off into the brush without hesitation, straight to the spot where he found his lost jacket suspended from a shrub. And then there's that arresting detail, in which Gerry found a pencil inserted through a buttonhole of his jacket, and tightly wrapped around the pencil was a note. He then proceeded—still in his trance—to remove the pencil, unwrap the note and *burn it without reading it*, the smoke from which seemed to snap him back to his senses. This episode *does* bear some resemblance to the above description of fugue states. Could that be what Gerry experienced?

Turning again to the broader category of amnesia, we find that there are three clearly documented incidents of this in Gerry's hospital records. In the first of these, dated March 20, 1959, Dr. Valentine reported on

---

23 "Fugue State." *Wikipedia*. Wikimedia Foundation, Inc., 26 Jan. 2017. Web.

24 There are discrepancies in the record regarding this timeline, as we'll see in Chapter 8.

25 Lorenzen, L. J., 22.

Gerry's amnesia and 24-hour blackout that occurred at the time of his original incident in Utah. Valentine's second report, (cited earlier in this chapter) from April 28, documented the March 15 blackout and amnesia episode which preceded Gerry's 32-day treatment at the hospital.

There's also a third report, which was written by a different doctor (the ward supervisor, a major), nearly two and a half months later (July 9). It states that Gerry was checked into WBAH on July 5, 1959, following an episode in which Gerry had approached El Paso police in a state of confusion. He reported that he was unaware of his identity or any other information about himself. Then the doctor revealed a fascinating detail, reporting that Gerry "allegedly bought a newspaper to *find out what city he was in.*"[26] (emphasis added)

According to the doctor, when Gerry was readmitted to Ward 30 (his *third* admission, no less), he claimed that he had no recollection of ever being there before and that he still didn't know who he was. By the next morning, he'd recovered most his memories, except for those of the events leading up to his current admission. However, the memory gaps he'd reported in his earlier hospital admissions were still in force. The doctor commented on the lack of any explanation for Gerry's "repeated attacks of memory loss."[27]

Jim Lorenzen had his own encounter with Gerry's amnesia. He wrote that he stayed in touch with Gerry's orderly room (i.e. his Army company HQ) during Gerry's 32-day admission at WBAH. When Jim was finally able to speak with Gerry by phone, it took considerable effort to refresh Gerry's memory, as Gerry had no recollection of their earlier discussions.[28]

Friends Downtown

The July 9th report contains another intriguing statement. Gerry had claimed that, "he had 'friends downtown' who are also interested in this matter and he was going to be in contact with them." The "friends" mentioned here is undoubtedly a reference to the civilian psychiatrist in

---

26 This incident was almost certainly unknown to the Lorenzens, who had lost contact with Gerry by then.
27 Hospital records.
28 Lorenzen, L. J., 24.

El Paso whom the Lorenzens had arranged for Gerry to meet. An initial consultation with the doctor—attended by Gerry and the Lorenzens—did take place, but apparently due to interference by his C.O., Gerry was unable to keep any of his subsequent appointments. This is a crucial point, because those blocked appointments had been scheduled for the purpose of using hypnosis to help Gerry recover his lost memories.[29] (More on this in Chapter 12.)

Dr. Valentine, Draftee

Incidentally, the doctor who prepared this report was Captain Valentine's superior officer on Ward 30. He is the only living witness to any part of Gerry's story (besides Gerry himself) that I have been able to locate. He spoke to me on the condition of anonymity. In spite of his advanced age (90), he was mentally sharp and quite articulate. Although he does not remember Gerry's case (and stated that he couldn't comment on it even if he did), he kindly offered some general background information.

The doctor told me the reason he was the one who wrote this final report, rather than Gerry's regular doctor (Captain Valentine), was that Valentine was a drafted doctor and had presumably been recently discharged. He surmised this because the report is from July and turnover among drafted doctors—who usually served a two-year enlistment—was in early summer. Of course, I tried to track down Dr. Valentine himself only to learn that had died in 2010 at age 80.

The Trauma Factor

Returning to the July 9 report, we read, "He expressed considerable resentment that the doctors had not discovered the cause of his memory loss and stated that it was the Army's responsibility to find out." It appears Gerry was angry, which is hardly surprising under the circumstances. Yet it seems reasonable to wonder, given Gerry's previously high marks for character by his superiors—as well as his notably disarming personality today—if this anger wasn't at least partly a symptom of PTSD (Post Traumatic Stress Disorder) caused by trauma from his Utah incident.

Besides anger, PTSD can produce feelings of mistrust and betrayal,

---

29 Lorenzen, L. J., 24.

depression, alienation, and suicidal thoughts and feelings. According to yet another—later—psychiatrist's report (which we'll see in another chapter) "...he described vague suicidal ideas which he characterized as a feeling that something was impelling him to jump in front of a vehicle. He also described some feelings that he would be harmed..."

In April, during his 32-day admission to WBAH, Gerry was referred for evaluation to a clinical psychologist. In her report, the psychologist first summarized Gerry's recent clinical history, including his two hospital admissions that were both precipitated by "a syncopal attack of unknown cause." She stated that Gerry "claimed amnesia for the past month." She further noted that Gerry had a "paranoid attitude" and was found "to be hostile, opinionated, and to oppose himself to the regimen of the psychiatrist, argumentative with respect to his treatment and feeling only he could treat his own case. *He implied there was some mysterious reason for what befell him* but refrained from voicing a theory." (emphasis added)

It looks like Gerry was having a rough time—to put it mildly—and one senses he wasn't receiving much compassion from his health care providers, either. To briefly revisit our list of PTSD symptoms, we find: feelings of irritability or anger, mistrust, betrayal, and alienation; in other words, a *dead ringer* for what the psychologist described. It makes sense that Gerry's condition would have made him difficult to deal with, and at the same time it's easy to see him receiving a frosty treatment from a skeptical Army psychologist.

One detail in particular—from the clinical psychology report—has special relevance for our story. As we saw highlighted above, Gerry reported *"there was some mysterious reason for what befell him."* Gerry voiced a similar suspicion to our unnamed doctor as well, whose July 9th report states: "he was sure that something happened to him when he had seen the unidentified flying object..." This is surely a vital consideration for our investigation. Regardless of what anybody else thought, *Gerry himself* maintained that his troubles *stemmed directly from his UFO encounter.*

Chapter 6: Atom Bombs and Space Brothers

*When a ground radar picks up a UFO target and a ground observer
sees a light where the radar target is located, then a jet interceptor is
scrambled to intercept the UFO and the pilot also sees the light and gets
a radar lock-on only to have the UFO almost impudently outdistance
him, there is no simple answer. We have no aircraft on this earth that can
at will so handily outdistance our latest jets.*
— Capt. Edward J. Ruppelt, 1956 [1]

For the purposes of our investigation, it will be helpful to take a step back for a moment in order to see how Gerry's story relates to the milieu in which he lived. The era in which these events unfolded was very different from the world we live in today, and it's worth a look, giving special attention to how the "flying saucers" in our skies were perceived in this schizoid decade of sock hops and bomb drills, just as humanity was mastering the secrets of nuclear annihilation.

Death from Above

Whereas in days of yore people quaked beneath lightning hurled by Zeus or Yahweh, Americans in the 1950s now feared the specter of Soviet hellfire raining down from above. As a Nike missile technician, Gerry played a crucial role in protecting the nation from this very threat. The Nike surface-to-air missiles (SAMs) were the last line of defense against

---

1   Ruppelt, Edward J. *The Report on Unidentified Flying Objects* (Garden City, NY: Doubleday, 1956), 225. Ruppelt was the first director of the Air Force's Project Blue Book (1952-1953).

airborne attack and were thus a key component of national security.[2]

Gerry's position as a missile technician made him privy to the Nike missile testing in the desert near Ft. Bliss. He witnessed these missiles launching and either hitting or missing the drone aircraft they were targeting.[3] Combined with his previous Air Force experience on the DEW Line,[4] it seems likely that Gerry's discernment in identifying various flying objects was probably better than most. This is a point worth bearing in mind concerning the reliability of his judgment on the night of his encounter.

Nike Hercules Missiles. (U.S. Army photo)

2 On that note, it's interesting to observe that in Gerry's previous service in the Air Force working on the DEW Line, he was also working to defend against Soviet air attack; except then he was on the defensive front line, at the other end of the safety net (see Chapter 3).

3 I was surprised to learn that drones were in use back then. In fact, a quick internet search revealed that development of military drone technology dates all the way back to World War 1.

4 See Chapter 3.

But strategic bombers weren't the only skyborne objects competing for attention. There were also overflights of the U2 spy plane. This top-secret, ultra-high altitude CIA reconnaissance jet entered service in 1955, and during his service in Alaska in 1953-54, Gerry told me he had observed overflights of what were almost certainly secret prototypes of this aircraft. Sightings of this incredibly high-flying jet plane were frequently mistaken for UFOs, according to the CIA.[5] But the CIA's claim is almost certainly overstated. The U2s could perhaps explain some UFO sightings of points of light high up in the sky, but certainly not disk-shaped objects seen low overhead, or objects making sharp right angle turns, etc.

Other newcomers in our skies were the world's first artificial satellites. Beginning with the launch of Sputnik 1, on October 4, 1957, and quickly followed by Sputnik 2 on November 3rd (bearing Laika the space dog), the Soviets won the first round of the Space Race. Strategically speaking, this was a frightening development for Americans, who had ample reason to fear not only space-based reconnaissance, but also the logical next step—satellite-launched weaponry. President Eisenhower responded in due haste with the creation of NASA in 1958.

And last but not least on our short list of man-made flying objects from the 1950s are the missiles. Of course, these had been around since the German V1 and V2 rockets of WW II, but the technology had been developing quite rapidly. There were short and medium range ballistic missiles at the ready, as well as surface-to-air missiles like the Nike, air-to-air missiles, anti-tank missiles, etc., but starting in February 1959, less than two weeks before Gerry's encounter, a frightening new breed arrived on the scene. And this one was a real nightmare. Called the ICBM (intercontinental ballistic missile), this was a trans-oceanic nuclear thunderbolt. The early models were aimed mainly at large targets, i.e. cities, due to their limited accuracy, which no doubt served to ramp up the terror index to ever higher levels. The first ICBM unit was deployed in the Soviet Union on February 9, 1959, followed by its first U.S. equivalent

---

5   David, Leonard. "CIA About UFOs of the 1950s and '60s: 'It Was Us'" *Space.com*, 14 Jan. 2015.

about seven months later.[6]

It Came from Outer Space

So clearly, there were plenty of man-made things to fear buzzing through the skies of the 1950s. Consequently, humanity was looking up in earnest—both in dread and in fascination—toward these new wonders. But people were seeing *other* things up there as well; both night and day and with alarming frequency. These things seemed intelligently guided but didn't fit into any known category of airborne object. These "flying saucers" fueled a whole new mythology, which in turn surely influenced perceptions of these allegedly celestial visitors. Thus, two closely related spheres of human intrigue circled each other in a kind of otherworldly dance; the realm of science fiction and the world of real-life UFO encounters.

The Fifties are widely considered to be the golden age of sci-fi movies. Classics like *Forbidden Planet, Invaders from Mars, The Day the Earth Stood Still, Plan 9 from Outer Space, It Came from Outer Space* and *Earth Versus the Flying Saucers* are some of the more memorable examples, for better or worse.

Some also consider the fifties to be the true golden age of science fiction literature.[7] Whether one agrees with this or not, it's hard to dispute that the genre was fairly bursting at the seams, exploding with fantastic ideas and imagery. Greats like Ray Bradbury (*The Martian Chronicles* was published in 1950), Arthur C. Clark, Philip K. Dick, and Isaac Asimov were all coming to the fore. A common theme in the science fiction then (as now) was alien invasion. On that note, it's interesting to observe that Gerry's encounter took place more than 20 years after Orson Welles' radio production of H.G. Wells' *War of the Worlds* (1938), and six years after the book's first major film adaptation (1953).

Science fiction was popular in electronic media as well. In radio, there was *Dimension X* (1950-51), *Exploring Tomorrow* (1957-58) and *X Minus*

---

6   "Intercontinental Ballistic Missile." *Wikipedia.* Wikimedia Foundation, Inc., 26 July 2016. Web.
7   Silverberg, Robert. "Science Fiction in the Fifties: The Real Golden Age."
     American Science Fiction, Classic Novels of the 1950's. Library of America, n.d.
     Web.

One (1955-58). On television, there were shows like *Tales from Tomorrow* (1951-53) and *Science Fiction Theater* (1955-57). And Gerry's real life visit to the twilight realm was preceded, less than three months earlier, by Rod Serling's teleplay *The Time Element* (November 24, 1958). This science fiction special was later regarded as the pilot for *The Twilight Zone* TV series, which premiered in October of 1959.

No discussion of fifties sci-fi would be complete without mentioning the pulps, many of which blurred the line between science fact and science fiction. Though pulp magazines as a whole were declining, there were sub-genres like men's adventure magazines that thrived in the fifties. The most famous and influential of the pulp magazine publishers of the time was Ray Palmer.

While often compared to P.T. Barnum, Palmer was a complex and multifaceted individual. He certainly had a flair for the sensational, yet he also published many serious articles by reputable authors. He is credited as a major force in popularizing the "flying saucer craze," beginning with a story he published in 1948 in *FATE* magazine (which he co-founded with Curtis Fuller) titled "The Truth about the Flying Saucers."

This article, written by pilot Kenneth Arnold, told of Arnold's sighting of a formation of flying disks over Mt. Rainier in 1947 (in fact, it was Arnold's report that led directly to the coining of the term "flying saucers"). And, significantly for our story, it was Palmer who first published Gerry's full story —as far as it was known at the time, anyway. "Where is Private Irwin" by Jim Lorenzen, appeared in Palmer's *Flying Saucers* magazine in the November 1962 edition.

Saucer Mania
This brings us to the modern UFO phenomenon as a whole, which officially begins (according to many ufologists) in 1947, with the Maury Island (Puget Sound) incident and the sighting of Kenneth Arnold just mentioned, with both the "Crash at Roswell" and the enormous UFO sighting wave of 1947 following close on its heels. (This beginning date is rather arbitrary, as a number of authors have pointed out that encounters

with otherworldly craft and beings have been reported for millennia.[8])
These incidents were at the leading edge of widespread reports of strange
lights and flying objects in our skies performing impossible maneuvers.

The 1950s saw at least two massive waves of sightings, the first of
which was the 1952 wave which was "one of the largest UFO waves
of all time"[9] and which prominently featured the "Washington Flap."
Incredibly, this flap—which occurred over the course of two consecutive
weekends over Washington D.C. in July of that year—featured tracking
of unidentified targets on radar confirmed by visual sightings of air traffic
controllers, as well as eyewitness testimony by both high-level military
personnel and fighter pilots.

As if that weren't enough, this was all happening in and around the
most restricted and well-defended airspace in the U.S., and probably in
the world for that matter! Yet somehow, in the face of all the high-profile
media coverage supported by very convincing evidence and testimony,
the whole affair was basically swept under the rug by Major General John
Samford, Director of Air Force Intelligence.

In a press conference at the Pentagon on July 29, 1952, Samford
attributed all of the observed and documented strangeness to natural
phenomena (i.e. "temperature inversions").[10] Somehow this seemed to
calm the furor that had arisen in the media. As summed up by author
William Birnes, "Our nation was locked in a stalemate war with Korea
and the government was ever fearful of what the nuclear-armed Soviets
and Chinese might do if there was one mistaken calculation, one slight

---

8   *See*: Vallee, Jacques. *Passport to Magonia: From Folklore to Flying Saucers* (1969.
     Reprint. Brisbane, Australia: Daily Grail Pub., 2014). A landmark study of this
     historical material going back to ancient times. Importantly, this book also included
     a summary of Gerry's story, which presumably afforded it a wider audience than
     Palmer's magazine could have reached.
9   Hall, Richard. "Radar-Visual Sightings Establish UFOs As A Serious Mystery." *The
     1952 Sighting Wave*. NICAP, 15 Dec. 2005. Web.
10 United States. Department of Defense. *Minutes of Press Conference held by Major
     General John A. Samford, Director of Intelligence, U.S. Air Force, 29 July 1952*,
     NICAP (nicap.org) n.d. Web. 21 May 2017.

miscommunication."[11] It would appear that in the grip of all this tension, America, or at least the media, was more than willing to be reassured, true or not, that there were no aliens invading our airspace. In spite of this, the sightings continued.

Brother from Another Planet

In a much different vein that same year, a man named George Adamski began making some rather fantastic claims about contact with a man from Venus named Orthon. He went on to tell tales of travels aboard spacecraft with his new Venusian friends. His first book on the subject, *Flying Saucers Have Landed*, was published in 1953, generating considerable controversy and publicity. Over time it became apparent that Adamski was making statements that were demonstrably false and some of his purported photographs of UFOs were exposed as blatant fakes.

However, to those who believed him, Adamski was among the first of the 'UFO contactees,' to be followed by a slew of others in the fifties and beyond. The contactees spoke of the "space brothers" coming to offer assistance and guidance to the people of Earth. They gained a following that would develop into a significant subculture, whose participants gathered by the thousands at events like the annual Giant Rock Interplanetary Spacecraft Conventions in California, organized by contactee George Van Tassel.[12]

Aside from these flamboyant figures and their often dubious claims, there is another side to the contactee phenomenon which is quite fascinating. The maverick UFO researcher John Keel did an in-depth investigation into what he called the "silent contactee" phenomenon. These were contactees who were unknown to the public and wanted to remain that way, shunning media attention. They spoke with Keel only on the condition of anonymity. Eventually Keel developed connections with hundreds of these individuals, and he was astonished at what he learned from them.

---

11 Birnes, William J. *Aliens in America: A UFO Hunter's Guide to Extraterrestrial Hotspots Across the U.S.* (Avon, MA: Adams Media, 2010), 81.

12 Doore, Kathy. "Integratron's George Van Tassel and the Giant Rock Spaceship Conventions" *Labyrinthina*. kathydoore.com, n.d. Web.

A great many of them reportedly had some kind of ongoing telepathic connection with entities who typically claimed to be from other planets (a claim Keel doubted, instead favoring a hypothesis that they were an unknown intelligence from Earth—what he called "ultraterrestrials"). In this way, they would receive messages which they passed on to Keel. Although these individuals were unknown to each other, they would often make the same exact predictions, down to quite specific details. More startling still, these predictions often came true—at least according to Keel.[13]

Ufology Takes Off

In stark contrast to the sometimes circus-like atmosphere surrounding the contactee phenomenon, a number of serious, dedicated UFO investigators entered the field in the 1950s in a concerted effort to separate fact from fiction. One of the early standouts was Major Donald Keyhoe who published his breakthrough book *The Flying Saucers Are Real* in 1950. This book made a strong case that UFOs were physical, intelligently guided flying objects posing possible risks to the nation's security. He argued that the Air Force was aware that the UFOs were probably extraterrestrial in origin but, concerned about a possible panic, actively discouraged public interest by claiming that all sightings could be explained by natural causes.

Keyhoe went on to serve as Director of the National Investigations Committee on Aerial Phenomena (NICAP) from 1957 until 1969. NICAP, with Keyhoe at the helm, proved to be an effective and influential group, with high level military and government officials on its board of governors. NICAP was a leader among the many voices clamoring for a review of the Air Force handling of UFO investigations, and they succeeded in getting one...with a little help from their otherworldly friends: "... the House Armed Services Committee convened the first formal hearing on UFOs on April 5, 1966, as a direct response to the highly publicized UFO sighting wave then in progress and widespread journalistic criticism of

---

13 Refer to Keel's *Operation Trojan Horse* (1970) and *The Mothman Prophecies* (1975) for more on these subjects. (see Bibliography for publishing details).

the Air Force UFO project."[14] As a result of the hearing, an independent study group headed by physicist Edward Condon at the University of Colorado was commissioned.[15] Among the participants in the study were NICAP and APRO, the Aerial Phenomena Research Organization, headed by the husband and wife team of Jim and Coral Lorenzen (whom we met in Chapter 2). Founded 1952, APRO made important and lasting contributions to the field of ufology.

It was a truly international organization, receiving reports from field representatives in over 40 countries, as well as the contributions of dozens of scientific consultants. All of this was coordinated and managed by the Lorenzens with a tiny staff on a shoestring budget—they weren't even able to afford a full-time employee and an office outside their home until 1969.[16] And importantly for our story, it was APRO that put the Gerry Irwin story on the map of ufology.

What was it that the Lorenzens found so compelling about Gerry's case, anyway? The answer to that question probably has to do with the fact that Gerry's experience was strongly suggestive of a new phenomenon in the world of UFO research. This phenomenon was completely unknown to the public at the time, and indeed, even the Lorenzens themselves had only recently heard of cases that seemed to feature it. In later decades however, it would be known by a term that has since become a household word.

---

14 Hall, Richard. "Congressional Interest in UFOs." *Journal of UFO History* 1.5 (2004): 2. NICAP. Web.
15 Ibid.
16 Clark, Jerome. *The UFO Encyclopedia, Volume 2* (Detroit: Omnigraphics, 1992), 14.

Chapter 7: Alien Abduction and APRO

According to African lore, Credo [Mutwa] says, "star people" have come from the heavens in "magic sky boats" for thousands of years... Even the great Zulu warrior king Shaka was "kidnapped" by the "mantindane." — Dr. John E. Mack[1]

What was known of the UFO abduction phenomenon, named or unnamed, in America circa 1959? It is a crucial question for a number of reasons, not least of which is the question of hoaxing. In a case like Gerry's, with no other witnesses to his sighting, this is a question that naturally arises. As we saw previously, papers found by the sheriff in Gerry's car indicated he was due back at his base that same day (i.e. Friday, February 20). One might be tempted to ask: *did he fake the whole thing as a cover for being late getting back from leave*? Based strictly from the available evidence, it's a possibility we cannot rule out.

But first, let's consider the notion that hoaxes must be imitative of something—a perspective that author Patrick Harpur brings to bear on the mystery of crop circles, when he writes:

...as William James reminds us, imposture is always imitative. Just as one swindler imitates a previous swindler, but the first swindler of that kind imitated someone who was honest, so it seems likely that hoaxers need "real" crop circles to copy. "You can no more create an absolutely new trick than you can create a new word without any previous basis.

---

1   Mack, John E. *Passport to the Cosmos: Human Transformation and Alien Encounters* (New York: Crown, 1999), 192.

You do not know how to go about it."[2]

Following this line of thinking, if one were to perpetrate a hoax of an alien abduction in 1959, what prototype was there to mimic?

The first cases of "alien abduction" as the phenomenon later became known, did not receive significant publicity until the mid-1960s with the publication of stories about Antonio Villas Boas (1965) from Brazil, and Betty and Barney Hill (1966) from New Hampshire, although the actual events reported had occurred several years earlier (1957 in the former and 1961 in the latter.) This chronology clearly demonstrates that whatever it was that Gerry was talking about, he could not have been inspired by any existing abduction stories, as it appears there simply weren't any.

Abduction vs the Contactee Phenomenon

So what exactly constitutes an "abduction" type of close encounter? Basically, these are the stories that involve themes such as missing time, amnesia and/or paralysis somehow induced by the UFO occupants, and being forcibly taken aboard an alien craft, etc. The late Richard Hall of NICAP listed a number of important differences that distinguished the abductee from the contactee phenomenon. Among them were the fact that in abductions, the UFO occupants seemed to initiate the contact, with a specific purpose that seemed to center on physical examination, and it involved a relationship that was not voluntary for the human participant—who was typically in a trance. Contactees, on the other hand, gave tremendously variable accounts of willing participation with "beautiful and friendly human-like mentors from other planets" bearing messages. By contrast, the abductor-type entities were "businesslike diminutive humanoids with a hidden agenda," and abductees seemed to refer to "a phenomenon with consistent and recurring properties."[3]

---

2 Harpur, Patrick. *Daimonic Reality: A Field Guide to the Otherworld* (Enumclaw, WA: Pine Winds, 2003), 163.

3 Hall, Richard. *The UFO Evidence: A Thirty-Year Report* (Lanham, MD: Scarecrow, 2001), 511.

Villas Boas and APRO

In the history of alien abduction, the Villas Boas case is generally regarded as the 'ground zero' of the phenomenon, and it has special relevance for our story. This event took place in the remote countryside of the state of Minas Gerais, Brazil, near the town of Sao Francisco de Salles. At exactly 1 a.m. on October 16, 1957, a young farmer named Antonio Villas Boas was out ploughing his field when he noticed something like a bright red star in the sky, slowly growing larger as it moved in his direction.

After a few moments, he realized it was moving "at a terrific speed," and shortly, what now appeared as a brilliant egg-shaped object was hovering directly above him. The light it gave off was so intense that it drowned out his tractor headlights completely. Soon the object landed, whereupon short, humanoid occupants, wearing bizarre, helmeted suits emerged, chased him down, and dragged him back to their craft.[4]

Villas Boas was taken into a room where he was forcibly undressed and sponged down with a clear gel-like substance. He was then brought to another room furnished with a "couch" of some kind, where blood samples were drawn from beneath his chin. Then he was left alone while a strange gas filled the space, causing him to vomit. After a long while, a door opened, and a short young blonde woman—completely nude—strolled in. Apart for some odd features, like "hardly visible" lips, and cheekbones that yielded to the touch, she seemed human-like.[5]

She made it clear by her movements just what it was she wanted from him, and soon they engaged in what Villas Boas described as a "normal act" with the woman reacting typically; the main exceptions being that there was no kissing, and she occasionally uttered disturbing, animal-like growls. (Villas Boas had also commented on the barking dog-like language spoken by the crew members.)[6]

After two rounds of these "normal acts," the woman suddenly gave Villas Boas the cold shoulder, which he understood to mean that he was

---

4   Creighton, Gordon. "Even More Amazing: Part I" *Flying Saucer Review* July-Aug. 1966: 25.

5   Creighton, Gordon. "Even More Amazing: Parts II & III" *Flying Saucer Review* Sept.-Oct. & Nov.-Dec. 1966.

6   Ibid.

merely being used like "a good stallion to improve their own stock." Before leaving him, the woman gestured at her belly, then at Villas Boas, and lastly up towards the heavens. At this point, Villas Boas was given his clothes, and when he had dressed he was taken on a tour of the craft before being escorted back outside to his farm field. He then watched in wonder as the object rose up in the air and "shot off like a bullet towards the south," disappearing in a few seconds. The time was now 5:30 a.m., and thus he estimated that he'd spent about four-and-a-quarter hours aboard the "strange machine."[7]

This information was drawn from testimony provided in person by Villas Boas to journalist Joao Martins and physician Dr. Olavo Fontes on February 22, 1958, (about four months after the incident, and interestingly, almost exactly one year before Gerry's encounter). Fontes was at that time Brazil's leading UFO investigator, as well as APRO's Brazilian correspondent.

According to author and researcher Jerome Clark, although Fontes found Villas Boas to be a highly credible witness, he declined to publish his story, choosing instead to send a "private report" to the Lorenzens. The Lorenzens also chose not to publish, but they did apparently discuss it privately with fellow ufologists. Now we come to a detail that clearly demonstrates just how volatile this subject matter must have seemed in the staid and serious atmosphere of 1950s era UFO studies. As Clark wrote:

> Nonetheless, when a critic learned of its existence, he attacked the Lorenzens for associating themselves with a man (Fontes) so gullible as to have listened to a story about an "alleged rape...by a somewhat uninhibited female from space." [cit.] Defending Fontes (regarded by most ufologists as a sober researcher), Coral Lorenzen retorted that the story was not about "rape" but "seduction"; in any event, it "was never published in the *APRO Bulletin*, nor was it mentioned in my book for the simple reason that we do not feel it was sufficiently authenticated." [cit.] In fact, Lorenzen privately considered the story intriguing. [cit.][8]

---

7   Creighton, Gordon. "Even More Amazing: Parts III & IV" *Flying Saucer Review* Nov.-Dec.1966 & Jan.-Feb. 1967.

8   Clark, Jerome. *The UFO Encyclopedia, 2nd ed.* 2 vols. (Detroit: Omnigraphics, 1998), 833-834. Reproduced with permission from publisher.

In 1962—four years after speaking with Fontes—Villas Boas agreed to be interviewed by a pair of Brazilian ufologists, who went on to become the first to publish his remarkable tale. The story appeared in the *SBEDV Boletim*, April/July, 1962. Clark continues:

> Though written in English, the article drew little attention outside Brazil. But in its January/February 1965 issue England's *Flying Saucer Review* (FSR) afforded prominent treatment to what it called "the most amazing case of all." Between then and 1972 FSR's Gordon Creighton wrote no fewer than eight articles on the Villas Boas affair. Soon the Lorenzens, abandoning their reservations, published Fontes' full report in their 1967 book *Flying Saucer Occupants*. By the end of the decade, the Villas Boas episode would become one of the best known of all CE3s [Close Encounters of the Third kind.][9]

Sitting on a Bombshell

The important point here is that while Gerry could not have known of the Villas Boas case—the world's first documented alien abduction—the Lorenzens certainly did. Not only was Dr. Fontes their trusted point man in Brazil; he was essentially passing the ball to them.

In fact, it seems downright uncanny that the people who were in the preeminent position to publish the Villas Boas case—who were basically just sitting on this bombshell—were physically located so close to Gerry's duty location (Alamogordo is a mere 86 miles from El Paso), and thus were ideally situated to jump on Gerry's story. They had been holding the Villas Boas story for less than a year when they got wind of Gerry's encounter, and it must have sparked some real excitement. Would this turn out to be the world's second known alien abduction?

Gerry Enters the APRO Files

Although it would be many years before the term "alien abduction" was even coined, the outlines of this phenomenon were definitely taking shape in Gerry's story. While the Lorenzens never made any explicit claims of this sort regarding Gerry encounter, they were openly exploring a number

---

9   Ibid.

of possible abduction-like scenarios. In her *APRO Bulletin* article, Coral conjectured that unknown entities associated with Gerry's UFO sighting were somehow responsible for his unconsciousness and memory loss, and that these entities may have interacted with him (including physically) during the time occluded by his amnesia. Here Coral speculates on how Gerry's sports jacket could have gone missing:

> When he came to 24 hours later in the Cedar City Hospital, he was talking about, 'jacket on the bush' but doesn't know why he mentioned it. There is one important point, however, and that is the fact that Irwin was wearing, besides the normal clothing, a sports jacket with an overcoat buttoned over it. He had it on when he left the car, and said that his overcoat was on and buttoned when he got to the hospital, according to hospital attendants, but that his jacket was missing. The jacket was just simply not on him when he was undressed by attendants at the hospital. Nor was it found during the air and ground search, nor was it in the car. It can be theorized that the jacket was stolen, but by whom and when, except during the period that he was lying unconscious near that lonely road...[10]

Here she pursues this line of inquiry further, obviously troubled by the implications:

> When removed to the hospital, a piece of his apparel was missing—an ordinary sports jacket. What would anyone want with a sports jacket? The ordinary thief would have taken any other things of value, but none were missing—not even money.[11] Even if other valuable articles had been taken, we would have some sort of explanation, but none for the light that Irwin had observed before losing consciousness. The light and his unconscious state must be connected. But how? It is evident that his overcoat and his sports jacket were taken from him while he was unconscious, and the overcoat put back on and buttoned up again. But why? Was it an oversight?

---

10 Lorenzen, Coral E., 1, 10. Reproduced with permission from Larry Lorenzen.
11 For some reason, this detail had changed by the time Jim's article came out. He wrote, "Thirty dollars in bills which he had been carrying in his shirt pocket was also missing." See: Lorenzen, L.J., 20.

After considerable thought on this problem, the possibility that the jacket being left off was just an oversight seems reasonable. When he was regaining consciousness, Irwin was mumbling about "jacket on the bush." Was his conscious mind momentarily concerned with a memory of something which had stuck in his mind during the time he was unconscious? Had he, while he was in his state of unconsciousness (or whatever the state was) been worried because he saw his jacket hanging on a bush?

The jacket was not found during the air and ground search, so it was taken away by someone. Why? It does not seem logical that a man would be knocked unconscious for the purpose of stealing his sports jacket. It seems more correct that the jacket was an oversight, and that it was taken away later—perhaps after Irwin was taken to the hospital and the searchers were gone.

Taking into consideration all the strange coincidences and facts about this incident, there is a strong possibility that Irwin saw a UAO [unidentified aerial object] by accident, attempted to approach it and was incapacitated *by some means not yet known to men*, thoroughly examined, and the examiners, *whoever or whatever they were*, not being familiar with a man's conventional clothing, overlooked putting the jacket back on Irwin. Perhaps they were interrupted when another car approached, or when the conservation agent and the police started searching for Irwin, and had to take the jacket along rather than attempt to get it back on their unconscious victim.[12] [emphasis added]

So clearly, Coral Lorenzen is poking around the edges here of the phenomenon that we now call alien abduction. She's considering a hypothesis involving non-human entities who incapacitated Gerry by unknown means, removed his clothing, and then "thoroughly examined" him. She even goes so far as to suggest that these entities must be unfamiliar with human clothing, since they forgot to put his jacket back on! While this does not necessarily imply abduction, it is certainly in the ball park.

Jim's Analysis
Now let's look at what Jim Lorenzen had to say in this regard, in his

---

12 Lorenzen, Coral E., 10.

article published three and a half years later.[13] Note that in what follows, Lorenzen seems to accept Gerry's return visit story at face value—surely a solid vote of confidence for Gerry's sincerity and credibility. This is an important point to consider in view of the fact that Gerry is our only witness to the event.

Jim speculates that when Gerry crested the ridgeline, whatever he laid eyes on must have motivated him to write the second note, which he attached to his jacket. Then he left his jacket on a bush where he hoped it would be found by searchers.

Jim goes on to remark on the role psychological shock plays in forming amnesia—i.e. confronting a situation that one simply can't bring oneself to "face or accept"— implying that this may be what happened to Gerry. He suggests that although Gerry initially believed he was looking for a plane crash, what he actually found was something jarringly different; something which made him afraid he'd be long gone by the time the searchers got there. Thus he felt compelled to leave the second note.[14]

Intriguingly however, after having just proposed this relatively conventional explanation for Gerry's amnesia, Jim abruptly switches tracks; expressing his intuition that Gerry was subjected to "some bizarre influence which caused his hysteria—and later, amnesia." Continuing with this line of thought, Jim proposes that this "influence" installed "memory blocks" of some kind—after Gerry left his jacket behind with the note on it—producing Gerry's repeated blackouts and "progressive amnesia." He reasons that these "blocks" were designed to accentuate Gerry's amnesia "or otherwise complicate matters to prevent solution," whenever Gerry tried to retrieve his buried memories.[15]

As far as Gerry's motivation for returning to Utah and destroying the note, Jim relates that initially he suspected the Army of overtly manipulating Gerry via post-hypnotic/post-amytol suggestion to get rid of the evidence. But he discards this notion as being too inexact and too unlike his expectations of Army behavior. Rather, he finds it more reasonable to think it could have been the unintentional result of a poorly

13 Lorenzen, L. J., 25-26.
14 Ibid., 25.
15 Ibid., 26.

articulated suggestion to get rid of whatever might be troubling him.

Jim elaborates that what he actually *would* expect from the Army, would be for them to send a detachment of men to the locale of Gerry's incident to look for evidence. He reasons that if Army intelligence had gotten involved, they might have indeed utilized a "post-amytal suggestion" to achieve their aims, but he quickly discounts this possibility since there was no evidence of anyone other than Gerry's doctor and a medic in attendance at Gerry's amytal interview. In addition, Jim relates his view that the Army was dismissive of Gerry's case from the very beginning; a stance reflected by Army regulars who assumed Gerry was just "bucking for a discharge," as well as medical staff who seemed to regard his stories as mere fabrications. Jim suggests this mindset was another likely factor impelling Gerry's decision to absent himself without leave.[16]

Ultimately however, Jim seems to favor the explanation that the "influence" he spoke of was largely responsible for Gerry's strange behavior via the "blocks" it had planted and the "mental mechanism" they triggered. By contrast, human intervention merely activated the mechanism already in place whenever Gerry got too close to remembering.[17]

For a comparison to Gerry's case, Jim calls attention to a series of Brazilian reports brought to APRO's attention by Dr. Olavo Fontes— whom we've just discussed in connection with the Villas Boas case. These cases all involved children who vanished in areas of simultaneous UFO activity. When they reappeared, sometimes after days had elapsed, the children had no recall of what they'd experienced.[18]

In his assessment, Jim Lorenzen comes ever so close without saying it outright—that Gerry was abducted. But what he proposes explicitly is astonishing enough—that Gerry's mind was manipulated by non-human entities.

---

16 Ibid.
17 Ibid.
18 Ibid.

Chapter 8: Two Locations

The fate of all explanation is to close one door only to have another fly wide open. — Charles Fort [1]

Of all the haunting questions woven into the fabric of the Gerry Irwin story, one of the most vexing and provocative of all is what I have come to call the "Two Locations Conundrum," or TLC for short. It lies at the very heart of the mystery, and any attempt to make sense of it only leads to confusion and more questions.

Briefly stated, here is the problem. All the newspaper accounts I have found report that Gerry's UFO sighting occurred on Highway 20, which intersects with Interstate 15 (known as U.S. 91 in 1959) about 37 miles northeast of Cedar City. According to the Lorenzens on the other hand, Highway 14 (which comes off of I-15 right in Cedar City) was the location of both the UFO sighting and Gerry's return visit in April.[2] These two locations are roughly 30 to 35 miles apart as the crow flies, and nearly 50 miles by road. What could account for this glaring discrepancy?

As we proceed, I will refer to this conundrum in two parts. "TLC I" will refer to the problem of two different locations reported for the UFO sighting. If, after examining the evidence, we decide to trust the version of events printed in the newspapers, then we come to "TLC II" the problem of the UFO sighting location being different from the location of Gerry's return visit to Utah in April—the place where he finds his missing jacket.

---

1   Fort, Charles. *The Book of the Damned* (New York: Boni and Liveright, 1919), Ch. 3.
2   Lorenzen, L. J., 22.

But First, a Word from Otto Fife

More than three years after beginning this project, I happened to stumble across an entry on the Irwin case in a massive UFO history written and privately published by a researcher named Loren E. Gross. Reading his summary of Gerry's story, I was amazed to discover that one of his sources was a document that, until that moment, I had not even known existed. It was a letter from the Iron County Sheriff—Otto Fife—to one C.H. Marck Jr. of Wheat Ridge, Colorado. In the letter, the sheriff recounts what Gerry told him about his recent adventure.

Within the narrow confines of my research project, this was a bombshell. I had gone to considerable trouble three years earlier tracking down living friends and relatives of the late sheriff, in order to quiz them concerning anything he may have shared about Gerry. Eventually I was able to speak with two nephews, one grand-nephew and two good friends of Mr. Fife, but as luck would have it, none of them could remember him mentioning a single word about Gerry's case. And so, I was forced to surrender yet again to one of the big challenges of chasing down old stories; namely, that witnesses die, taking their secrets to the grave. But now suddenly, here were tantalizing quotes taken directly from one of Sheriff Fife's letters!

Luckily, Mr. Gross had duly noted the source that had provided the document, which was the Center for UFO Studies (CUFOS). After contacting their very helpful team, I soon received scans of not one but two of Fife's letters. Most of the important information is contained in the first letter, dated March 4, 1959, and is worth reproducing in full. (Spelling errors have been retained; it certainly looks like the work of a busy, small-town sheriff typing his own letter.)

Dear Mr. Marck:

 With regards to your request for a report on Bernard G. Erwin; I will tell you the story as he told it to me.

 Mr. Erwin was returning to Ft. Bliss, Texas from his home in Nampa, Idaho. He was going south on U.S. highway 91 and he desided to go over the range of mts. east to highway 89. The State highway no. 20 connects these two U.S. highways and is located about 40 miles north of Cedar City.

It was dusk on the evening of Feb. 20, 1959 and about five miles into the mountains that Mr. Erwin saw a large object flying from south to north almost directly overhead. He thought it was an airoplane but couldn't tell the shape on account of the streams of light shooting out from it. He said it was very large and on account of the light radiating from it he thought it was on fire. He drove up the road for a few hundred yards and turned around and came back to the place where the object had flown over him. He could see the light to the north shinning up into the sky and thought the plane has crashed and was burning.

At this point Mr. Erwin wrote a note and left it on his car, stating that he had gone to investigate a plane crash. He started to climb the steep mountain in about a foot of snow. And the closer he came to the top of the hill, the brighter the light became. He figured the plane had crashed just over the top of the hill and he would be able to see it from the top. As he reached the top of the hill he blacked out and was out for about twenty three hours.

A passing motorist saw the note on the car that Mr. Erwin had left and called our department. I took a group with me including an ambulance, we hiked to the top of the hill following his tracks and found him passed out at this place. We brought him to the Iron County Hospital in Cedar City where he came to the next evening.

Mr. Erwin is a soldier stationed at Ft. Bliss Texas. When we notified his C.O., they flew in and took him back to Texas on the 24th of Feb.

I am very much interested in the stories you told in your letter and would like to learn more about such things.

I hope this information is what you wanted and I wil be willing to help in such matters all I can.

> Very truly,
> OTTO FIFE Sheriff of Iron Co.[3]

This letter is invaluable to our investigation, as it contains Gerry's earliest testimony. Since Fife was the first to hear Gerry's full story— almost immediately after he woke up from his long "sleep"—this letter arguably contains the most reliable and unadulterated version of events that Gerry could have provided. Considering all the problems Gerry suffered with his memory in the wake of his encounter, this first telling

---

3   Fife, Otto. Letter to C.H. Marck, March 4, 1959. [CUFOS archives].

becomes all the more critical. We observe details here that do not appear anywhere else.

For example, it's the only record we have of Gerry commenting on the size of the object, which he reportedly said was "very large." Also, whereas our previously quoted sources indicated that Gerry was unable to describe the object's shape, here we find out why: "...[he] couldn't tell the shape on account of the streams of light shooting out from it"—certainly a vivid image for the mind's eye!

The "crash" is remembered differently as well. Rather than the light flaring up from the "crash" site and then fading away, Fife records that Gerry "could see the light to the north shinning [sic] up into the sky and thought the plane has [sic] crashed and was burning." Then, not only did the light remain visible, but the closer he got to the top, "the brighter the light became." This is surely a critical detail to ponder. For anyone tempted to dismiss Gerry's sighting as some transitory hallucination produced by a brain anomaly, this would be strong evidence to the contrary. If he could still see the light—perhaps a half hour or more after the initial sighting—and it was only getting brighter with each step, then it would seem likely that he saw something that was really there.

Then, when he reached the top of the hill—where he'd expected to see it—he blacked out. In other words, at virtually the same instant he should have laid eyes on the object, he lost consciousness; just as you would expect if the mystery object was the cause of his condition, as Gerry himself had maintained.

Another important point is that the sheriff matter-of-factly confirms that the location of Gerry's incident was along Highway 20, specifically "five miles into the mountains." Having personally driven this route, I can add that this would place Gerry's encounter about six miles from the turnoff, since the mountains begin rising up from the valley floor after about a mile.

One further detail worth mentioning is that the sheriff uses the "Erwin" spelling, a point which seems to have influenced the conjectures of Loren Gross—as we'll see shortly.

All told, this account surely contains some of the most vivid details we've seen so far. Furthermore, I think it adds to the credibility to the case, given that Sheriff Fife, like the Lorenzens after him, shows no indication of doubting Gerry's story. And considering the sheriff's role as the proverbial "Johnny on the spot" in organizing and leading Gerry's rescue through the foot-deep snow, his "boots on the ground" perspective certainly lends some weight to his words.

A Necessary Deception?

Having introduced our "new" evidence, let's return now to the Two Locations Conundrum. One proposed solution to this has been put forth by the aforementioned Loren Gross. In his summary of Gerry's case, he notes "a few slight changes" made by the Lorenzens in their article, possibly in order "to grant the confused young man some privacy, or they may have wanted some way of screening out anyone claiming to be Erwin [sic] at a future date."[4] The changes he specifically mentions are: (1) The spelling of Gerry's last name: Gross thought the correct spelling was "Erwin," based on the sheriff's letter and some newspaper articles. As we know, the spelling was in fact "Irwin," just as the Lorenzens had written it; (2) The spelling of the sheriff's name, which he correctly noted was "Fife" and not "Pfief," as the Lorenzens rendered it; and (3) The highway, which Mr. Gross observes was Highway 20 and not Highway 14 (in accordance with both the newspapers and Fife's letter).

To recap then, Gross' proposition is that the factual discrepancies were introduced by the Lorenzens essentially as a form of misdirection, to either protect Gerry's privacy or to screen out potential Gerry Irwin imposters. To address the imposter/caller screening notion first, it's likely that Gross got this idea from a note—captioned "An Open Letter to Gerry Irwin"—that Jim Lorenzen tacked onto the end of his 1962 article, asking Gerry to call him if he happened to read it.[5] Looked at from this angle, it would potentially make sense for Jim to give out some false details that the real Gerry Irwin could correct—if and when he called—in order to prove his identity.

But there are some real problems with this caller screening idea. To

---

4   Gross, Loren E. *The Fifth Horseman of the Apocalypse—UFOs: A History, 1959 January-March* (Fremont, CA: ©Loren E. Gross, 1999), Fn. 73.

5   We'll discuss more of this note in the next chapter.

begin with, how likely would it be for the Lorenzens to be bombarded by phone calls from imposters in the first place? And even if they actually did have a problem of that sort, how hard would it be to identify the real Gerry? After all, they knew him personally, so one would think that even just his voice and mannerisms would provide all the confirmation they needed; and if not, a few carefully worded questions would probably take care of the rest.

And as far as the proposal that Jim Lorenzen was protecting Gerry's privacy, I think we can safely dispense with this on the grounds that Gerry's last name was in fact spelled correctly in the article, contrary to what Gross believed.

There's another point against the idea of intentional deception—whether for screening callers or for protecting privacy. When the Lorenzens finally got around to publishing Gerry's story in their book *Encounters with UFO Occupants* in 1976—14 years after Jim's 1962 article appeared in *Flying Saucers*—they left all the information unchanged. Presumably by then they would have had very little concern about potential Gerry Irwin imposters, especially since this time around they omitted the note requesting Gerry to call them. It would have been a simple matter to include the correct data in this later publication—along with a brief explanation for the previous need for deception—but they didn't.

In any case, I think it goes without saying that the actual location of an event is of critical importance. What are the first questions we ask about *any* event? They're always the same ones; once we know *what* happened, we want to know *when and where*? It seems hard to believe that these dedicated researchers would falsify this critical information—which would be handed down to posterity—merely to avoid the possibility of an unwanted phone call!

A Convergence of Routes?
Another possible answer to the TLC emerged from a conversation with a friend who suggested a scenario that could have provided a simple solution to both TLC I and TLC II. She pointed out that route numbers frequently change, so it's possible that in 1959 the configuration of the highway route numbers was different—in other words that the two routes

might have run together over that stretch of road at that time.

To explore that possibility, I was able to locate a 1961 Utah state highway map (being published only two years later, it's probably close enough for our purposes). The map shows that not much has changed since then except that, as noted above, Interstate 15 at that time was still known as U.S. 91. Highway 14 and Highway 20 were in the same places

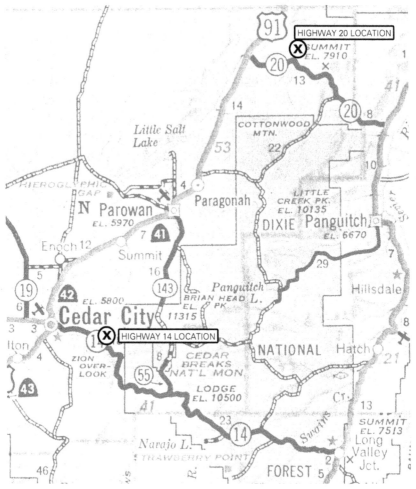

1961 road map showing Cedar City and the approximate locations of the two sites.
(Utah State Road Commission map)

then as they are now, roughly parallel east-west roads intersecting with Interstate 15 about 37 miles apart. And besides, as we proceed it will become clear that geographical clues in the existing reports also confirm that the highways in question were in fact in the same positions then as they are now.

A Short Cut vs. the Scenic Route

In other words, the respective sources are *internally* consistent in regards to location. Looking at Jim Lorenzen's report first, there seems to be no question, given the context, that Gerry really did mean Highway 14. Jim writes,

> At Cedar City he turned left (southeast on route 14) without hesitation. Though little traveled, it afforded a convenient link between highways 91 and 89. It was a time-saving route which had become a habitual part of his returns to Ft. Bliss from Nampa, Idaho. Recalling the wild beauty of this mountain country, he found himself wishing that he had been able to accomplish this leg of the trip in daylight.[6]

First off, it is important to note that Highway 14 is the only highway one *can* turn left on in Cedar City (when heading south). Next, I can personally vouch for the beautiful mountain scenery one encounters along Highway 14, as I have driven that route as well as Highway 20 on a site visit as part of my research. Highway 14 features curvy, steep grades, a 10,500-ft. mountain pass, and spectacular views. But a shortcut? Compared to what? The only real competitor is Highway 20 which is much lower in altitude (by nearly half a mile) as well as only half the distance (21 miles versus 41 miles), and thereby well over twice as fast. So, given a choice between the only two reasonable routes in the area, Highway 20 wins hands down as a shortcut.

One further point in this regard is that Gerry had good reason to seek out a shortcut. The sheriff found papers in Gerry's car indicating that Gerry was due back at his base that very day, which would mean he was running late. In that case Gerry's primary concern would be speed. Thus,

---

6 Lorenzen, L. J., 18.

it would seem a strange decision indeed to go out of his way to take a high, winding mountain road stretching twice as long, in the dark of night no less, rather than the obvious choice of Highway 20.

The newspaper articles as well as Fife's letter—which all name the Highway 20 location—provide geographical context as well. Several articles mention that Gerry was taking a shortcut between 91 and 89. Also some of the newspapers along with Fife's letter mention that Highway 20 is north of Cedar City, with Fife giving a figure of "about 40 miles north of Cedar City."

Additionally, it's worth noting that the newspaper stories certainly did not all come from a single source; there were, at minimum, five different reporters involved. It's clear from the differing content and typos, that the articles carried by the AP and the UPI came from different "stringers" (as the wire service contributors were called), and there were also independent articles (i.e. not merely rewrites of the AP and UPI stories) in the *Deseret News and Telegram* (Salt Lake), The *Idaho Free Press* (Nampa, Idaho), and the *Salt Lake Tribune*.

The many articles that appeared were published in three waves over the course of about four days; the first wave appeared while Gerry was still unconscious, a second after he woke up, and a third smaller wave when he was being prepared to be shipped back to Ft. Bliss. The number of different articles on different dates and by different reporters would all seem to argue against a simple mistake. In all of that media attention, Highway 20 is the only highway mentioned by name.

Troubling Discrepancies

Now we come to a very thorny problem. If we set aside the possibility of a cover-up for the moment, then we have to ask, *why would the normally reliable Lorenzens have gotten the location of the sighting wrong?* We know that they had access to the newspaper accounts because Coral Lorenzen actually mentions, "the press, in their reports..."[7] In fact, it seems reasonable enough to presume that those reports are what led them to the story in the first place. It's worth repeating that the Lorenzens and APRO had an international reputation for their dedication and integrity.

---

7   Lorenzen, Coral E., 1.

How could they have made such an obvious blunder? This problem becomes all the more interesting now as we move ahead to Gerry's return visit to Utah in April and TLC II.

Remember that on Saturday April 18, Gerry entered a trance and felt a strong urge to return to the scene of his encounter. Going AWOL, he hopped on a bus to Utah and disembarked in Cedar City at the intersection of Highway 14. He followed this highway five or six miles out of town, veered off into the desert scrub, and found his jacket with the note attached, which he promptly burned without reading.[8]

The Lay of the Land

Assuming these events actually occurred the way Gerry remembered them, it is completely logical and consistent with the local geography that it happened along Highway 14. First off, he could not have gotten off the bus in Cedar City at the Highway 20 intersection, because it's not there; that intersection is 37 miles to the northeast. In other words, he could not have walked 5 or 6 miles from Cedar City and been anywhere near Highway 20.

A hill north of Highway 20. (Photo by David Booher)

---

8   Lorenzen, L.J., 22-23.

I have driven through Cedar City and turned onto Hwy 14 (from Main St.), following it out of town and up Cedar Canyon. Going that way, one reaches the edge of the town quickly, after only several blocks at most. Five or six miles takes you well up into the canyon and the rugged countryside thereabouts. This detail about the walking distance is vital, because it makes it possible for the story to unfold as it does. After Gerry leaves the location of his jacket, *he still has enough time to walk back to Cedar City before dark.*[9]

Near Highway 14, about six miles east of Cedar City. (Photo by David Booher)

This bears repeating. Gerry simply could not have walked from Cedar City to the location of his original incident and back even in a full day of walking, or *two* days for that matter! In fact, even covering that distance *one-way* in a single day (roughly 43 miles) would hardly be possible for the average person, given that the typical rate of walking (3 miles per

---

9   Ibid., 23.

hour) would make for a grueling 14-hour day! Could Gerry have hitch-hiked then? Yes, undoubtedly, he *could* have, but that would completely negate his memory, which hinges on him walking out from Cedar City to find his jacket and walking back again in one afternoon (a round trip of about four hours, quite doable in other words). Likewise, there is nothing in the record to suggest he took the bus to Highway 20 and back either.

In short then, the three sources (i.e. the newspapers, Fife's letter, and the Lorenzens) are (mostly) internally consistent regarding locations. If the Lorenzens are correct all the way, then we have no location conundrum, neither TLC I nor TLC II. However, their one inconsistency, as we've seen, is in referring to Highway 14 as a "shortcut." And since we have the wild card of Gerry's memory problems to take into consideration (Gerry being their primary source, at least for the return visit) we're really left with a dilemma.

For the moment, let's take the path of trusting the authority of Sheriff Fife and the newspapers and accept that the UFO was seen on Hwy 20, putting us on a collision course with TLC II. Now we're directly confronted with the troubling question: *How on Earth did Gerry's jacket get to the second location? And how would Gerry have known it was there?* We'll attempt to wade through that patch of proverbial quicksand shortly.

Later on in our story, we'll be examining some handwritten notes in detail that the Lorenzens were keeping as they investigated Gerry's case, but for now we'll just take a peek at them. Although some of the notes are badly faded and partially illegible, I was able to make out the timeline they recorded at least. Interestingly, this timeline is slightly different than what's written in Jim's 1962 article. We'll compare what the Lorenzens wrote—indicated by an (L)—to what the Army records state, as indicated by an (A):

- April 17: "Discharged." [from WBAH]. (L) and (A)
- April 18: "Developed urge to go back to Utah." (L)
- April 20: "Returned to scene." [of incident] (L)
  First day of AWOL. (A)
- April 21: "Turned self in." [to police] (L)
- April 25: Last day of AWOL. (A)

- April 26:   First day of confinement. (A)
- May 3:   Last day of confinement. (A)
- May 4:   "Returned to Bliss." (L)
- May 5:   "Article 15" [non-judicial punishment]. (L)
             Demotion from SP4 to Pfc (A)

Taking all of this into account, we can suggest a timeline that holds together fairly well, as follows: Gerry was released from WBAH on April 17. The next day he developed an urge to return to Utah. But apparently—in contradiction to Jim's 1962 article—he did not act on this urge until two days later, i.e. April 20; as Army AWOL records confirm.

The next day, April 21—as Jim's article points out as well—Gerry turned himself in to local police. Gerry spoke with Sheriff Fife the next day, and Fife contacted the Army. But MPs from Fort Ord did not arrive until a few days later, indicated by the fact that Gerry's AWOL didn't officially end until April 25. (AWOL time doesn't end until the offender is back under Army control, and it's not uncommon—from what I've read—for the Army to take its time in collecting AWOL offenders.)

It appears that on April 26, the MPs picked up Gerry and escorted him to Ft. Ord, thus beginning Gerry's confinement, which didn't end until he arrived back at Ft. Bliss on May 3. The Lorenzens have him returning on May 4, but this minor discrepancy could possibly be chalked up to the way the time was accounted for. Then the Lorenzens note that Gerry received his Article 15 (non-judicial punishment)[10] on May 5, which corresponds exactly with the Army records of his demotion. Elsewhere, the Lorenzens note that Gerry's punishment amounted to a fine and a demotion in rank.

In summary then, the dates provided by the Lorenzens are all quite plausible, setting aside the two-day discrepancy between Jim's article and the handwritten timeline regarding the beginning date of the return-trip to Utah (which we'll take a closer look at later in the book). A discrepancy that is a little harder to reconcile though, concerns the date of the original incident. The newspapers all list the date as February 20. The *APRO Bulletin* article by Coral Lorenzen states that it happened on February 22. Jim's 1962 article provides a date of February 28. Is this nothing more

---

10 This type of punishment is administered directly by the C.O.

than sloppy journalism, or is there something more going on here?

The Fruit Left Hanging

How could these researchers have gotten both the location and the date wrong (of the sighting at least, and possibly the return visit), when that information was readily available? I think it is obvious enough that the goal of any investigation is at least to try to find answers to the basic questions of: Who? What? When? Where? How? and Why? The first step would be to nail down the facts that are already established in the case, or at least the version of the facts currently known and/or reported, as a jumping off point. In Gerry's case, "Where?" and "When?" seem to have had clear and credible answers already. We're talking about low-hanging fruit here—why didn't they grab it?

The fact that they apparently got these few simple and obvious facts wrong is all the more interesting in view of what they got right. Here is a list of facts they reported that are corroborated by Gerry's service records:

- The fact that Gerry's initial, as well as subsequent, physical examinations by the Army could find nothing wrong with him.
- The fact that Gerry was found unconscious in downtown El Paso on March 16, taken to Southwest General Hospital, and then transferred to WBAH. Upon awakening he thought he was in Utah and that the date was the same as when he had the UFO sighting. This delusional date is given by the service records as February 20, but is reported as February 28 by Jim Lorenzen, which although incorrect, at least matches the date that he gave for the sighting.
- The name of Gerry's attending physician at WBAH (Valentine).
- The ward number (30) at the hospital, as well as the fact that it was a locked psychiatric ward.
- The dates of his 32-day admission to the hospital.
- The fact that Gerry was interviewed under the influence of sodium amytal during his admission.
- The fact that Gerry's actual rank was SP4 (Specialist 4), one rank higher than Private First Class, which was the rank reported by

the newspapers. This rank reflected his specialized credential as a Nike missile technician. Oddly enough, even most of the Army's own documents fail to note this higher rank, even though there is no question that he held it at that time.[11]

- The name of Gerry's physician (Broadbent) at the hospital in Cedar City, although Jim Lorenzen gives the name of the hospital as "Cedar City Hospital" when in fact it was called "Iron County Hospital." Broadbent is not actually mentioned by name in Gerry's records, but I did confirm that there was a Dr. Broadbent working at the hospital then.
- The date in July that Gerry went AWOL for the second time—just one day off here; actual was July 31 (Lorenzen reported August 1). Here Lorenzen was only repeating what Gerry's "orderly room" (the administrative office for Gerry's company) had told him.
- The fact that Gerry was listed as a deserter after 30 days.
- The fact that following Gerry's AWOL in April, Dr. Valentine was consulted, and that he gave his opinion that Gerry was normal and therefore responsible for his actions.
- The fact that (probably as a direct result of Valentine's opinion) Gerry was reduced in rank to Pfc soon after this same AWOL.[12]

Other Explanations

There are certainly some mundane explanations that could account for the Lorenzens' departures from the facts reported in the newspapers. We've already discussed one of these—the caller screening idea. What are some other possibilities?

For one, what if it was just sloppy journalism? Could it be that simple? It sounds believable at least. After all, the Lorenzens were researching and reporting on an enormous number of cases; perhaps they were simply overworked and they got a little careless. On that note, one might ask, *how much did they really care about accuracy?*

I found an interesting anecdote in an article on APRO's history that

---

11 Army Service Records.
12 Ibid.

may shed some light on this question. According to the article, when Coral read the new bestseller, *Flying Saucers-Serious Business* (by Frank Edwards—published in 1966), she said she was "appalled." Coral elaborated: "I counted 13 gross errors in his recounting of the Zamorra case (Socorro, New Mexico, April 24, 1964) alone."[13] She explained that she knew the correct details quite well because she and Jim had gone to the scene and investigated the case in person.[14] So Coral was appalled by reporting errors. Not exactly what you would expect from a careless researcher!

There are a couple of other points relevant to the carelessness/ sloppiness question. One is that—within the arc of the Lorenzens' UFO investigating careers—their work on this story took place during what should have been their prime. That is to say, by that time they were veteran researchers with lots of experience, and yet they were still relatively young and thus presumably energetic (they were both still in their thirties.) In addition, it should be clear by now that for the Lorenzens, Gerry's case was no ordinary case. They understood that it was potentially a game-changer, with far-reaching implications. So if they were going to be sloppy, you'd think they would have picked a less important case!

The other explanation for the discrepancies that comes to mind is that the Lorenzens simply assumed the newspapers were mistaken. Initially this sounds promising. But there's actually a big problem with both this and the other solution just mentioned.

Even if the Lorenzens were getting sloppy, or even if they dismissed certain facts from the newspapers in favor of Gerry's testimony, this simply cannot explain away the central mystery of Gerry's return visit to Utah. It all comes back to the jacket.

---

13 Ironically, this scathing critique of errors contains an error. The correct spelling of the name is Zamora (as in police officer Lonnie Zamora--the main witness in the case). As it turns out, however, this mistake was made not by Coral but by the interviewer.

14 Ruhl, Dick. "A History of APRO." *Official UFO* Vol. 1, No. 5, January 1976, 24. Print. Republished on: *Internet Archive Wayback Machine*, 02 Feb. 2005. Web. 11 May 2017.

Jacket on Bush

As we've seen, in order for Highway 20 to be the correct location for Gerry's return trip to Utah, we would have to rewrite a critical segment of Gerry's story to make it work. Along these same lines, Jim's article reports that Gerry found his jacket near Highway 14; and both times he mentions this highway, he provides identifying details that make it crystal clear he really means Highway 14. In other words, Jim is practically broadcasting that this was no simple reporting error. He might as well have said, "We are definitely talking about Highway 14, and *not* Highway 20." Regarding Jim's reporting here, sloppiness probably would not be the first word that springs to mind.

In any case, it looks like this conundrum is just not going away. Is there a way around this apparent impasse?

Here's an intriguing solution: What if *both* locations are correct? What if Gerry was somehow transported to a second location where he intentionally left his jacket on a bush with the note attached? Then at some point he was brought back to the first location. What if, even under the presumably extreme duress of the situation, he'd still been able to remember the one piece of evidence that could prove the reality of what he'd experienced? Could it be that—even though his mind had been shocked to its core by what he'd encountered—he'd retained just enough wherewithal to make himself remember the words *"jacket on bush?"*

Gerry certainly demonstrated clear and quick thinking under the gun when he wrote "STOP" on his car in shoe polish before setting off on his rescue attempt. Perhaps he still retained enough of his grace under pressure to manage this other, hypothetical feat. We already know that he was heard to be mumbling the phrase "jacket on bush" in the hospital while he was still unconscious; and in fact, this detail was in print before he even woke up.

Given that he had such a long blackout followed by amnesia, and that he was transported to Cedar City in the dead of night and unawares, it seems possible at least that he might have begun to conflate the *one important thing to remember*—the place where his jacket was located— with the place where his sighting occurred. That could explain in part why the Lorenzens—for whom Gerry was their primary informant—never even mentioned Highway 20.

In support of this scenario, recall that the searchers found no sign of Gerry's missing jacket. Since Gerry had attached a note to it, presumably he would have wanted someone to find it; therefore he would have left it in plain sight. And given Gerry's clear trail through the snow, it would have been quite obvious where he had wandered and thus where his jacket *should* have been. But Gerry knew exactly where his jacket was, and according to him, he found it near Highway 14, i.e., nowhere near Highway 20!

On the matter of leaving his jacket in plain view, I found some fascinating "new" speculation from Coral Lorenzen—contained in correspondence between Swedish author and researcher K. Gösta Rehn and Coral that I had received. In a letter dated June 5, 1959, Coral gave an account of the ongoing investigation into Gerry's case. On the subject of Gerry's original incident, she offered her conjecture about what happened during the time obscured by his amnesia. "...He took off his jacket, wrote the note describing what he had seen, wrapped it around a pencil, put it in the buttonhole of his jacket and *spread it on a small tree to attract attention, if searchers came, and if he was unable to contact them.* It seems apparent that Gerry knew he was facing something possibly dangerous and probably alien."[15] (emphasis added)

Returning to the detail about snow cover, one would think this would have made it relatively easy to determine if others had been in Gerry's vicinity, and thus could have meddled with him in some way. But according to the news articles, Sheriff Fife had said, "there were no marks of violence or any indication of foul play."[16] So clearly if Gerry was transported to our proposed second location, *it was not on the ground!*

UFO Airlift Down Under

In considering the airlift possibility, it would be logical to ask, *have there been other UFO cases featuring this phenomenon?*

In my research, I ran across a well-documented incident of this sort,

---

15 Lorenzen, Coral E. Letter to K. Gösta Rehn, June 5th, 1959. [Archives for the Unexplained (AFU), Sweden]

16 See Chapter 4.

half way around the world in kangaroo country. This is the case of a Finnish couple's close encounter in Queensland, Australia in 1971, investigated by researcher Bill Chalker.

The couple was driving home late one night through the countryside, when they saw two unidentified green lights just above the treetops. At that point they both experienced a kind of altered awareness in which the appearance of the road changed and it seemed as if they were continuously repeating the same lines to each other. Soon they caught sight of another strange object, hovering above them this time. This one had a circular arrangement of lights like those on a merry-go-round.[17]

They passed landmarks that were in actuality quite far apart in surprisingly quick succession, and arrived at a gas station in their destination city in less than half the time it should have taken. There were at least four towns on their route that they should have passed but saw no sign of. This last detail is takes on added importance in light of the fact that they had been hoping to refuel in one of those towns, since they had feared they were too low on gas to reach their destination.[18]

A motorist who had passed them early on in their journey was amazed when he eventually pulled into the same gas station, only to find the couple there before him. They had actually been there for a while already, lingering in puzzlement over the strange events and discussing them with the gas station attendant. The attendant, along with the couple, observed some strange markings on the hood of their car, as well as evidence of what looked like heat damage.[19]

All told, it makes for a fascinating case. Could something of this sort have happened to Gerry?

The Hoax Angle

On the other hand, what if Gerry just made it all up? What if it was all a hoax? What if he didn't see anything strange, but instead just waited for help to arrive that night and then had lain down in the snow and feigned

---

17 Chalker, Bill. "Australian 'Interrupted Journeys'" (©Bill Chalker, 1979). Published in *MUFON UFO Journal* No. 150, Aug. 1980.

18 Ibid.

19 Ibid.

unconsciousness? And after the initial hoax, what if he just kept faking more blackouts and amnesia and ultimately a return to Utah, cooking up all those interesting details?

We've previously considered the imitative aspect of hoaxes and how that doesn't seem to fit with Gerry's story. Now we'll pursue this line of thought a little further. Since there was no existing model to imitate, what are the chances that Gerry could have just invented the whole story on his own? Well, if he did, then we're looking at a degree of inventiveness and forethought that would make any science fiction writer proud.

Just look at the vivid story elements; the mysterious glowing object in the night sky crash-landing nearby, the quick-thinking soldier writing STOP on his vehicle before setting off on his search, the unconscious mumbling about the jacket on the bush, and the return to Utah in a trance. And then there's that truly riveting "scene"—the pencil with a note wrapped around it and inserted into a button hole, and then burning the note without reading it. It's like a Hollywood screenplay, and a good one at that!

Seriously though, what evidence would there be to suggest that Gerry had the predisposition necessary for masterminding such an elaborate hoax? Sure, it's clear that Gerry had more than enough smarts, but the question is: Did he have the kind of personality that gravitated towards things of a fantastic or theatrical nature, or in the arts of deception?

From everything I've gathered so far, including talking extensively with him as well as speaking with one of his daughters, Gerry is and always has been a very down to earth, nuts and bolts kind of guy. He has a lot of technical know-how and a knack for repairing electronic devices and rebuilding old radios, as well as fixing up his house. But with the exception of the curiosity Gerry demonstrated regarding his own UFO experience (as documented by the Lorenzens in the spring of 1959), I've seen no indication that he's ever taken an interest in either UFOs or science fiction. He seems to regard the whole subject of UFOs as utter nonsense, and he sees nothing especially interesting about his story. On that score at least, the hoax theory seems unconvincing.

Toeing the Line

The nail that sticks up will be hammered down. — Chinese Proverb

Besides, reporting a UFO is not a good excuse for anything whatever the need, considering the withering force of ridicule and ostracism endured by the typical UFO witness. UFOs are dismissed by all of our major institutions. The U.S. government, while secretly studying UFOs—which has been clearly documented—pursues a public policy of denial and ridicule,[20] with the media following suit. The scientific establishment, for reasons of its own, ridicules and marginalizes scientists who dare to conduct research on this phenomenon. It's no surprise then that—as Jacques Vallee has observed in the phenomenon as a whole—only one in ten UFO witnesses comes forward with a report.[21]

Just as important as our institutions, however, is the context of society as a whole. As much as we are loath to admit it, Americans are largely governed by the pressure of social conformity—and thus the constraints of socially acceptable beliefs—like any other society (perhaps this is why we tend to idolize rebels and mavericks). Along these lines, societal attitudes play a big role in determining what qualifies as reality, and from this, what passes for sane and/or appropriate behavior. Seeing and reporting UFOs does not generally make the cut. Therefore, those who engage in this behavior are thought to be either lying or mentally unsound, and should be shunned and/or humiliated as a result.

Of course, social conformity ebbs and flows over time, and in this regard the fifties were arguably the high-water mark of post-war America. Author Jay Stevens illuminates this point quite well, in his commentary on Ken Kesey's inspiration for writing *One Flew Over the Cuckoo's Nest*. Referring to Kesey's experience working on a veterans' hospital psych ward, Stevens writes:

...Kesey was not unaware that a mental hospital had wonderful

---

20 See Chapter 12.
21 Vallee, Jacques. *Confrontations: A Scientist's Search for Alien Contact* (New York: Ballantine, 1990), 18.

possibilities as an extended metaphor for the America of the 1950s. Here the game was simpler: one conformed or was made to conform via drugs and electroshock therapy. There was no room for either personal assertiveness or mild eccentricity. Anything that fouled the smooth workings of the system was crushed.[22]

And in what segment of society is conformity pressure the greatest? The obvious answer is the military, where "stepping out of line" results in immediate and harsh consequences. So there was Gerry, in a double social straightjacket—enlisted in the U. S. Army during the tightly controlled culture of 1950s America. Seen in this light, perhaps we can begin to perceive what he must have been up against. It's hard to imagine anyone in his situation making claims about UFOs lightly.

22 Stevens, Jay. *Storming Heaven: LSD and the American Dream* (NY: Grove, 1987), 227.

Chapter 9: No Return

People have always, it seems, had a way of vanishing without a trace along the River of No Return. Old man Campbell himself, owner of Campbell's Ferry, walked out his kitchen door one day to bring in firewood and was never seen again.[1] — Harold Peterson

What became of Gerry Irwin when APRO lost track of him and he deserted his post two months later? Where did he go when he fell of the edge of the map?

Jim Lorenzen wrote that his final meeting with Gerry occurred on May 30, when Gerry came to the Lorenzens' home in Alamogordo for a weekend visit. He said that due to Gerry's contact with the Army I.G., Gerry was to be admitted yet again to WBAH come July 10.

After that, wrote Jim, "I never saw him again." Gerry had promised the Lorenzens that he would keep them in the loop, but he never contacted them again. Jim later learned from Gerry's post that Gerry had disappeared from the base on August 1, and that 30 days later he was listed as a deserter.[2]

Somewhat poignantly, Lorenzen ends his piece with an "Open Letter" to Gerry himself. It begins, "If you read these words, please contact me by telephone collect…" Jim goes on to express his wish to know how Gerry is doing and whether he has "solved the mystery." He offers assistance for whatever Gerry might need and assures him there's no need for him to

---

1   Peterson, Harold. *The Last of the Mountain Men* (New York: Scribner, 1969), 36. Print.
2   Lorenzen, L.J., 25.

disclose his location if he'd prefer not to.

So where did Gerry go? As the old saying goes, *thereby hangs a tale;* one which I was fortunately able to reconstruct by combining the scattered details that Gerry recalled in our interviews with some vitally important documents I later received with Gerry's help.

It begins on July 31, when Gerry went to the Ft. Bliss Exchange and cashed a counter check for $50—drawn on El Paso National Bank—from a non-existent account. He needed some extra cash for the kind of Hail Mary he was planning. He had decided, apparently, that his only hope of healing his broken mind was to get away from the Army for a while and go back to his old haunts in the Idaho wilderness. That would take some money, and he must have been a little short. It would seem to be a true measure of his determination, if not desperation, that he was willing to resort to such an act in order to execute his plan, something clearly out of character for him.

That very day he would have also collected his pay, $141 per month at the time. So with paycheck money and pilfered cash in hand, Gerry made his escape. It's a long way from Ft. Bliss to McCall, Idaho—around 1300 miles. Gerry has no memory of how he got there. He had no car—he had not owned one since he had abandoned his vehicle in Utah more than five months previously. After talking it over with Gerry, the best guess we could come up with is that he took a bus.

When Gerry arrived in Idaho, he somehow managed to get a rucksack together and some supplies (but apparently, no gun), in the McCall area. As he vaguely remembers, he borrowed some things at his oldest sister's house, as she was living there with her husband at the time. The rucksack would have been quite Spartan by today's standards. "You just have a tarp," said Gerry, "and if you're going to move around you wrap all of your goods that you want to take with you in the tarp into a bundle and pack it on your back. And you'd have matches and, articles you could cook in, maybe tin cans that you could heat water in—we didn't necessarily have pots and pans with handles on them."

He brought along other essentials, like fish hooks and fishing line, and a bedroll. The tarp would serve as a roof for the simple lean-to type of shelters he was accustomed to building from sticks and branches. With his supplies ready, he set out into the woods, headed for the Big Creek/ Monumental Creek area that he was familiar with from his days working for the Forest Service, in the heart of what was officially called the Idaho Primitive Area (now The Frank Church-River of No Return Wilderness).

It was a trek of 70-to-80 miles to get to that area, first on Forest Service roads and then hiking off road across *very* rugged terrain, but for Gerry, this was home. His route along Lick Creek road had him cross the South Fork of the Salmon just ten miles south of the Irwins' old homestead. Like the salmon had done for untold millennia before him, he was returning to his headwaters. And being in the middle of the largest tract of roadless terrain in the lower 48 states, it would be hard to imagine a better place to go if one wanted to become lost to the outside world.

A History of Protection
This awe-inspiring expanse of wild country has a fascinating history. The area was originally the domain of Sheep Eater Indians as well as the Nez Perce (of Chief Joseph fame)[3]. Miners moved into the area starting in the 1860s, which led to the Indian wars and Indian removals of the 1870s. Eventually much of the area was set aside as federal timberland as a result of the Forest Reserve Act of 1891, passed by the U.S. Congress, which gave the President the power to create Forest Reserves, later renamed National Forests. A large portion (nearly half) of what is now the Frank Church-River of No Return Wilderness is comprised of a special area that was delineated within the National Forests called The Idaho Primitive Area (as it was known during Gerry's time there). The stage was set for the emergence of some truly remarkable legislation championed by an equally remarkable senator.

It just so happens that Frank Church (U.S. Senator- Idaho, in office 1957-1981), whom we mentioned previously for his role in reigning in intelligence agency abuses, was an energetic and tireless advocate of wilderness preservation. He sponsored the Wilderness Act of 1964, which

---

3   Some of the earliest armed clashes leading up to the Nez Perce War (1877)
    occurred in the vicinity of Warren and the Salmon River country. See: Edmunson,
    Cletus R. *A History of Warren, Idaho: Mining, Race & Environment*. Boise, ID:
    Boise State University, 2012. Print, Web. 48-49.

protected nine million acres of U.S. wildlands. In 1968, he sponsored the Wild and Scenic Rivers Act, which, among others, protected the Middle Fork of the Salmon River, and ensured that designated rivers remained free from development and were maintained in a free-flowing state, even in sections that were not federally owned.

Near the end of his life, Church's career culminated in the passage of the Central Idaho Wilderness Act in 1980. This act created the River of No Return Wilderness by combining the Idaho Primitive Area with two adjoining parcels—the Salmon River Breaks Primitive Area and the Magruder Corridor—for a combined area of 2.3 million acres (at 3700 square miles, that's the largest roadless area, and the second largest protected wilderness area, outside of Alaska). It also brought 125 miles of the Main Salmon River under the protection of the Wild and Scenic Rivers Act. In 1984, as Frank Church was dying of pancreatic cancer at age 59, Congress renamed the wilderness as The Frank Church- River of No Return Wilderness in his honor.

Frank's Creatures, Great and Small

The wilderness, known locally as "The Frank," is home to a robust variety of wildlife. Big game species include moose, elk, bighorn sheep, mountain goats, mule deer, and white tail deer. Black bears, mountain lions and wolves roam throughout much of the area, along with red fox, lynx and coyote. Otters feed on the resident fish, which include three species of trout and at least two species of salmon. It also serves as a critical habitat for wolverines, a species that was recently under consideration for protection under the Endangered Species Act.

It was into this wild province that Gerry returned, instinctively, to apply the healing balm of pristine nature to the mysterious wound in his mind. It would be easy to imagine that under the circumstances, he would have been distracted and apprehensive, and perhaps he was. He certainly didn't seem to have a lot going in his favor. There he was, a deserter on the run from the Army, struggling to overcome problems that officially did not exist, stemming from a cause (a UFO) that also officially did not exist.

However, whether the wilderness welcomed him with a warm embrace, or whether it is simply a matter of seeing the past through rose-colored lenses, Gerry now remembers that he enjoyed his wilderness walkabout. When I asked him why he chose that area, he replied: "I knew that area. *It wasn't somewhere that anything was going to happen that I knew was dangerous* or something like that... [emphasis added] The place was quiet; you didn't hear any airplanes going over or anything... And the fishing was good...plenty of trout." (As far as the safety level of the area, we'll soon see that actually there *were* serious concerns in the backcountry. Gerry's fond recollection here may reflect more on the relief he likely felt at having gotten away from his oppressive situation in the Army—for a while at least—and arriving back in his old haunts.)

For a while, Gerry camped where he saw fit, and provided for himself by fishing in the abundant trout streams of the area. He would fashion a simple fishing rod from a willow branch or whatever was at hand. Beaver ponds were particularly good, as the slow-moving water harbored abundant insects which in turn attracted fish.

Here he remembers a close brush he had with some wildlife:

> I ran into a mama bear with cubs- I knew just how to treat that. I looked up and about 40 feet ahead of me was a cub going up a tree... I knew that there must be a mama... and I looked around and there was mama standing up on her hind feet smelling around trying to catch my sent.... and I stopped in my tracks and I started walking backwards facing her rather than turn around and run, because we were trained to do that when I was younger. You keep your eyes on, and you stop and you walk backwards, and when I got far enough away she called the cub down and [makes clicking sound] gone.

After wandering around for a while, Gerry made the acquaintance of an older couple inhabiting the backcountry along the West Fork of Monumental Creek. They lived in a little cabin and seemed to be living off the land for the most part. Gerry took up residence in a vacant hunter's cabin somewhere nearby, where he stayed for the remainder of his time in the wilderness. As he recalls it was quite basic, but serviceable.

At some point the couple expressed their desire for some venison, and Gerry arranged to borrow their rifle in order to shoot some, apparently on the understanding that the three of them would share the catch. As agreed,

Gerry then shot a deer and hauled a portion of it to the couple's place, keeping the rifle in his cabin for the time being. He remembered with a laugh that the next morning while he was still asleep, the woman snuck into his cabin to retrieve the rifle. This was due in part, he said, to the fact that she was nervous about the possibility of being implicated in the crime of poaching.

Trouble in Paradise

Gerry does not remember much else from that period until October, when three factors converged to put an end to his sojourn. First, he remembers that he heard from someone (whose identity is forgotten) that the local sheriff had gotten wind of his AWOL status and that he knew roughly of Gerry's whereabouts.

"I think one of my sisters ratted me out," said Gerry. "whether it was Rita or one of them. They knew where I was at, and they knew that I was probably AWOL...They were all concerned about me, you know for my welfare and whatever. It wasn't something they did to be vindictive. They had some concern that I might get hurt—there was some pretty tough people back in those areas..."

This reference to "tough people" was evidently no idle boast. The legendary mountain man Sylvan Hart, a.k.a. Buckskin Bill—whose homestead on the main Salmon was about 20 miles north of the Irwins' place—had a lot to say about the rough and tumble life in the Salmon River country. And he should know—he lived alone on an isolated stretch of the river for 50 years. He called it the "easiest country in the world to murder anyone."[4]

Del Davis: The South Fork's own John Wayne

The second factor impinging on Gerry at this time was that it was getting cold in the high country—time to think about getting out before the heavy snow came.

And then came the clincher. It involved Buzz Davis, son of the legendary packer and hunting guide Del Davis—an upstream neighbor of the Irwins on the South Fork. (More about the clincher in a moment.)

4 Peterson, 36.

I heard about Del Davis from Gerry's brother John. John knows very little about Gerry's wilderness solo, due to his enlistment in the navy at that time, but he did know about one dust-up Gerry had during his sojourn. John recalled: "He, and somebody else was with him for a while, some other guy. I know they got tangled up with a packer by the name of Del Davis, over in the Middle Fork. And Davis threatened to shoot 'em and... he [Gerry] never talked much about it other than getting scared to death, when the guy took a few shots at him! I don't know what they did. They probably did something that irritated him."

If the altercation between Del, whose shooting skills were legendary (he even served as an elite sniper in WW II)[5], and Gerry actually took place as John recalls, then it is one of an amazingly large number of details from that year that have fallen through the hole in Gerry's memory. Regarding the story, Gerry commented that he didn't remember it, and he didn't think it was likely, but he did remember that Del could be a "real hothead."

On this last point at least, I was able to find some corroboration. I spoke with a hunting guide named Casey Kuenzli—Del's protégé—who eventually took over Del's hunting concession from Del's son Buzz. In general, Mr. Kuenzli spoke very highly of Del's skills and character traits. When I asked him about Del's incident with Gerry—which would have taken place long before his time—he said that he'd never heard about it. But he did have this to share:

> "I've heard a lot of stories about Del, that he'd pull out a gun pretty fast, or a knife... he was really short tempered when he'd been drinking. When I knew him, it was the last years of his life so he had mellowed out a lot, and he didn't hardly drink. But they say that you didn't ever want to give him whiskey, that he would turn on people on a dime, at the drop of a hat. I never did witness that—just the stories I've heard. I haven't heard that story about Irwin, but it kind of sounds like something Del would have done.[6]

---

5 Wilson, Greg. "Del Davis: A Life in the Saddle." *Sun Valley Magazine* Summer 2004: 107-09. Web.

6 Author's communication with Kuenzli.

A Surprise Eviction

Back to the clincher involving Buzz Davis and his hunting friends in tow. I gathered from what Gerry told me, though he seemed reticent to explain, that he and Buzz were not on the best of terms. Anyway, the hunters were determined to take over the cabin for their own use and Gerry resisted. As a result, Gerry exclaimed, "I got the hell beat out of me!" (On a side note, I suspect that it was this same bunch who clued Gerry in that the sheriff was onto him, simply because it's hard to imagine anyone who knew him actually traipsing all the way out there to find him and tell him that—if they could find him at all!)

This violent expulsion from the cabin provided all the impetus Gerry needed to finally clear out of the back country. He set out on his 80-mile hike to the sheriff's office in Cascade, stopping along the way in McCall to see his sister and brother-in-law. He was already intending to turn himself in, but she persuaded him that time was of the essence. He paid heed to her advice, going straightaway to Cascade, but he never got the chance to make good on his intentions.

Chapter 10: The United States v. Gerry Irwin

He thought that if he could get away and remain in solitude for a short period of time, he might conquer this problem himself.
— Gerry's defense counsel

L ate one night I was listening to some recordings of interviews with Gerry from my second visit to his home, when we were reviewing his service records that we'd recently received from the National Archives. We were going over the dates of his promotions and reductions in rank and the locations where those took place. It can be a tall order to decipher all the various abbreviations and acronyms the Army employs in its paperwork, and progress was slow.

After plodding through these for a while, I heard myself ask (on the recording), "Now that's odd, why does it say you were at headquarters in Ft. Lewis, Washington? Do you ever remember going to Ft. Lewis? Supposedly you were in Ft. Leavenworth at that time." Gerry responded, "Maybe that was just a typo, I don't know. I have no idea." Given the fact that Gerry remembers so little from that time period, his response was hardly surprising. Anyway, something about this odd tidbit got me thinking that there was something here worth looking at.

I pulled out the service records and found the page I'd been reading from that day. It was the Army form DA 20 under a section captioned "Appointments and Reductions." There were three columns: "Grade," "Date of Rank," and "Authority." On one line under "Rank" was the designation "RCT E1." This indicates he was demoted to the level of recruit, in other words, no rank—the bottom of the pay scale. Under

"Date of Rank" it said "22Jan60." Here's where it gets interesting. Under "Authority," it says, "GCMO 15 HqFLewis Wash 1960." So what, I wondered, does "GCMO" stand for?

After a quick search on the web, there it was: GCMO is the abbreviation for "General Court-Martial Order." Further reading brought home the full gravity of the situation. There are three levels of court-martial: Summary court-martial, Special court-martial, and General court-martial, in order from least serious to most serious. A General court-martial, also referred to sometimes as a felony court-martial, is reserved for the most serious crimes and requires the largest number of court officials. Along with that, it has the authority to mete out the most severe punishment. So there it was, staring me in the face for months, but I had not known what I was looking at—clear documentation that Gerry had been court-martialed at the highest level. This was an interesting development to say the least.

Naturally, I called Gerry to quiz him about this revelation. As with so many other things from that time period, Gerry remembered nothing at all about a court-martial. As I mulled over my options, it seemed like a good bet that those records were being preserved somewhere. I had learned the hard way that you can't take anything for granted when you're dealing with 55-year-old documents, but I had a hunch that this just might pan out. The next day I began calling around to various federal offices to track down the location where old court-martial records are stored.

Pay Dirt on the Paper Trail

Although I was accustomed to, and thus expecting, the bureaucratic run-around, luckily this time was different. Within a couple of hours, I was talking to a friendly man at the Army Court of Criminal Appeals office at Ft. Belvoir, Virginia. He didn't have the records from that time period—at least, not anymore. But he knew exactly where to direct me, because he himself had sent those records to their current home—the National Archives in St. Louis, aka The National Personnel Records Center. This is the very same institution that had provided Gerry's service records, just a different department. We had asked for "any and all records" but, wouldn't you know, the court martial files are housed separately—albeit in the same building—and require a separate procedure to get access.

Even with all the bureaucratic hoops that had to be jumped through though, within a month those records were in the mailbox. This is approaching light speed in terms of government correspondence! And it was worth the effort. Now the months missing from our existing records and Gerry's memory were beginning to take shape.

A Parallel Reality

There are actually two versions of the events leading up to Gerry's court martial, which begin with Gerry being taken into legal custody at the end of his two-and-a-half-month-long AWOL episode. The difference between these versions is dramatic—which serves to highlight the severity of the memory lapses and distortions that Gerry has continued to experience.

We'll look at Gerry's story first. Up until we received the court martial records, this was the only version of the story I knew of. In this version, Gerry turned himself in to the sheriff in Cascade—with a nudge from his sister to do it ASAP. Gerry maintained that since he came willingly, and also because the sheriff knew the Irwins, that his confinement while waiting for the MPs was very relaxed. As Gerry remembered it, the door to his cell was not even locked. Also he said that while he was staying in Cascade, he filed assault charges against one of the guys who had beaten him up (i.e. Buzz Davis or one of his cohorts).

According to Gerry, when an MP (just one) finally arrived, he escorted Gerry to Ft. Leavenworth (the Army base) via regular civilian bus service. Gerry evidently believed that, because he had turned himself in, he was never even punished. He recalled that he was simply reinstated and assigned to Ft. Leavenworth as his new duty station. He remembered only being there for a short time before he was shipped overseas to serve in Germany, as per his own request.

Even his memory of deserting Ft. Bliss was sketchy to say the least. Gerry had told me quite clearly that he had in fact deserted—but he only said this once. All the other times it came up, he remembered that he had merely overstayed a leave of absence that he'd been granted.

So that's the story as Gerry remembered it. When the court martial documents arrived however, a very different picture emerged. The records show that Gerry was apprehended by police in Cascade, Idaho, on October

14, 1959, (i.e. officially, he didn't actually turn himself in. We'll see later, however, that Gerry's defense made an interesting argument in this regard. If there is some truth to it, it may explain—in part at least—some of Gerry's later confusion). He was held for two days and then released to military police from Mountain Home Air Force Base near Boise. On October 23, Gerry was released back into the custody of the Valley County sheriff in Cascade in order to complete his legal case pertaining to the assault charges he'd filed (which, as we've seen, Gerry *did* recall). Then he was released once again to the Air Police from Mountain Home on November 18. On November 26, Gerry was transferred to the Army base at Ft. Lewis, Washington, where he was confined while awaiting charges.

The Court Martial

On December 8, Gerry's newly appointed commanding officer filed court-martial charges against him, which were then forwarded to the commanding colonel, who recommended trial by general court-martial. Following approval by the commanding general, the date was set and then postponed by two weeks to January 15, 1960. The title of the case is given as "The United States v. Bernard G. Irwin."

Gerry was arraigned on two charges—Desertion and Larceny (the latter pertained to cashing a bad check for $50 at the Ft. Bliss Exchange on the day he abandoned his post: July 31, 1959).

Gerry's defense then requested an out-of-court hearing for a plea-bargaining session with the Law Officer, who is analogous to the judge in civilian courts. The result was that he pleaded guilty to larceny and not guilty to desertion, but guilty of the lesser crime of AWOL. At that point, the main bone of contention became the question of intent—did Gerry intend to remain away permanently or did he intend to eventually turn himself in? In order to provide evidence for the former, the Trial Counsel (the prosecution in civilian courts) submitted a copy of the Morning Report from Ft. Bliss, signed by Gerry's former commanding officer, which showed that Gerry was dropped as a deserter on August 29, 1959.

The Law Officer proceeded to inform the court that they should not be influenced by the term "deserter" in the report, because in this sense the word has a strictly administrative meaning, having no bearing on the legal determination of desertion—which requires proof of intent to remain away permanently.

Gerry's defense counsel (DC in the transcript) addressed the court regarding what he considered was the appropriate way for them to approach their deliberations (and in the process revealing something perhaps, of the outmoded attitudes of that day and age). He then submitted two interesting documents, Defense Exhibits A and B, which are labeled "stipulations" (I have omitted the names of Gerry's relatives to protect their privacy):

```
DC: Gentlemen, you have before you two charges
and a specification under each. The only issue
with which you are confronted is that of the
intent of the accused. A charge of desertion is
something like a charge of rape - it is easy to
make, hard to prove, and awfully hard to defend.
We would like you to consider the evidence which
comes before you very, very closely. I request
the reporter mark these as Defense Exhibits A and
B for identification.

DEFENSE EXHIBIT A:

STIPULATION

Trial Counsel and Defense Counsel with the
express consent of the accused, PFC (E-3) Bernard
G. Irwin, in order to avoid the necessity of
requiring the appearance in court of the witness,
stipulate that if XXXXXXXX of McCall, Idaho were
present in court, he would testify substantially
as follows:

I am the brother-in-law of PFC Bernard G. Irwin.
In early October 1959 Irwin came to our home
after having been beaten quite severely in a
mining fracas. At that time he stated that he was
```

absent without leave from the Army, and intended to return, after prosecuting the persons who had attacked him.

I further have a letter from Irwin which he had not mailed, but had on his person which stated that he intended to return to the Army.

DEFENSE EXHIBIT B:

STIPULATION

Trial Counsel and Defense Counsel with the express consent of the accused, PFC (E-3) Bernard G. Irwin in order to avoid the necessity of requiring the appearance of the witness in court, stipulate that, if XXXXXXXX of Nampa, Idaho were present in court, he would testify substantially as follows:

I am the brother-in-law of Bernard G. Irwin. In early October 1959 Bernard G. Irwin stated to me that he was absent without leave from the United States Army because of a problem of a personal nature.

He further stated that he fully intended to return to military control, having conquered his problem.

Both of these documents were signed by Gerry, the Trial Counsel, and the Defense Counsel, but significantly, not by the named brothers-in-law—who apparently were not even contacted. This seems like a rather curious form of evidence, and it came under intense scrutiny by the Trial Counsel as well as the Law Officer. An out-of-court hearing was called to discuss the instructions to the court (i.e. the jury), and a spirited debate about these stipulations ensued. The debate focused mainly on whether the stipulations amounted to anything more than "hearsay."

Afterwards, the Law Officer asked the two counsels if there was anything that they would like to see added to the instructions for the court (as prepared by the Law Officer). This resulted in some more jousting between the prosecution and the defense. The Trial Counsel (i.e. prosecution) said that he *did* have a request:

```
TC: … In your statement that begins as follows,
"Thus, in deciding whether the accused intended
to remain away permanently, you may consider
evidence," I have something I would like to
insert. (1) The distance between McCall, Idaho,
and Fort Bliss, Texas; (2) The fact that the
accused committed the crime of larceny on the
day he went AWOL; (3) The fact that the accused
committed the larceny on pay day --

DC: I object to that, unless you can prove that
he was paid on that day.

TC: I think this court can take judicial notice
of the fact that the 31st of the month is pay
day.

DC: I will object to it, sir, no matter how you
rule.

LO: I believe the objection is well taken.
```

After a little more debate in this vein, the court was reconvened to receive the instructions of the Law Officer before meeting to discuss the verdict. The Law Officer gave them an overview of their task and then explained that since Gerry had already pleaded guilty to the charge of larceny, there was really nothing left to decide on that point. The only point they need to resolve pertained to the charge of desertion, since he had already plead guilty to the lesser charge of AWOL. So it all came down to whether Gerry intended to remain away permanently.

> LO: In order to find the accused guilty of the
> offense of desertion, you must be satisfied by
> legal and competent evidence beyond a reasonable
> doubt:
>
> (1) That on or about 31 July 1959, the accused
> absented himself from his organization, to wit:
> Battery F, 1st Regiment, School Brigade, U.S.
> Army Air Defense School, located at Fort Bliss,
> Texas, without proper authority, as alleged; (2)
> That the accused intended at the time of absenting
> himself, or at some time during his absence, to
> remain away permanently from his organization;
> and (3) That the accused's desertion, if any,
> continued until he was apprehended on or about 18
> October 1959 and returned to military control on
> or about 16 October 1959...
> ...However, the accused's plea has established,
> without the need for proof, two of the three
> elements of desertion, leaving in issue only the
> element of his intent to remain away permanently.
> With respect to this issue, you are instructed
> that no inference to remain absent permanently
> arises from any admission involved in the plea
> and to warrant a conviction of desertion, the
> evidence must establish this intent beyond a
> reasonable doubt.

Here he discusses some of the particular facts and circumstances of Gerry's case which should be taken into account:

> In this connection you are advised that this intent
> on the part of the accused may be proved not only
> by direct evidence of the accused's statement
> of such an intent, but also by circumstantial
> evidence, that is, by evidence of facts and

circumstances from which, according to the common experience of mankind, the accused's intent may reasonably be inferred. Thus, in deciding whether the accused intended to remain away permanently, you may consider evidence such as, for example, that he committed the offense of larceny at his duty station, Fort Bliss, Texas, on the same date that he is alleged to have gone absent without leave. You may further consider evidence that he was apprehended at McCall, Idaho, which is located at a distance from Fort Bliss, Texas, which evidence may cause you to infer that he intended to remain away permanently; or, on the other hand, you may consider an inference such as the statements attributed to the accused, which were shown in the stipulations of expected testimony of the individuals, that the accused stated he intended to return, which evidence might raise a reasonable doubt that he intended to remain away permanently. However, proof of no one fact may be equated to proof of the accused's intent; and, in the final analysis, you must determine in your own mind, based on all the evidence and the natural inferences to be drawn therefrom, whether the accused intended to remain away permanently. If, under all the evidence, including proper inferences, you are satisfied beyond a reasonable doubt that the accused, either at the time of absenting himself or at some time during his absence, intended to remain away permanently, you should find the accused guilty of desertion as charged. Otherwise, you must find the accused not guilty of desertion, but you should, in view of the accused's plea, find him guilty of the lesser included offense of absence without leave.

The Law Officer then went on to describe the court's responsibilities in determining the verdict under a provision of the UCMJ (Uniform Code of Military Justice), whereupon the court adjourned for their deliberations.

The Verdict Arrives

The court, composed of ten officers ranging in rank from Lt. Colonel to Captain, took exactly 19 minutes to decide Gerry's case:

PRES: [President or head of the jury]: The court will come to order.

TC: All parties to the trial who were present when the court closed are again present in court.

LO: Has the court arrived at its findings?

PRES: It has.

LO: The accused and counsel will stand before the president of the court.

PRES: Private Bernard G. Irwin, it is my duty as president of this court to inform you that the court in closed session and upon secret written ballot, two-thirds of the members present at the time the vote was taken concurring in each finding of guilty, finds you:

Of the Specification of Charge I: Guilty, except the words, "and with intent to remain away therefrom permanently" and the words "in desertion"; of the excepted words, not guilty.

Of Charge I: Not guilty but guilty of a violation of Article 86.

Of the Specification and Charge II: Guilty.

Gerry Gets to Tell His Side of the Story

The verdict could not have gone any better for Gerry's side, since it was exactly what they had argued for. There was still a huge question left to decide though—the sentence. At this point, the defense counsel was allowed to make a statement to the court in hopes of influencing their decision for the best. This is where Gerry was able to tell his story, via the Defense Counsel, of what transpired beginning with his going AWOL on July 31st:

DC: Gentlemen, by means of an unsworn statement, the accused wants you to know a little bit about how he came to go AWOL, where he went, and what he was doing when he was apprehended. The accused, prior to going AWOL, had been subjected to a series of spells of dizziness and black-outs. As a result of these, he was hospitalized for a period of time at the Beaumont Hospital at Fort Bliss, but the doctors were unable to lay a finger on anything physical as the cause for his condition. He became worried about his condition and he did in fact write the fifty-dollar check as a means of obtaining money so that he could leave. It was at no time his intention to remain away permanently. What he did was to take the money and return to basically what is his home area in Northern Idaho as he is well known there. He thought that if he could get away and remain in solitude for a short period of time, he might conquer this problem himself.[1] He felt that he had not received any help from the Army medics, and that is precisely what he did—he removed himself to a spot near his home and went into the mining country in Northern Idaho. It is pretty rugged up there. He was in a mining camp with a friend and he had a job which was only for room and board, strictly a temporary

---

1 We recall the report of the clinical psychologist in April (Chapter 5), that Gerry felt that "...only he could treat his own case."

job.[2] One day, just prior to his apprehension,
he was alone on the property, the owner and his
wife having gone elsewhere to do some shopping,[3]
and at that time a party of hunters came through
the area. There were several of them and they
decided they would use the house to camp out
in. He attempted to defend his friends' property
and in the process got himself pretty thoroughly
beaten up. At this time, through various persons
he knew and who knew where he was, he learned the
sheriff had knowledge that he was absent from the
Army and was in fact going to apprehend him.[4] He
knew this and at this time too, he was prepared
to turn himself back in. This man was gone for
a total of 81 days. There had been no recurrence
of the dizziness, so he prepared to turn himself
in. By the use of radio and telephone, he got in
touch with the Valley County Sheriff at Cascade,
Idaho, this being the sheriff, to his knowledge,
who was looking for him. He informed him that he
was coming out and wanted to see him. He worded
his message to say that he wanted to see him in
regard to a beating and did not think it was
necessary for him to say he was turning himself
in for the AWOL charge for the simple reason that
he knew this sheriff knew it. He left word where
he would be and where he was going. He came out of

---

2   Gerry does not remember the friend mentioned here, nor the mining job. He thinks
that perhaps he and his defense counsel may have fabricated these details with the
idea that it made his case sound more sympathetic for one reason or another. This
sounds plausible, considering Gerry's recollection of staying in the vacant hunter's
cabin (which was not near a mine), and then getting literally thrown out, as we saw
in the previous chapter. It is intriguing however that he mentions a friend in the
above document, and that Gerry's brother John remembers that Gerry was with a
friend for a while, i.e. the time when he was supposedly shot at by Del Davis.
3   Here again is an interesting parallel. While Gerry told me he did not remember a
mine and thus no mine owners, as we saw in the previous chapter, he did remember
an older couple whose cabin was nearby to where he was staying.
4   This is exactly as Gerry had told me, before either of us had seen this document.

the back country, left an additional message at
the general store for the sheriff, and proceeded
to Cascade and was then apprehended by the city
police before he had an opportunity to keep his
appointment with the sheriff.

He wishes that you know, first of all, that he
knew he would have to return the money someday.
He stole the money. He doesn't question that and
he pleaded guilty to it. However, he wants you
to recall that he did sign his own name, his own
service number, and he cashed the check at a place
where they were sure to find out that he did not
have an account. He did not attempt to hide that
fact. He desires that you also know that during
the period of relative solitude that he spent, he
had a good deal of time to think over the entire
affair and that he realizes he has done a very
wrong thing. He further requests that you consider
whether or not his mistake, and it is his first
mistake, in the light of four years of previous
service in the United States Air Force, has never
been in any disciplinary difficulty prior to this
matter, and he asks that you consider that and
that this is his first offense. He also further
wishes that I make the statement for him that he
is, in fact, sorry and not just because he will
be punished, because he knows he will, but more
because he has done something wrong and because
he has turned his back on those who were superior
to him and who had faith in him.

It's interesting to note that Gerry and his defense counsel studiously
avoided mentioning Gerry's UFO encounter at any stage of the court
martial. It probably says a lot about the general attitudes of the time, to
observe that they must have thought it would do more harm than good to
his case.

A Plea for Leniency

The Defense Counsel then made one last appeal for good sense and restraint in the sentencing, emphasizing Gerry's spotless record beforehand, his contrition for his misdeeds, and his desire to complete his full term of enlistment:

```
You have here a man who has had a good deal of
previous good service, and what we would like
the court to consider is whether or not this
first offense is of such magnitude as to ruin
any further use of this man to the service. He
would like to be restored to duty. He would like
an opportunity to make amends for his wrong...So
often men appear before a general court who have
no desire to remain in the service whatsoever,
and I think it warrants more than just a little
consideration when a man does desire to finish out
his tour honorably.
```

The Law Officer then instructed the court as to the parameters of the sentencing—the maximum sentence being a dishonorable discharge and two years confinement at hard labor—as well as what criteria they should consider in their deliberations.

The Sentence is Delivered

As with the verdict, the court's deliberations over the sentence lasted exactly 19 minutes—an amazingly brief period for deciding a man's fate!

```
PRES: Private Irwin, it is my duty as president
of this court to inform you that the court in
closed session and upon secret written ballot,
two-thirds of the members present at the time the
vote was taken concurring, sentences you:

To forfeit all pay and allowances,
to be confined at hard labor for one year, and
to be reduced to the grade of Recruit (E1).
```

Adjustments

With the sentence pronounced, Gerry's fate was sealed. Although he received a harsh sentence, he was granted his wish to remain in the Army, and his confinement was only half of the maximum penalty. He was sent from Ft. Lewis to the U.S. Disciplinary Barracks at Ft. Leavenworth, Kansas, on orders of the temporary commanding general of Ft. Lewis, Brigadier General W.O. Blandford (filling in for Lt. General Louis Truman), in order to fulfill the General Court Martial Order resulting from the proceedings. General Blandford upheld the sentence of one year at hard labor and reduction to the grade of Recruit (E-1), but he only approved a forfeiture of pay of $70 per month instead of all pay, as the court had adjudged.

On February 23, 1960, the U.S. Army Board of Review further reduced Gerry's forfeiture of pay down to $40 per month, for the duration of his confinement, while upholding the rest of the sentence.

According to the records, that was the final adjustment to the sentence in Gerry's court-martial order. As it turned out, however, Gerry's confinement officially ended on August 22, 1960, so it appears he was granted clemency. His total period of confinement was given as 312 days, of which approximately seven months was served at Ft. Leavenworth.

An Angry Young Man

One pre-trial document is worthy of our attention here. In December of 1959 (at Ft. Lewis), Gerry was given a neuropsychiatric examination by one Major Heber S. Hudson, of the Mental Hygiene Consultation Services, Ft. Lewis. Apparently, this was done at least in part to determine if Gerry was psychologically fit to stand trial. In his report dated December 22, Dr. Hudson began by summarizing the events leading up to the present situation, according to Gerry. He noted Gerry's sighting of a "bright light crossing his path" in February 1959, and how Gerry went to look for it; whereupon he passed out for "48 hours." (An interesting variation!) The history continues, covering basically the same information as recorded elsewhere, such as Gerry's recurring problems with blackouts and amnesia, his various hospital stays, etc., and then we see this:

He stated that no basis for his symptoms was found and that he was told that he should continue his duty, pending an administrative separation which had been recommended. Dissatisfied with this decision he absented himself from military control and financed his journey with a fraudulent check. He denied any further symptoms, stating that rest in an isolated part of his home state had led to complete recovery from his prior condition.

The doctor then launched into his assessment, noting that Gerry "was in good reality contact" and that he was not showing any signs of "disorder in thinking." However, he records that in the lead-up to committing "his offense," Gerry "described vague suicidal ideas which he characterized as a feeling that something was impelling him to jump in front of a vehicle. He also described some feelings that he would be harmed…" It continues:

He reported that he knew he should not cash a check and that it was wrong to leave the Army but that he felt he was justified in so doing, since in his opinion, he had not received proper treatment. In general terms he stated that he felt society was "a mess, so what I do is OK". He expressed the belief that he thought he had the right to do what he thought was right, despite the rules…."

Dr. Hudson goes on to diagnose Gerry with "Emotional Instability Reaction" as the main condition, "with no evidence of serious mental disorder." He therefore concludes, "There is no psychiatric bar to trial."

Fortunately for Gerry, it would appear that neither the trial counsel nor the court were privy to this report. It certainly does not convey the image of the contrite, well-behaved soldier who had a regrettable slip, so carefully cultivated by the Gerry's defense counsel. Rather, it seems to suggest that, at the time, Gerry was an angry young man, and it would seem he had good reason to be.

After all, he had recently been through a bewildering ordeal that had somehow disrupted the workings of his mind. And the organization that he depended on for both his livelihood and his health care (the Army) not only failed to help him—it treated him with suspicion, disbelief, and dismissal to boot. All this while they were reducing his rank and threatening to discharge him.

Consistent Themes

In regards to both the court-martial proceedings and Dr. Hudson's report, one important conclusion we can draw is that Gerry remained consistent regarding his encounter in February and the after-effects he experienced. From the earliest reports at Ft. Bliss until nearly a year later at Ft. Lewis, some 1700 miles distant, Gerry kept repeating the same points: (1) He saw a glowing object come out of the sky and apparently crash nearby, he went looking for it, and he became unconscious, with no memory of what had transpired upon awakening. (2) He then had recurring blackouts and amnesia. (3) Although it's not recorded in Dr. Hudson's report, Gerry is on record at least three times at Ft. Bliss as stating that he believed the UFO had caused his symptoms. And (4) Gerry consistently maintained that the treatment he'd received from the Army had not helped his condition, and that he was disappointed with their treatment of his problem.

Another repeated theme that emerges in the court martial proceedings is that Gerry had a plan to help himself. He expressed the belief that if he could return to his old wilderness haunts for a while, his condition would have a better chance of improving, and he acted accordingly. As far back as April (i.e. eight months earlier), a psychologist evaluating Gerry's condition commented on him "feeling only he could treat his own case."[5]

His plan included obtaining funds for his trip both legally (from his paycheck) and illegally (bad check). And it appears that his plan worked— that his symptoms were largely cured, at least from the perspective of being able to move forward, face consequences, and get on with his life. He certainly thought so himself, at least as he testified in court; as well as what he reported to Dr. Hudson, who wrote, "He denied any further symptoms, stating that rest in an isolated part of his home state had led to complete recovery from his prior condition."

The Hoax Question Again

If we return now to the question of whether it was all a hoax, the obvious question to ask is, how did it help him? What did he gain from it? In other

---

5 Hospital Records.

words, what was the motivation? Just for the sake of discussion, let's say it started as a hoax, staged for the purpose of avoiding discipline for an AWOL (i.e. returning past due from his 30-day leave). Then why did he keep the hoax going? After all, he was already "off the hook" in a sense. It had worked—no punishment for his tardiness, just several days in the psych ward. At this point his goal (in this scenario) was accomplished. So, if it was a hoax, then why did he persist, feigning more blackouts and amnesia? What was the payoff?

First, he was re-admitted to the psych ward for 32 days. As we have seen, Ward 30 was no Club Med. And what of the social stigma attached to those who suffer mental illness? Who would choose that? To continue this possible hoax scenario, his next step was to go AWOL and hop a bus to Utah, later claiming he was in a trance. What did this get him? Special favors? Hardly. His commanding officer fined him and cut him down a rank. But this persistent "hoaxer" was not finished yet. He then sought intervention from the Army Inspector General, which earned him another stay in the psych ward.[6]

But before the reported admission date arrived (to continue with our thought experiment), we see that Gerry then faked another blackout and amnesia spell, causing him to be admitted a few days earlier than planned. Soon after, his doctor relegated him to the care of the Mental Hygiene Clinic[7] (a separate Army facility), which in turn apparently discharged him at some point in the days or weeks that followed. But Gerry had one more trick up his sleeve—desertion paired with larceny. As we have seen, he reaped quite a reward for this last stunt.

So again, what was there to gain? Frankly, it just doesn't add up as a hoax. But equally, it doesn't add up as a conventional psychological or medical case either. His doctors did not believe that he actually had amnesia. They stopped just short of claiming that it was all an act, but the

---

6 Lorenzen, L.J., 25.

7 The anonymous doctor mentioned earlier informed me that the William Beaumont Army Hospital falls directly under the command of the U.S. Army Surgeon General, and thus is considered to be at the top tier of Army medical care. By comparison, the Mental Hygiene Clinic falls under the jurisdiction of the Ft. Bliss command, i.e. a lower level of facilities and services.

implication was clear enough. Gerry just did not fit their criteria. Since they could not find anything wrong with him according to their defined categories, they seem to have assumed that he was either pretending or imagining his trouble. There are two points that seem relevant here.

The first point is that Army doctors have a long history of dealing with soldiers bucking for a discharge, often of the "Section 8" variety (mentally unfit for service). It is quite possible, or even probable, that this was the presumption made by Gerry's doctors. But considering all the known facts, this scenario just doesn't hold water. For one thing, it's probably a safe bet that the majority of these cases occur among draftees during wartime, but Gerry was a *volunteer* during *peacetime.*

Next, Gerry had re-enlisted in the armed forces less than a year and half earlier, and going by the available evidence (excellent evaluations, rising in rank, no disciplinary problems), he was thriving in the Army. In that regard, Gerry is on the record elsewhere as stating his wish to pursue his Army career. In a phone interview with Coral Lorenzen on March 11, Gerry matter-of-factly stated that he was a "career man" who enjoyed his work, and he wanted to make sure that all the hubbub resulting from his recent incident didn't ruin it for him. [8]

In that same vein, let's consider a detail from Gerry's interview with Dr. Hudson: "He stated that no basis for his symptoms was found and that he was told that he should continue his duty, *pending an administrative separation* which had been recommended. Dissatisfied with this decision he absented himself from military control..." (emphasis added) Avoiding administrative discharge by going AWOL may seem a bit counter-intuitive, but as we have seen, Gerry also had his own logic in in regards to "treating his own case." And to top it off, when Gerry stood for his court martial, he actually asked to be allowed to stay in the Army. The bottom line is that Gerry consistently expressed his wish to continue his military service. At the very least, he hardly fits the profile of someone "bucking for a discharge."

It's All in Your Head

The second point here—pertaining to the Army doctors' perspective—is

---

8 Lorenzen, L. J., 20.

that, for me, this is getting into familiar terrain. As a health care provider, I have often served patients with symptoms for which doctors could find no cause or diagnosis. In this scenario, typically the patient is said to be suffering from psychosomatic symptoms. Often, as time goes by there will eventually be enough research completed in order to give names to and/ or establish better protocols for assessing and treating these conditions, thereby validating the hapless, afflicted souls who were previously brushed off.

Two recent examples that come to mind are fibromyalgia and chronic fatigue syndrome. In the past these conditions often went undiagnosed and patients were basically told it was all in their heads. I don't know how widespread this was, but I personally know of several cases where this absolutely did happen and it made the lives of the affected individuals almost unbearable. Functionally disabled on one hand, and labeled by the medical establishment as psychological cases or sometimes even (essentially) fakers on the other hand, the suffering was immense. Thankfully, for these two particular syndromes, things have improved, with established screening criteria and treatment protocols.

The important point here is that *doctors, like people in general, tend to dismiss or ignore what they don't understand.* And one could hardly blame them for not understanding, if the cause of Gerry's condition originated from beyond the human realm altogether.

Chapter 11: Amnesia from Space?

In his book on the folklore of Celtic countries, Walter Evans-Wentz reports that the mind of a person coming out of Fairy-Land is usually blank about what has been seen and done there. The mind of Private First Class Gerry Irwin was blank indeed when he woke up [in the hospital, the day after his UFO encounter]. — Jacques Vallee [1]

D id Gerry encounter a real UFO? If so, how does it relate to his amnesia? Did he even have amnesia? In this chapter we'll explore these questions in light of some fascinating new evidence.

The Amytal Interview
As we know, Gerry was interviewed under the influence of sodium amytal by his attending psychiatrist, Captain Valentine. According to hospital records, this occurred on March 27, 1959—11 days into his 32-day admission at WBAH—following his blackout and subsequent amnesia in downtown El Paso. Captain Valentine recorded the results, stating that Gerry's thoughts were "very bizarre and unusual." The report continues:

> [Gerry] *stated there was a "special intelligence" that he couldn't explain to me, since it would be incomprehensible to me, which has directed him not to remember or not to tell me about any of the events in Utah.* He says that if he tells what was behind the incidents in Utah there will be a "big investigation" that he does not want to be bothered with and also because it will harm many people and he doesn't want that to happen. *He states "it" all began at the age of three years,* although he will not

---

1 Vallee, 1988, 115.

reveal how or what began, stating that it would provide a clue to me as to what is behind all this. Also, he informed me that he could leave this hospital any time if he wanted to by invoking a special force...Following this interview the patient stated he could remember nothing of what he said during it...[2][emphasis added]

It's intriguing that Gerry speaks of an intelligence which "directed him not to remember or not to tell me about any of the events in Utah." As we know, in the decades that followed this would become a very common theme in the alien abduction literature, i.e. having memories blocked and/or being warned against telling others about the experience. This makes Gerry's statements all the more convincing, considering that, as we've seen, there simply were no abduction stories circulating in 1959, and thus no one he could have been mimicking.[3]

In this light, Gerry's peculiar statement, "it all began at the age of three years..." provides further support for an abduction scenario. This type of assertion would become all too familiar to UFO researchers in the decades to come, i.e. the long-term or even lifelong involvement with the abducting entities so often reported by abductees.

With that in mind, consider the following report from the NICAP archives:

Feb. 20, 1948; Emmett, Idaho 1:15 pm. local. Six surveyors saw a small flat, heart-shaped UFO flying in the sky. It was fuzzy across its back edge as if "dipped in cream", and was flying point first below the cloud level at between 2,000 and 4,000 feet. [cit.][4]

Now, it just so happens that Gerry and his family were living in Emmett at the time of this sighting. And note the date: February 20 is the same exact date that Gerry had his encounter in Utah 11 years later. If nothing else, this strikes me as an odd coincidence. The maverick UFO researcher John Keel sifted through many thousands of UFO reports and

---

2   Hospital records.
3   See Chapter 7.
4   Ridge, Francis, and Joel Carpenter. "1948 UFO Chronology." *Nicap.org*. NICAP, 15 Dec. 2005. Web. 11 June 2016.

was able to discern recognizable patterns emerging from the apparent chaos. He noted, "These events are staged year after year, century after century, in the same exact areas and *often on the same exact calendar dates.*"[5] (emphasis added)

Just seven and a half months earlier, there was another multiple witness sighting that occurred over Emmett, this time by the pilot and crew of a United Airlines DC-3 passenger plane on July 4, 1947. This was a well-documented and highly credible sighting of multiple objects performing seemingly impossible maneuvers in a clear sky. As one report on this incident began, "Former skeptics joined the ranks of the believers as the flashing objects glittered before their eyes."[6]

On July 6, *The Brownsville Herald* ran a front-page banner headline that read, "Flying Disc Mystery Baffles America – Army, Navy Deny Experiments with Planes, A- Bombs." America was in the midst of its very first modern UFO flap, and hundreds of reports were pouring in from all over the country. However, the July 4 Emmett sighting was considered one of the more credible cases due to the long experience and excellent reputation of the witnesses; and more than 20 years later it was submitted as evidence by Dr. James McDonald to the Symposium on Unidentified Flying Objects in Washington.[7] It also entered Project Blue Book archives as their "Incident No. 10" of 1947.[8]

The Hoax Question Continued: Car Trouble or Close Encounter?
There is an important detail reported in the news coverage from the night of Feb. 20 that might bear on the question of hoaxing. Sheriff Fife commented that he had found papers in Gerry's car signed by his commanding officer indicating that Gerry was due back at his base on

---

5   Keel, John. *Operation Trojan Horse: The Classic Breakthrough Study of UFOs* (San Antonio, TX: Anomalist, 2013), 331-332.

6   "Perplexity Deepens." *Billings Gazette* [Billings, MT] 6 July 1947: 2.

7   U.S. House of Representatives. Committee on Science and Astronautics. *Symposium on Unidentified Flying Objects.* Washington D.C.: U.S. Gov. Printing Office, 1968. Print. Pdf at nicap.org.

8   Wilson, Daniel. "July 4, 1947; Near Emmett, Idaho (BBU 34)/ AVCAT." *Nicap. org.* NICAP, 19 Nov. 2010. Web. 13 May 2017. <http://www.nicap.org/ reports/470704emmett_report.htm>. [Contains links to the Blue Book documents.]

Friday. It would seem safe enough to assume that by "Friday" he meant that same day, i.e. Friday the 20th of February. Assuming that's true, then Gerry was definitely going to be late getting back, since he still had to cover a distance of roughly 800 miles, and it was already at least 7 PM. Clearly, he was going to be late. Taking stock of his situation, his thinking could have gone in a couple of different directions.

On one hand (to revisit a scenario we explored briefly in Chapter 8), he could have cooked up some crazy hoax about getting knocked out somehow after going to look for a mysterious, noiseless, and non-existent plane crash, in order to avoid punishment back at his base. In this scenario, he would have left a note and written STOP on his car in order to ensure his hoax would go according to plan. Then all he had to do was hide out somewhere about a quarter mile to a mile away, and wait for his rescuers to find his note and follow his tracks in the snow. When he noticed they were getting near, he could have just lain face-down and feigned unconsciousness.

But who would go to all the trouble of concocting such an elaborate story, which was bound to create such a huge commotion including mobilization of all the emergency services as well as a whole lot of probing questions, just to avoid irritating the C.O.? Why not just make up a story about car trouble and be done with it? And it's not like he was already on thin ice—in fact there is no evidence of any previous disciplinary problems in Gerry's record at all. Certainly there would have been consequences, but it seems unlikely they would have been very serious (e.g. kitchen duty, cleaning latrines, confinement to barracks, etc.).

A more likely scenario is that he had already resigned himself to his fate, to whatever punishment would result from his tardiness. Or perhaps he had already thought up a believable excuse (e.g. car trouble). But then, when he saw the strange glowing object in the sky that brought to mind a possible plane crash, he thought that whatever assistance he could provide in the event of a tragedy outweighed any other consideration.

Now, if Gerry was the only person in the world to ever report such an experience, his superiors would perhaps have felt justified in assuming that Gerry was either crazy or lying. And in fact, that is pretty much what happened. Both that his story was unique, and that he was received as a kook and/or a liar. With the benefit of hindsight, however, we can now look back over the many thousands, or even hundreds of thousands of reports[9] in the intervening 55 plus years and notice that his experience was marked by several key elements that are now seen as typical features of the abduction phenomenon: inexplicable unconsciousness, amnesia, blocked memories and/or warnings against speaking about them, reported long-term involvement, and trance-like states.

The Islands of Memory

Returning now to the report of the amytal interview, Captain Valentine follows his account with some interesting commentary:

> He persistently maintained amnesia for the period previously delineated, although at times there seemed to be inadvertent lapses in his stated amnesia when the patient would seem to remember an event or person but would quickly manage to explain away the memory.[10]

This observation struck me as sounding quite familiar, because this is exactly the pattern that I noticed over the course of my interviews and discussions with Gerry. I found that on so many occasions, he would remember a very important detail that he had earlier denied, or the converse, he would deny a detail that he had previously remembered. I never got the sense that there was deception or dishonesty involved. It seemed as if the individual memories he has for that period in his life (at least, what remains of his memories) are like islands, far removed from

---

9　Strieber, Whitley. *Breakthrough: The Next Step* (New York: HarperCollins, 1995). By the time he published this book, Whitley Strieber had received nearly 140,000 letters from people who had experienced abduction type phenomena. This is quite likely just the tip of the iceberg. First, bear in mind that this incredible number is from just one single source, while there are many, many other reputable authors and researchers who have collected similar stories. Also, consider the words of Jacques Vallee—written five years *earlier*—from his book *Confrontations*, 1990, p. 18, "The total number of unexplained UFO cases on record worldwide is well in excess of 100,000, yet we are fairly certain on the basis of opinion polls that only one witness in ten comes forward with a report." Granted, he is referring here to unexplained UFO cases *in general*; nonetheless, it's an astounding number to contemplate.

10　Hospital records.

one another. It appears as though these islands are so far apart that he can't see one from another. So it seemed to be the luck of the draw as to which island or islands his mind would alight upon on any given day.

Here's an example. In our very first interview over the phone, Gerry told me that he was given "truth serum" when he was brought back to Ft. Bliss after his original Utah incident: "They put some sort of drug and put you out and it's like a truth serum, and I couldn't recall what I said or who asked me what…They wouldn't say anything about it."[11] I didn't know of this detail at the time, though I was able to corroborate it a few weeks later when I finally got hold of Jim Lorenzen's 1962 article. Therefore, there is no way I could have led him to remember this by inadvertently suggesting it. When I followed up with a question the next day, Gerry confirmed and elaborated a little on this subject: "I think they gave me some sort of a drug, or something like a truth serum or something to relax me, because I was unconscious. Whatever it was, it put you to sleep." Then, a few months later when I interviewed Gerry in person and brought up the truth serum and sodium amytal, Gerry replied: "Did I say that?"

There is no question in my mind that he honestly didn't remember. When he asked me if he said that, it was with sincere curiosity and some confusion. He clearly couldn't remember it. This is just one instance of many similar examples.

Amnesia: Real or Fake?

In the conclusion of his report, Dr. Valentine offers an assessment which appears to have strongly influenced Gerry's subsequent treatment by the Army:

> Discussion: In spite of the patient's stated amnesia, it is my opinion that this man does not have amnesia for the period in question, and that he would be responsible for any of his actions during this period. *We have checked on this man's recent history as thoroughly as we can and we cannot find that he has committed any breaches of civilian or military law nor has he had known difficulty in the emotional sphere.* The material obtained on Amytal interview would certainly make one think

---

11 See Chapter 2.

of paranoid schizophrenia but there was absolutely no other evidence to support this single finding. Psychological testing produced data most consistent with a normal mental structure... [emphasis added]

Besides the "Islands of Memory" phenomenon, it would seem that Dr. Valentine was influenced by another, quite significant factor. The anonymous doctor whom we discussed previously (who was the ward supervisor at that time and thus Valentine's superior officer), told me there had been a number of patients who claimed to have amnesia in order to avoid punishment for crimes they had committed. Valentine seems to be clearly signaling this concern when he reports they couldn't find any evidence that Gerry had been broken the law.

Certainly the problem of faking might well have given the doctors rather jaded eyes in assessing for amnesia. It's an interesting consideration in light of the hoax question. Right off the bat though, the thought occurs that if Gerry was planning to use amnesia as a cover for his later misdeeds (i.e. the two AWOL incidents and the larceny) the degree of forethought required would have been extraordinary, to say the least.

A Smoking Gun?

Having said that though, there *is* this very provocative line from the supervising doctor's report dated July 9: "He claimed that if he were to commit a crime during the blackout spells, that he would have to consider the Army responsible." Now, this was written only about three weeks before Gerry cashed the bad check and deserted his post, and it certainly does lead one to wonder. In fact, it appears quite likely that at this point Gerry had already made his decision to leave and was indeed trying to create some cover for his planned actions. If there is a smoking gun regarding a hoax of some kind, this would be it. In that case we must ask: just how much of Gerry's story *was* a hoax, i.e. how far back in time did it originate?

This is surely a crucial question. But taking into account all the various clues and evidence we've looked at, it seems hard to believe that Gerry was pulling a fast one from the very beginning. To what end? It just doesn't add up. As we discussed in the previous chapter, who on earth would go to all the trouble of masterminding an elaborate hoax involving a UFO, amnesia, a missing jacket etc., for a mere $50 and the privilege of dodging the police as a deserter five months later? Sure, $50 was worth more back then, but not that much more, considering that it was only about a third of his monthly pay. Hardly a "get rich quick" scheme!

It would make more sense to think that he really was having problems after an event that really did take place. Then, as things progressed and his condition was not improving, he tried to use his history in this regard to run some interference for himself, for plans that were recently hatched. In support of this idea, recall that in Dr. Hudson's report of December 22 (at Ft. Lewis), Gerry mentioned he was facing a pending "administrative separation," and that "he was dissatisfied with this decision." In other words, he was about to be discharged, and he didn't like it.

First of all, what exactly does the term "administrative separation" mean? Basically, this is the Army equivalent of firing someone. We can narrow this down further by looking at the July 9 physician's report from WBAH. In it, the doctor mentions a request for a new evaluation of Gerry's case in preparation for a "209 type administrative discharge." Confronted with yet another inscrutable Army code, I searched online for a translation.

I found the answer in an Army Board of Review document discussing a case from 1962. At that time, Army Regulation 635-209 governed discharges due to "unsuitability" for service, which included "character and behavior disorders." This designation was typically issued under the broad category of "General Discharge, Under Honorable Conditions" as opposed to the much more desirable "Honorable Discharge," which is what Gerry actually ended up with years later. The General Discharge, had he received it, could have negatively impinged upon his civilian career opportunities as well as his veteran's benefits.

So it makes sense that Gerry was not exactly thrilled about this development. After all, his "behavior disorder" was due to something beyond his control, something which the Army was either unable to help him with, or worse, was even possibly contributing to. It seems as if Gerry was just being tossed away—after six years of exemplary military service—since he was no longer convenient to have around.

If Gerry thought the administrative discharge was a bad deal though, he made an interesting choice by going AWOL instead. There's a wide gulf between the relatively mild consequences of an administrative discharge and the severity of a General Court Martial verdict sentencing him to a year of imprisonment at hard labor. Yet ultimately, that is exactly what Gerry's choice led to, and he surely would have been aware of the kind of trouble he was courting.

What was going on in his head at that pivotal moment? What internal pressures could have led him to such a fateful decision? Was tossing his discharge and going AWOL instead just his way of telling the Army to "Discharge *THIS*"? Or did he just truly believe that his only real hope for a cure lay in returning home to the Salmon River country?

A List of Things Gone Missing
My interviews with Gerry revealed that there are a striking number of details from the years 1959 and 1960—many quite significant—that still remain lost from his memory, and many others which are misremembered. Some of these are quite astonishing, as they would seem to be the kind of things that would be impossible to forget. And I must emphasize once again the sincerity in Gerry's demeanor during our discussions that revealed these memory gaps. Here is a partial list of these items:

Not remembered: (Unless otherwise noted, these items were not recalled in any of our interviews.)

- That he wrote STOP on the side of his vehicle.
- That he wrote a note requesting that police be notified about a possible plane crash.[12]
- That he had recurring blackouts and amnesia after he returned to Ft. Bliss.

---

12 Regarding this item and the preceding one, in our initial interview Gerry seemed to vaguely confirm them in a kind of a blanket acknowledgement (along with several other details) after hearing me read a paragraph of Coral Lorenzen's report (see Chapter 2.) In subsequent conversations he denied these details, stating that it didn't sound like something he would do.

- That he was admitted to the psych ward at William Beaumont Army Hospital on three separate occasions, or that he spent any time there at all.
- That he ever talked to the Lorenzens.
- That he carried the rank of SP4 before his reductions in rank began.
- That he went AWOL in April 1959.
- That he returned to Utah where he found his missing jacket (as he told the Lorenzens).
- That he cashed a bad check at Ft. Bliss.
- How he travelled from Ft. Bliss to Idaho when he deserted his post on July 31.
- That he was held at Mountain Home AFB before and after his legal proceedings in Cascade, or that he was even there at all.
- That he was held in confinement at Ft. Lewis for nearly two months pending his court-martial, or even that he was ever in Ft. Lewis at all.
- That he was tried in a general court-martial at Ft. Lewis.
- That he served seven months at hard labor at Ft. Leavenworth in the U.S. Disciplinary Barracks.

Misremembered:

- That he turned himself in when actually he was apprehended.
- That he served as a soldier at the Army base of Ft. Leavenworth when in fact he was a prisoner in the disciplinary barracks there.
- That he was given leave after his original incident in Utah and simply overstayed his leave, when he really just deserted his post.[13]

It may sound like a litany, but the point is to establish just how severe Gerry's amnesia is. It serves as a clear indicator of just how strongly his encounter in Utah seems to have affected him, in ways that can still be

---

13 This is actually another "islands of memory" item, because on other occasions Gerry did recall going AWOL when he went back to Idaho.

seen to this day. And again, regardless of what anyone else thinks, the record is quite clear that Gerry himself consistently expressed his belief that the UFO caused his amnesia.

Gerry's testimony clearly indicates he was struggling with a severe case of amnesia, which is only underscored by how much he remembers from his life both before and after what must have been a very painful and difficult time for him. It bears repeating just how weird it was to have Gerry tell me he didn't remember being either court-martialed or being in prison for the better part of a year—with seven months of that at hard labor! There are thousands of things in life that are easily forgotten to be sure, but it seems safe to say that doing hard time in prison would not be among them. What else could account for this memory gap in a man who had no history of such problems?

Treatment protocols for amnesia in general, as well as our understanding of how mental/emotional trauma can impact the functioning of the mind, have undoubtedly improved in the intervening decades. At least, one would hope that if Gerry's incident happened today, he would have a better chance of getting the kind of help he should have gotten back then.

But what if the lack of help was actually deliberate and designed to keep something secret?

Chapter 12: A Saucerful of Spies

Perhaps, as Lorenzen suggests, there has been a military investigation [into the Irwin case] *that has been kept secret. If so, secrecy on the part of the authorities, if they are really concerned with the nation's peace of mind, is not the best course...* — Jacques Vallee[1]

One can't help but wonder just how large a role official secrecy has played in Gerry's saga. There is certainly no denying that official secrecy has to some extent woven its way in and out of Gerry's life in the military. As we saw previously, Gerry observed top secret aircraft flying from Alaska into Soviet airspace at extremely high altitudes on numerous occasions. These flights officially did not exist, and it was expressly forbidden for Gerry and his team members to speak about them.

Years later, Gerry observed a UFO in Utah, another observable that the military categorized as non-existent. In fact, as we'll see shortly, if Gerry had called it a UFO rather than a suspected plane crash, he would have been breaking the law by talking to the media about it. Then, when Gerry tried to get access to *his own memories* about his encounter through hypnotic regression, the Army blocked his attempts. It would almost seem as if his memories were classified as state secrets, with Gerry lacking the requisite clearance to gain access to them.

Then, a year and a half later, as soon as Gerry was released from his confinement at hard labor in August 1960, he was immediately shipped to

1   Vallee, Jacques. *Passport to Magonia: From Folklore to Flying Saucers* (1969. Reprint. Brisbane, Australia: Daily Grail Pub., 2014), 87.

Germany, a move which under ordinary circumstances would seem rather unexceptional. But considering Gerry's recent history, it could provoke a raised eyebrow or two. Was Gerry shipped overseas in order to keep him from talking to the American media?

Finally, after several years of service in Germany, Gerry was sent to Austria, disguised as an American tourist, on an officially non-existent mission. And again, it was something he was supposed to keep quiet about. By this time, he was probably getting pretty good at it.

Were (Are) UFOs Really an *Official Secret*?

Following the general ruckus stirred up by the 1952 UFO Wave, the U.S. Joint Chiefs of Staff engaged in a little "information management," i.e. they lowered the boom on public access to 'all things UFO.' In December, 1953, they issued "JANAP [Joint Army Navy Air Force Publication] 146" followed by "JANAP 146(C)" on March 10, 1954, subtitled: "Communication Instructions for Reporting Vital Intelligence Sightings from Airborne and Waterborne Sources" (contracted into the acronym "CIRVIS," aka "MERINT" apparently standing for "Merchant ship Intelligence"). They identified the types of sightings that were required to be reported, including missiles, aircraft, submarines and "Unidentified flying objects." Then under "Section III—Security", item "308" reads:

308. MILITARY AND CIVILIAN
a. All persons aware of the contents or existence of a MERINT Report are governed by the Communications Act of 1934 and amendments Thereto, and Espionage Laws. MERINT reports contain information affecting the National Defense of the United States within the meaning of the Espionage Laws, 18 U.S. Code, 793 and 794. The unauthorized transmission Or revelation of the contents of MERINT reports in any manner is prohibited.[2]

---

2   JANAP 146(C). The last version of this regulation I've seen is JANAP 146(E) from 1977, posted at cufon.org. However, John Greenwald of *The Black Vault* has revealed more recent UFO reporting regulations, including AFI 10-206, which was active until 2011—at which time the UFO reference was dropped, right after a *Huffington Post* article publicized Greenwald's discovery!

The gist is that military *and civilian* personnel ("U.S and Canadian civil and commercial aircraft,"[3] among others) were required to report UFOs to the government. However, these same personnel were expressly prohibited under threat of prosecution—under both the Communication Act and the Espionage Act—from sharing with the public any information contained in those official reports, which were now classified.

Having considered military UFO secrecy in general, what about Gerry? Was there a military investigation of Gerry's incident that's been kept secret? Was there an attempt to cover-up his UFO report? Or could it be that that there *was* secrecy around Gerry's incident; but rather than for the purpose of covering up UFOs, it was meant to obscure a covert military operation of some kind?

The Cover-Up Question
Let's return for a moment to that fateful night of Gerry's encounter. As we recall, his incident occurred on a Friday evening, and it was already being reported in Saturday's newspapers. This means that if there was a cover-up, it would have to have been executed with considerable speed and efficiency. If government agents were involved, they would have had a fairly brief timeline to get things "sorted out," considering Gerry didn't even get to the hospital until around midnight. That might seem like a short timeframe for a cover-up scenario, but not necessarily.

Let's say, for instance, that the Air Force was testing a top-secret experimental aircraft of some sort, and an inquisitive motorist (i.e. Gerry) noticed and decided to investigate. Or alternatively, that Gerry saw a genuine UFO that had been tracked on radar, and government agents were dispatched to the site where the craft touched down— not a big leap considering the oft-reported phenomenon of unmarked helicopters or jets suddenly appearing in the vicinity of UFO sightings.

In either case, whether the project operatives were already on site and "at the ready," or dispatched and soon to arrive, it seems credible that a cover-up could have kicked in immediately. It would make sense that they would have wanted to divert the public's attention away from where the

---

3   "Janap_146.pdf." *NSA.gov.* National Security Agency/Central Security Service, 2 May 2006. Web.

operation actually took place, and instead point the media to a second, false location. In other words, in this scenario the media unwittingly reported the wrong highway (Utah 20) due to a disinformation campaign orchestrated by government agents. To accomplish this, perhaps they "leaned" on the sheriff—under the pretext of "national security"—in order to secure his cooperation in throwing reporters off the trail.

Move Along, Nothing to See Here

One further point in favor of a cover-up is that Gerry's Commanding Officer repeatedly blocked Gerry's access to the civilian psychiatrist with whom he was scheduled to undergo hypnotic regression.

According to Jim's 1962 article, when Gerry's first hypnosis appointment was drawing near, he was given a "barrack cleaning detail" for that evening. When Gerry asked to switch duties with a fellow soldier—normally a perfectly acceptable practice—his request was met with suspicion from the sergeant in charge. The sergeant put Gerry in front of his C.O., who gave Gerry a stern warning about pursuing his private quest to retrieve his memories. He reminded Gerry that until recently, his record had been exemplary, so why would he want to throw that away? He told Gerry that if he would just cut out the shenanigans (in so many words), then they would let the matter drop. But if he persisted, they could "make it plenty rough" on him.[4]

It appears this was no idle warning. As if to show Gerry that he meant business, over the course of the following two weeks Gerry was given extra duties almost every evening. As a result, Gerry simply gave up. He never showed up for any of his appointments.[5]

Was there a coordinated effort from "on high" to keep the lid on Gerry's memories and shut him up? It certainly raises the question. Why should there have been any problem with Gerry pursuing answers for what caused his condition while he was off-duty (or at least *should have been* off-duty)? Looked at another way, was Gerry being denied access to the contents of his own mind because, according to someone higher up, he lacked proper security clearance? In that case, who did have access? One

---

4 Lorenzen, L.J., 24.
5 Ibid.

would apparently be Dr. Valentine—who administered the sodium amytal interview—as well as whomever he may have shared it with (which, as we know, did not include Gerry).

PSYOPs

This bears emphasizing: some UFO sightings are covert experiments in the manipulation of the belief systems of the public. — Jacques Vallee [6]

Previously, we have discussed the possibility of Gerry being subjected to secret government mind control programs. There is considerably more to explore in that regard, which we'll begin examining shortly. At this juncture however, we'll turn our attention to another, closely related sphere of black ops that walks hand in hand with mind control; this is the disturbing domain of psychological operations. Whereas mind control programs target individuals, "PSYOPs" or "psychological operations" are aimed at the masses. They are covert government programs to manipulate perceptions, emotions and beliefs—and thereby the behavior of—targeted populations. Typical tactics include the notorious "disinformation" campaigns, which exploit unwitting government officials, media outlets, and unsuspecting researchers and journalists (among others) to promulgate their deceptions. In essence it is mind control on a grand scale.

In fact there are very troubling implications for ufology arising from both mind control programs and PSYOPs. Vallee, and more recently, author Mark Pilkington among others, have covered this angle extensively, documenting the fact that besides planting rumors, government agents actually execute elaborate UFO hoaxes in order to encourage belief in UFOs, when such a belief happens to serve their interests. [7] America's intelligence community has been aware of the potential to exploit the UFO phenomenon in this manner at least as early as 1952, as shown by the following memo from CIA Director Walter Bedell "Beetle" Smith:

---

6   Vallee, Jacques. *Revelations: Alien Contact and Human Deception* (1991. Reprint. San Antonio, TX: Anomalist Books, 2014), Kindle Ed., loc. 128-129.
7   See Vallee's: *Messengers of Deception: UFO Contacts and Cults* (1979, 2008) and *Revelations: Alien Contact and Human Deception* (1991, 2014).

1. I am today transmitting to the National Security Council a proposal (TAB A) in which it is concluded that the problems connected with unidentified flying objects appear to have implications for psychological warfare as well as for intelligence and operations.
2. The background for this view is presented in some detail in TAB B.
3. I suggest that we discuss at an early board meeting the possible offensive and defensive utilization of these phenomena for psychological warfare purposes.[8]

In order for the disinformation component of PSYOPs to be effective, it needs to contain some actual truth mixed in with the falsehoods and half-truths. The end goal is to so thoroughly confuse and obfuscate the real situation that members of the public don't know *what* to believe anymore, or worse, they get caught up in chasing after the provocative crumbs thrown to them and assembling them into elaborate conspiracy theories or even cults. The wackier the theories get, the more the UFO phenomenon, as well as the idea of government conspiracies in general, are discredited and dismissed by the mainstream culture. As Jacques Vallee has commented:

> If you cannot force a train to slow down, there is another way of stopping it: you can speed up the locomotive until it goes crazy and jumps the track. Was that sort of action deliberately taken against UFO researchers when it became obvious that censorship and cover-up were no longer effective? Was that the reason for the leaking of false revelations, the deliberate fomenting of absurd beliefs in crashed saucers, alien autopsies, and Short Grays?[9]

Given this paranoia-inducing climate, one can never be too sure of anything. It's a precarious situation that UFO researcher Linda Moulton Howe has described as "A fractured hall of mirrors with a quicksand floor,

---

8 Smith, Walter B. *CIA Memo ER-3-2809*. Washington D.C.: Central Intelligence Agency, Feb. 10, 1952. Web. (accessed at the CIA's Electronic Reading Room as of 5 Jan 2017).
9 Vallee, 1991, 2014, loc. 1155-1158.

that nobody knows exactly what the truths are, and everybody has found themselves completely suspicious..."[10]

Villas Boas Revisited

As we have previously noted, if Gerry's experience was actually an alien abduction, then it would be the second documented case of this phenomenon in modern times. The first is generally agreed to be the case of Antonio Villas Boas from 1957. But was this Brazilian case really an alien abduction, or something else?

In recent years, there has been renewed speculation that the entities who captured Villas Boas may have originated not from some remote planet, but from somewhere a lot closer to home. Was it really a PSYOP? That possibility may be difficult to dismiss.

There are three main sources for this hypothesis, which taken together, certainly lead one to wonder. The first is the testimony of Bosco Nidelcovic, a Yugoslavian-born linguist and self-proclaimed former CIA agent. He made the claim—in a 1978 interview with an American UFO researcher named Rich Reynolds—that he'd worked under a CIA front organization in Latin America from 1956 to 1963, and that for part of this time he participated in a PSYOP known as Operation Mirage. This was a clandestine program of faking UFO events in locations around the globe. For his part, Nidelcovic maintained that he was on a helicopter team that traversed the same region of Brazil where Villas Boas lived, performing PSYOPs and hallucinogenic drug tests on unsuspecting locals. Nidelcovic claimed that Villas Boas was, in fact, one of their victims.[11]

Of course, it would probably be foolish to simply trust a self-described former CIA agent "any farther than you could throw him" to revive an old expression (liar's paradox, anyone?). But there are corroborating details to be found in at least two other sources. First, we have the testimony

---

10 Howe, Linda Moulton. Excerpt of interview from *Mirage Men: How the Government Created a Myth That Took Over the World.* Dir. John Lundberg and Roland Denning. By Mark Pilkington. Perception Management Productions, 2013. DVD.

11 Pilkington, Mark. *Mirage Men: An Adventure into Paranoia, Espionage, Psychological Warfare, and UFOs* (NY, NY: Skyhorse, 2010), 111-113.

of Villas Boas himself, in which he described elements of the alien's craft that sound suspiciously helicopter-like, including a "cupola" that kept spinning whether the craft was in the air or on the ground. While standing close by, Villas Boas felt the wind it generated, which escalated to "storm-like" proportions when it took off.[12] That certainly sounds like a helicopter. On the other hand, by the year 1957 you would expect just about anyone living in the modern world—including a poor farmer in Brazil—to have witnessed helicopters on occasion and thus have been able to identify one, by its characteristic noise if nothing else.

You would think so, but perhaps not, considering this interesting passage from an earlier account given by Villas Boas dated February 22, 1958 (as received by Dr. Olavo Fontes). After the vessel had risen up a certain distance off the ground:

> The whirring noise of the air being displaced became much more intense and the revolving dish began to turn at a fearful speed…At that moment, the machine suddenly changed direction, with an abrupt movement, making a louder noise, a sort of "beat"…[13]

So here we have what could pass for a reasonable description of helicopter noise. But then in the very next paragraph, we see a capability described that would presumably be impossible for a large military helicopter (or for that matter, *any* helicopter, especially for that day and age):

> Then, listing slightly to one side, that strange machine shot off like a bullet to the south, at such a speed that it was gone from sight in a few seconds.[14]

This "bullet" comparison is surely a timely warning against the temptation to latch on to the helicopter theory too quickly. In addition, although Villas Boas does describe whirring sounds and even a beat, he

---

12 Creighton, Gordon. "The Most Amazing Case of All." *Flying Saucer Review* Jan.-Feb. 1965: 17.

13 Creighton, Gordon. "Even More Amazing: Part IV." *Flying Saucer Review* Jan.-Feb. 1967: 26.

14 Ibid.

didn't comment on any sounds at all until the moment when the craft rose up off the ground, even though the "cupola" had never stopped rotating. In reading the entire Villas Boas deposition to Fontes (a good source, considering that this was only about four months after the incident), it's actually quite surprising how little he had to say about the sound, considering the deafening racket produced by helicopters in general.[15] And what are the chances that such a loud disturbance in the quiet countryside would have gone unnoticed by others, such as Villas Boas' own family members or neighbors?

The third source that can be marshalled in support of a PSYOP is a 2007 web magazine article written by Brazilian journalist Pablo Villarubia Mauso, who interviewed the living relatives of Villas Boas (who had died in 1991 at the age of 52.) The story that emerged, mostly from Villas Boas' sister Odercia, was fascinating. She recalled that after her brother had gone to Rio to be examined by Fontes and to give his deposition, a group of five uniformed men "from NASA" came and escorted him to the United States against his will, where they subjected him to questioning and a lie-detector test. They also showed him the purported remnants of a "flying saucer," as well as one that was completely intact, asking him if it was similar to what he had seen when he was abducted. He replied that indeed it was. The men also confirmed to him that extraterrestrials were visiting our planet.[16]

This account sounds suspiciously like a PSYOP as well (although it should be said that this was not the contention of the article's author). Whoever these mystery men were, what could possibly be their motivation for spilling the beans about such intelligence-sensitive topics to a Brazilian farmer, unless it was for disinformation purposes? It appears as if they were attempting to fortify an illusion they had already staged for Villas Boas (and thus for whoever was paying attention to him as well). In addition, the year 1957 was at the height of MKUltra activity, and there are strong indications that Villas Boas was dosed with some sort of mind-altering

---

15 The first "quiet" helicopter, the Hughes 500P (Penetrator) did not arrive on the scene until 1972.

16 Villarubia Mauso, Pablo. "Antonio Villas Boas: Total Abduction." *Inexplicata-Journal of Hispanic UFOlogy* 05 Nov. 2007: n. pag. Web.

drug—remember the gas that caused him to vomit?—which would jive with Nidelcovic's claims.[17]

One further piece of possible evidence in support of a PSYOP involves the physician, Dr. Olavo Fontes, who examined Villas Boas and took his deposition (along with journalist Joao Martins) in Rio de Janeiro. Fontes was also APRO's Brazilian consultant, and as such he shared the Villas Boas story with the Lorenzens. An article by Philip Coppens discusses how Fontes, who was Brazil's leading UFO investigator at the time, received a visit from officials claiming to be Brazilian Naval Intelligence officers, just four days after Fontes met Villas Boas. These officials "warned off" Fontes from pursuing his UFO research, but strangely they then proceeded to reveal to him the supposedly top secret international history of the UFO phenomenon—which had been purportedly withheld from the public.[18]

As Coppens points out, the material they shared with Fontes appears to contain the germ of what eventually became core elements of the modern UFO mythology: "…it was the first serious claim of the recovery of crashed UFOs and dead aliens. The case was also the first suggestion that military scientists were developing new technologies based on the captured craft—the so-called 'reverse engineering.'" [19] In retrospect it's easy to spot right off the bat just how suspect these claims are. Why would Fontes be warned off the UFO trail, only to be told the government's deepest and darkest UFO secrets, especially given the likelihood that Fontes would divulge those secrets (at the very least to other ufologists, which is exactly what happened). Isn't that a little counter-intuitive? It's hard not to see it for what it almost certainly must be: a counter-intelligence/disinformation program.

Was Fontes' unexpected visit somehow connected to the Villas Boas incident? Fontes himself seemed to think so, happening as it did right on the heels of his meeting with Villas Boas. Although he had been uncertain about the Villas Boas account initially, his meeting with the officials apparently led him to regard it as authentic. There is also a striking parallel

---

17 Pilkington, 2010, 112.

18 Coppens, Philip. "Doctoring Villas Boas and Aliens on Ice." *Philipcoppens.com.* N.p., n.d. Web. 30 Dec. 2016.

19 Ibid.

in the "secret" information that was shared—separately—with these two men. We saw how the "NASA" men supposedly confirmed the presence of ETs to Villas Boas and even showed him one of their purported craft; similarly, the "Naval" officers confirmed to Fontes that flying saucers existed, that they were extraterrestrial in origin, and that crashed saucers had been retrieved.[20] (Incidentally, I've seen no mention that Fontes was aware of Villas Boas' "NASA" men account. In fact, that story was uncovered only recently—in 2007 to be exact— by Villarubia Mauso.)

Looking at the total picture, the evidence favoring the view that the Villas Boas incident was a PSYOP is compelling, to be sure. At the same time, it's far from definitive, so it would seem to rate a solid "maybe."[21] But if the Villas Boas case actually *was* a PSYOP, would that suggest the possibility that Gerry's case was *also* a PSYOP? And if so, what evidence would there be for it?

A Gerry Irwin PSYOP?

What if the entire event—from Gerry's sighting onward—was orchestrated by a PSYOP team as an experiment of some kind? Using one of your own (a military man) would give you as much control, or more, over the situation as using a Brazilian farmer. No fake UFO would even be required.

Expanding on our cover-up scenario, what if Gerry was simply flagged down on the highway to help someone who seemed to be having car trouble? Then the hypothetical operatives could have moved in, used their repertoire of MKUltra techniques to implant false memories and erase others, and even written his note for him. At that point, they could have either given him a drug to knock him out for 24 hours or used post-hypnotic suggestion to achieve the same. In other words, could the entire incident have simply been planted in his mind? We'll explore this question further in Chapter 13.

---

20 Ibid.
21 I recommend that anyone interested consult the sources listed, and read Villas Boas'
entire deposition published by the *Flying Saucer Review* in 1966. The article, titled
"Even More Amazing," was printed in installments over the course of five issues,
which can be accessed on the web.

The Ghost of MKUltra?

Recall that Gerry's C.O. blocked his attempts to retrieve his own memories via hypnotic regression, with the civilian M.D. in El Paso. This raises the question of how far up the chain of command this action originated, and what exactly it was they were afraid of coming to light. How much further might they have gone in trying to prevent inconvenient memories from leaking out, or alternatively planting false ones? And if they did resort to mind control techniques, when and where would it have taken place?

One possibility is Leavenworth, where Gerry spent seven months in lockup in the U.S. Disciplinary Barracks—surely enough time to tamper extensively with his memories using whatever techniques were at their disposal (ECT, drugs, hypnosis, etc.). Prisons and psych wards were two of the preferred settings for the MKUltra experiments.[22] And as it turns out, Leavenworth is the *only* tentative Gerry/MKUltra connection I've been able to uncover in my research:

> Additional tests [of LSD on Army personnel] were carried out at the Aberdeen Proving Ground in Maryland; Fort Benning, Georgia; *Fort Leavenworth, Kansas*; Dugway Proving Ground, Utah; and in various European and Pacific stations.[23] [emphasis added]

The source quoted here goes on to note that by the middle of the 1960s, this LSD testing (which was carried out by the Army Chemical Corps) included almost 1,500 soldiers, some of whom have reported they were "coerced" into participating.[24]

22　More on this in Chapter 13.

23　Lee and Shlain, 39-40. Note: This figure only refers to LSD testing. Other chemicals—including the "super-hallucinogen" BZ (3-Quinuclidinyl benzilate)—were being tested in separate studies at other facilities. A 2012 *CNN* article revealed that soldiers at Edgewood Arsenal had in fact been exposed to BZ—as well as sarin nerve gas, LSD, and a host of others—to devastating effect. See: Martin, David S. "Vets Feel Abandoned after Secret Drug Experiments." *CNN*. Cable News Network, 01 Mar. 2012. Web. Importantly, these were not even MKUltra experiments—which highlights the fact that MKUltra was only one of several secret programs performing these studies.

24　Ibid.

The fact that LSD was being tested at Ft. Leavenworth and that this particular Army base was actually adjacent to the U.S. Disciplinary Barracks—where Gerry was imprisoned at the time—is certainly suggestive of a possible Gerry/MKULtra connection, but that's really all we have to go on at the moment. It must be remembered, however, that most of the information regarding MKUltra and related programs is gone, thanks to the massive MKUltra records purge of 1973. In any case, I believe my suspicion is justified—if you were a soldier *and a prisoner* at one and the same time, you were in double jeopardy, so to speak. As a soldier your rights would already be somewhat curtailed (to say the least), and your prisoner status would take you down yet another notch. In addition, soldiers had recently suffered a setback in their rights with the advent of the Feres Doctrine, resulting from a Supreme Court decision in 1950.[25]

No Recourse for "Guinea Pig" Soldiers

The Feres Doctrine prevents members of the armed forces from suing for injuries sustained in the performance of military service. The implications of the decision are far-reaching. If "service" is interpreted to include voluntary or involuntary mind control testing (as it has been so far[26]) then a soldier basically has no legal recourse to file a lawsuit for injuries sustained in that capacity. This is, of course, a recipe for abuse, effectively giving the mind control zealots free reign. And although we are discussing LSD at the moment, this was only one of many potential "psychochemicals" (as they were referred to) that were being tested, and these psychochemicals were only one category of the potential mind control weapons arsenal they were experimenting with—ECT and hypnosis being other examples. And since the Feres Doctrine has been in force since 1950, it was certainly in place at the time of Gerry's ordeal.

On the subject of places where Gerry could have been experimented

---

25 Feres v. United States. U. S. Supreme Court. 4 Dec. 1950.

26 United States v. Stanley. U. S. Supreme Court. 25 June 1987. In this case it was ruled that a soldier could not sue the government for injuries sustained from being secretly administered LSD as part of an experiment. The Feres Doctrine was cited as the basis for this decision, arguing that the injuries were service-related.

on, there are two other locations worth considering. The first is WBAH (William Beaumont Army Hospital). Of course, we do have the official hospital records to consult, which do not mention anything of the sort. However, Gerry was placed under a sodium amytal trance to extract information by his *regular* doctor, and who's to say there weren't other procedures—off the record—carried out by shadowy agents not affiliated with the regular hospital staff? (We'll see some troubling evidence for this very possibility in Chapter 13.)

The other location to consider is Ft. Ord, near Monterey, California. When Gerry made his return trip to Utah, upon finally coming to his senses he turned himself in to the sheriff at Cedar City. He waited there for a few days, and then M.P.s came to escort him to Fort Ord. On the face of it, this seems downright bizarre. Gerry's base was at Ft. Bliss, about 800 highway miles southeast of Cedar City, while Ft. Ord is about 680 miles west of Cedar City, *nearly in the opposite direction.* From Ft. Ord a military police escort drove Gerry back to Ft. Bliss a few days later, a distance of about 1100 miles. So, Gerry's return trip to El Paso, which should have been about 800 miles, ended up being around 1800 miles! Perhaps this is merely another example of the Army's inscrutable logic. But could it be something more sinister? Was there some special "program" in store for Gerry at Ft. Ord?

Chapter 13: The Jung-Lorenzen Letters—
Converging Clues

I think the confluence of military research and psychological trauma in the Irwin case are far more suggestive of a fairly sinister and secretive human agency. — Jeff Wells.[1]

At one point in my research, it looked like I had reached a dead-end; it seemed that I had simply run out of new leads to investigate. Faced with this impasse, I decided to mothball the project and move on to pursue other ventures. Then one day I was taken by surprise when a long-awaited package arrived in the mail. It was from the director of ICUFOR (International Center for UFO Research), which has been the custodian of the APRO files (reportedly amounting to 18 file cabinets full) since Coral Lorenzen passed away in 1988 (Jim had preceded her in death by two years). I had made a request to the director for copies of whatever documents there were in APRO's Gerry Irwin file, reasoning that, with all the questions swirling around Gerry's case, there must be some answers in that file. But in the end, who knew if anything about Gerry at all would be found in that massive archive?

The unexpected arrival of the package definitely stirred some excitement, and what was inside it did not disappoint. The envelope contained copies of several documents, which I was told represented the entire contents of the file. One document was a collection of handwritten notes taken during the Irwin investigation. A significant portion of these

---

1   Wells, Jeff. *Rigorous Intuition: What You Don't Know Can't Hurt Them* (Walterville, OR: TrineDay, 2008), Kindle ed., loc.13-14.

are faded to the point of being unreadable, but there is some fascinating information recorded in the readable parts, as we'll see. Another document was a copy of a letter sent by Jim Lorenzen to an attorney, seeking legal advice for Gerry's rather tenuous situation with the U.S. Army in the spring of 1959. Along with this was the attorney's letter of reply, giving his advice.

The Coral-Carl Letters

The real attention-getter in the packet, however, was a letter from Coral Lorenzen to Carl Jung. Three single-spaced typewritten pages long and undated, the letter begins with the very intriguing statement, "Thank you very much for your comments in your letter of 20 June," with the context indicating that the year was 1959. I was aware from reading the *APRO Bulletin* of that time period that there had been some correspondence between APRO and Jung, and it was quite exhilarating to have the opportunity to see some of it first-hand.

And not only that, but Coral was giving her response to Jung's analysis of Gerry's case, which she had obviously requested in a previous letter. In other words, *Carl Jung actually consulted on Gerry's case!* Now this was truly "breaking news!" Unfortunately, there was no copy of the letter from Jung that Coral was referring to, but after I thought it over a bit, I realized that here was a document that was almost certainly preserved somewhere.

Luckily, I was able to track down and get copies of a number of letters from the Jung/Lorenzen correspondence—but most importantly I received the letter of Jung's that Coral had referred to—the one in which Jung weighs in on Gerry's case.

It's unclear how much information Lorenzen had provided Jung in order for him to form an opinion. Although I don't have a copy of Coral's letter describing the case to Jung, I was able to find out when she wrote it. In her letter dated June 5, 1959—from her correspondence with the Swedish author K. Gösta Rehn mentioned in Chapter 8—Coral said she was "writing to Dr. Jung today for advice."[2] Given the timing then, it's *possible* at least that she could have offered him a fairly thorough account.

---

2   Lorenzen, Coral E. Letter to K. Gösta Rehn, June 5ᵗʰ, 1959. [AFU archives].

Jung Considers Gerry's Case

Getting into the letter now, Jung begins his assessment with what is essentially a disclaimer for the opinion he is about to offer—owing to the fact that he has not observed Gerry in person. He then launches into his commentary by remarking on the strangeness of how the case begins. He finds it unbelievable that a person could *spontaneously* think of, and carry out, the preparations that Gerry performed, before going off to investigate an unknown phenomenon. Thus, he surmises that Gerry had planned out his adventure—albeit unconsciously—in order to avoid returning to his official duties.

He talks about a condition that translates as ambulatory automatism, which takes over a person's volition at some point after the person has unconsciously plotted an escape from a secretly (even to themselves) undesired situation—an escape which they cannot find the courage to carry out in their normal state. (This sounds a lot like a "dissociative fugue" as we discussed previously, and according to the article noted here[3] they are basically one and the same.) He recommends hypnosis as the correct form of treatment.

Jung provides a fascinating example for comparison. He speaks of a case from nearly 60 years earlier, which was treated at the psychiatric clinic where he worked in Zurich at the time (but not by him personally). The patient was a man from Zurich who had lived in Australia for a period of years. This man came down with dengue fever, and he suddenly disappeared from Australia leaving no hint of where he had gone. Then one day he found himself in a Zurich café reading a newspaper. He saw an article about a man who had mysteriously vanished in Australia, with no indication of where might he have gone.

Suddenly the man came to his senses and—afraid that he'd lost his sanity—rushed to the psychiatric clinic (where Jung worked) for help. There he was hypnotized and the complete story emerged, covering everything from the details of his trip to the motives for his disappearance. He was terribly homesick—it turned out—but he could not bring himself

---

3   Hacking, Ian. "Automatisme Ambulatoire: Fugue, Hysteria, and Gender at the Turn of the Century." *Modernism/modernity* 3.2 (1996): 31-43. *Project Muse.* John Hopkins University, Apr. 1996. Web.

to consciously accept it. Thus, when the fever struck, it weakened his conscious will and allowed his unconscious desires to take control.

Jung concludes that Gerry probably has a similar condition, and recommends hypnosis (again), with dream analysis as a backup plan. Regarding the latter, he recommends a particular psychiatrist he knows who's an expert in this area.

Jung then moves on to discuss other conditions that may accompany or complicate ambulatory automatism—most commonly hysteria he says, but occasionally latent schizophrenia in which case, he cautions, hypnosis would not be effective.

In closing, Jung says that he deems it unlikely the Air Force is secretly involved. And finally, he cautions Ms. Lorenzen not to get too deeply involved in the case, due to the high likelihood of psychopathology being a factor.

It's intriguing that Jung mentions hysteria as the condition most closely associated with ambulatory automatism, because according to Jim Lorenzen's article Gerry actually *was* diagnosed with hysteria in Cedar City by Dr. Broadbent.[4]

A Dr. Jekyll Scenario?

It's a fascinating proposal Jung has set down to explain Gerry's behavior. It's unsettling to reflect that as we're going about our lives—thinking and doing what we normally think and do—there could be some deep, hidden part of ourselves secretly plotting a mutiny of sorts. And then one day, when we least expect it, this rogue aspect (formed of our unconscious desires) could just take over and do with us as it sees fit, while our usual self is sidelined and oblivious. The case of the man from Zurich serves as a striking case in point.

Of course, we need to bear in mind that Jung's assessment is—necessarily—of limited value to our inquiry. As Jung himself warned, it's quite problematic to offer an analysis of a case that one hasn't seen firsthand. Also, even though the timing of Coral's June 5th letter would have allowed her to give a thorough report on the case, her follow-up letter to Jung contains a wealth of detail. This may indicate that perhaps,

---

4 Lorenzen, L.J., 19.

after all, Dr. Jung had only been given a rough sketch of the case until then.

Coral fills in Carl

In this undated letter from the APRO archives, Coral begins her discussion of Gerry's case by offering Jung a curious reassurance:

> Regarding the Irwin case. Do not worry—we do not intend to get involved— at least not publicly—and even then, not until we have exhausted every avenue of investigation. Our members in Irwin's home town of Nampa, Idaho are looking into his past, and we have a couple of people at El Paso investigating his habits, etc. in the Army. Your suggestion that his may be a case of "automatisme ambulatoire" is intriguing and may very possibly be the answer, but there are certain facts which do not indicate this.

Next, Coral discusses the need to determine whether or not there could be a "physical cause" for Gerry's "trance" and his "fainting spells." To accomplish this, she mentions a plan for Gerry to get an electroencephalograph, to rule out "the possible existence of epilepsy, brain tumor, etc."

Coral then notes that Gerry had visited them at their home several weeks previously, granting them the opportunity to record a taped interview with him "of 45 minutes duration. We covered all points thoroughly, gaining much more new information."

When Coral gets to her discussion of Gerry's UFO encounter, she provides a brief description of the object. The descriptions we've seen so far have been decidedly vague (with the possible exception of Sheriff Fife's account), and although this one follows suit, it adds a qualifier— which I've highlighted— that further illustrates the perceptual challenge Gerry was grappling with:

> The object which Irwin describes as a "bright object" with no particular shape, and which he claims was responsible for his trip into the wilderness, was *very evidently not a conventional plane*, although he thought it was at the time he saw it. [emphasis added]

Coral continues with a description of Gerry's original incident here, which hews fairly closely to the narrative we're already familiar with. When she gets to the part about Gerry being flown back to Fort Bliss, she adds the interesting detail that Gerry's car remained in Cedar City under the care of the sheriff. The sheriff didn't think to check the car's antifreeze, which it apparently lacked, "and consequently the car's radiator froze up and cracked the block. It will have to have a new engine."

The letter proceeds with a discussion about what happened when Gerry got back to Ft. Bliss, including him missing his appointment with the Lorenzens on March 13, and Gerry's blackout and amnesia two days later in El Paso—whereupon he was treated at El Paso General Hospital. When Gerry regained consciousness, he was...

> ...very puzzled about his whereabouts, and with no memory whatsoever about the time between his spotting of the object and the present. His stay at Cedar City Hospital, his trip to Fort Bliss, the initial hospital observation, etc. —are all forgotten—as if his memory was wiped clean, he says.

She mentions that Gerry was re-admitted to the hospital for 32 days, and then:

> On the Thursday before he was released, he was given sodium amytal, after which, upon questioning, the Doctor told him they had not gotten any information. He kept insisting he was all right, and was told he would have to stay in the hospital for several weeks. On the next day, he was called into the surgeon general's office and told that he could return to duty.
>
> This was on a Friday, April 17. On Saturday, Irwin claims, he was overcome by an urge to return to the place where he had had the experience. He took a bus, went to Cedar City, then to the area where the side road joined the highway. He got off the bus, proceeded to walk "five or six miles", then turned off the road into the wilderness. He walked directly to a small tree, about 1 ½ or 2 miles from the road, took his jacket off from it, took a pencil from a buttonhole, unwrapped a piece of

paper, and burned it without looking at it. [5]

At this point, Coral elaborates on Gerry's dream-like condition during the episode, and recounts that when he burned the note, "he said he felt 'relieved' and 'free' again." She gives the details of Gerry walking back to Cedar City and turning himself in to the sheriff, his roundabout return to Ft. Bliss via Ft. Ord, and then his Article 15 punishment upon arriving back at the base. Besides his demotion in rank and being fined, she also mentions that Gerry lost his security clearance and was reassigned to a different job.[6]

Making Things Rough

Next, Coral discusses meeting with Gerry and the appointments they made for him with the civilian doctor skilled in hypnosis. She mentions another new detail here; that she and Jim were actually footing the bill for these treatments. She then describes the conflict that broke out between Gerry and his CO, adding some new information:

> Irwin did not keep any of the appointments, so Jim and I drove to El Paso and met him again. He said that on the evening when he had the first appointment, he had been put on extra duty and asked his commanding officer if he could get away to keep an appointment (not telling him what it was), and suggesting that he could perform the extra duty the next day. The CO said maybe he could, if he would divulge the nature of the appointment. Irwin then told him that he had an appointment to see a Doctor off the Base, because he wasn't satisfied with what the Army doctors had done and had told him. The CO then told Irwin to forget the whole thing—that he couldn't stop him from seeing the Doctor, but that he could "make it rough" for him.
>
> The next day Irwin got a taste of "how rough" it could be. Dust on the table in the room he shared with another soldier was blamed on him, etc. – little picayunish things like that. When Irwin visited Mr. Lorenzen and me, he said he was afraid to visit Dr. T. because he didn't want to get

---

5   Note the distance from the road. We'll be looking that this intriguing detail shortly.

6   Interestingly, in Jim's 1962 article, this loss of clearance and reassignment (as a file clerk) happened following the original incident, not after the return-trip to Utah.

into any more trouble although he was still determined to regain his lost memory.

Coral wraps up Gerry's story, and promises to contact the doctor that Jung had recommended, if Gerry happened to share any relevant dream material with them at their next meeting (which of course never happened). She reassures Jung that she is confident the Air force is not involved. Her suspicions regarding "UFO secrecy," she elaborates, are mainly focused on the CIA. Then she makes some revealing comments on the Army's treatment of Gerry, and how it's affecting him:

> In Irwin's case, it is possible that there is not sufficient interest on the part of the Army psychologists to bring about a successful conclusion to Irwin's problem—whatever it is. This lack of interest is evident in the fact that Irwin is a changed man. He stutters, stammers, is nervous, etc. He is determined to regain his memory—I certainly hope he succeeds and we intend to do everything to help him, whether he saw a UFO or is merely a case of "automatisme ambulatoire" as you suggest. At least it is the humane thing to do and apparently no one is interested in his quandary.

Before we proceed with our discussion of Coral's letter, it's hard not to wonder what sort of insights Dr. Jung would have offered in his response—in light of what was presumably a lot of new information for him. Unfortunately though, if Jung wrote a response, I have not seen it; or any further correspondence between them for that matter—the other letters mentioned earlier precede the above exchange.[7]

Returning to Coral's letter, there's a lot to unpack here—including some intriguing details that are not given in Jim's magazine article (which would not be published for another 3½ years). We'll be getting to these details shortly. For the moment, we see a snapshot of Coral Lorenzen that

---

7   Jung took a very strong interest in the UFO phenomenon in general. An editorial note in his fascinating book on UFOs (first published in English in 1959, i.e. the same year these letters were written), remarks that Jung had been collecting reports of the phenomenon since 1946. See: [Jung, C. G., *Flying Saucers: A Modern Myth of Things Seen in the Sky* (Princeton, NJ: Princeton University Press, 1978), vii. Print.]

reveals something of her complexity and temperament.

She comes across, by turns, as skeptic, hard-hitting journalist, dogged investigator, independent thinker (effortlessly, though respectfully, brushing aside Jung's psychological hypothesis), objective scientist, and protective mother-figure. She mentions that she has APRO members and "a couple of people" essentially acting as amateur private investigators in Nampa and El Paso, and she outlines her plans to have Gerry tested for various neurological and physiological conditions, including epilepsy.

So What *About* Epilepsy?

Speaking of epilepsy, this brain disorder would certainly be a logical possibility to explore—especially the type known as "temporal lobe epilepsy." The seizures resulting from this condition can produce an array of symptoms, including some that sound especially relevant for our purposes. According to one article, those affected can experience "… strange sensations, or have hallucinations and see, hear, feel, smell, or taste things that are not real."[8]

Coral mentioned in her letter that she intended for Gerry to receive an electroencephalograph (EEG), in order check for this condition as well as other abnormalities. Unfortunately, she never got the chance to follow through on her intention. However—unknown to the Lorenzens—Gerry actually did receive an EEG after their last contact with him. In his report of July 9th, our anonymous doctor from Ward 30 (at WBAH) noted, "An EEG was done which showed no abnormality."

As it turns out though, an EEG—especially a *single* EEG—is far from definitive in ruling out epilepsy.[9] In that light, it would seem worthwhile to explore the epilepsy scenario a little further anyway. Returning to our discussion of temporal lobe epilepsy, it appears that the resulting hallucinations can be quite convincing, and that the seizures often conclude with a blackout. But evidently the seizures rarely last more than a couple of minutes, with a following period of confusion and/or

---

8 "Temporal Lobe Epilepsy." *Wikipedia*. Wikimedia Foundation, Inc., last revision on 11 Feb. 2017. Web.

9 "Seizure Disorders and Epilepsy." *Conditions We Treat*. University of Rochester Medical Center, 2017. Web. 5 June 2017.

exhaustion typically lasting only 15 minutes at most. Even allowing for the rare exception to the rule, Gerry's 24-hour blackout would seem to be a pretty extreme outlier.

Regarding seizure-induced hallucinations; both Coral's letter and Jim's article mention that Gerry had stopped and gotten out of his vehicle to watch the object as it came down. If this was a hallucination, it was a persistent one to say the least!

Not only that, but by the time Gerry completed all the steps he took before his hike into the wilderness (turning the car around, parking, note-writing, getting out shoe-polish, writing on car, etc.), he would have been far beyond the two-minute hallucination time-frame of a seizure. And if Sheriff Fife's letter was accurate, then Gerry walked all the way to the hilltop while observing the object's light before passing out—stretching the time frame considerably further. By the time we get to the episode of Gerry's return-trip to Utah, the epilepsy hypothesis would seem rather absurd. What are the chances of a seizure-induced hallucination lasting long enough for Gerry to get all the way to Utah on a bus and walk five or six miles into the desert?

On the other hand, maybe there are rare exceptions that would fit Gerry's case. Skimming through some online forums for those dealing with epilepsy, there does appear to be a very wide range of experience with seizures and resulting hallucinations, including reports of seizures lasting for days. So perhaps there is a possibility this was a factor for Gerry. But if so, then he must have had a spontaneous recovery—because evidently he never received any treatment for such a condition, and I've seen nothing to indicate he's had any similar symptoms since then.

How Far from the Road?

In Coral's description of Gerry' return trip to Utah we find a critical detail. She relates that "He got off the bus, proceeded to walk 'five or six miles,' then turned off the road into the wilderness. He walked directly to a small tree, *about 1 ½ or 2 miles from the road...*" (emphasis added) If he really did walk that far from the road, that would definitely support our speculations regarding the Two Locations Conundrum.

In all of the reports of Gerry's original incident, the largest estimate given for the distance he walked was one mile from the highway. So what is his jacket doing here, at least half a mile, *maybe even a full mile* beyond the farthest previous estimate? Gerry himself had estimated—in the note he left in the car—that the "crash" was only a quarter-mile away; and this same figure was given (in many reports anyway) for Gerry's distance from the road when he was found.

So if Gerry really walked "1 ½ or 2 miles from the road," it would certainly lend further support to the idea that Gerry "returned" to a place that was different from the location of his original incident.

And in Amnesia News...

Another new revelation from Coral's letter is this key piece of information concerning Gerry's amnesia:

> On Sunday night, while in downtown El Paso, he lost consciousness again, woke up in the El Paso General Hospital, very puzzled about his whereabouts, and with no memory whatsoever about the time between his spotting of the object and the present. His stay at Cedar City Hospital, his trip to Fort Bliss, the initial hospital observation, etc.—are all forgotten—as if his memory was wiped clean, he says.

We've already learned about Gerry's collapse in El Paso and his resulting memory loss, according to both Jim's 1962 article and Gerry's hospital records. The fascinating thing here is that Coral is speaking in the *present tense.* In other words, as of Gerry's visit on May 30, 1959 (two and a half months after his collapse), he *still* remembered nothing of what had transpired "between his spotting of the object"—February 20—and his blackout on the streets of El Paso on March 15, a period of 23 days! As Coral observed, it was "as if his memory was wiped clean."

Given the hole in Gerry's memory that so much of 1959 fell into, this should come as no surprise. But here we have a firsthand report of Gerry's awareness of his condition *during* that critical timeframe, giving us a discreet period for at least one crucial memory gap. All in all, it lends further credence and exactitude to Gerry's story—not to mention creepiness. Could it be that his expression "wiped clean" represented—unbeknownst to Gerry—something more than a figure of speech? As we'll see, this suspicion will soon become difficult to ignore.

The Lorenzen's Paternal Side

One passage in particular from Coral's letter seems to reveal a strong personal concern, where she says, "…Irwin is a changed man. He stutters, stammers, is nervous, etc." She concludes this paragraph with, "At least it is the humane thing to do and apparently no one is interested in his quandary."

Here we catch a rare glimpse of Coral expressing almost a maternal impulse toward Gerry, in a world where Gerry doesn't seem to have any other friends or advocates. He appears to be breaking down from his treatment at the hands of the Army command structure, which seems to range from indifference to suspicion, intolerance, and impatience. I am tempted to suspect that the mental-health treatment protocols of the day, as we discussed earlier, may have played a role as well. As we shall see, this was a concern shared by the Lorenzens.

Another example of concern of this sort appears in a letter Jim Lorenzen wrote to an attorney in Connecticut dated June 6, 1959. It's worth reproducing in full, since it tells Gerry's story from a legal perspective—providing an intriguing new angle from which to observe matters. He begins by summing up Gerry's situation:

> The situation briefly is this: Circumstantial evidence indicates that our subject—an enlisted man in the U.S. Army—is the victim of either medical malpractice or extreme incompetence. The young man concerned had a UFO experience. He was subsequently placed in the psychiatric ward for observation and examination. The standard psychologist indicated that he was an alert, normal individual; yet he had periods of unconsciousness and amnesia, for which the Army doctors could not account. Finally in an attempt (purported) to pierce the amnesia, sodium amytal was used.
>
> Abruptly after the "truth serum" session he was released from the hospital. The following day he became victim of an overwhelming compulsion to return to the scene of the UFO incident, even though this being A.W.O.L. In the vicinity he found and destroyed evidence supporting the reality of his original story. Upon destruction of the evidence, the compulsion dissolved

and our subject returned to his original state of mind. He turned himself in to law officers as soon as possible and was returned to station where he was administered punishment for misconduct under "article 15" and resultantly demoted in rank. This was on the testimony of two Army doctors that our subject had been in full command of his facultys [sic] and there[fore]— responsible for his actions. They also advised him that he should "learn to control his urges". On the basis of this latter remark our boy went to the Inspector General of his post. He told the I.G. he felt he had been punished unfairly and that instead he warranted help in learning to control these "urges" if what they said was true. The I. G. agreed and our boy is scheduled to return for another medical consultation on 10 July.

1. Can an Army enlisted man be penalized for seeking civilian medical help?
2. Does he have any recourse against the Army medicos should malpractice be indicated?
3. Can he legally refuse sodium amytal should they want to try it again? (concerning the first treatment, the doctor, a Captain, had remarked "it didn't work")
4. Can he insist on having a witness of his own choice present at any future truth serum sessions?

You see, it is possible he has already been made to destroy important evidence through post-hypnotic suggestion. I'm afraid of what they might do to him if they ever got him under again. The boy is cooperative but not a little confused. If we can only have a little time to work this out it may turn out to be a very important case. Any thoughts you may have on the subject will be welcomed. In the meantime would you please keep the information confidential?

One can sense a paternal, protective impulse in the barely contained outrage just below the surface of Jim's words, as well as an almost fatherly pride in his description of "our boy" taking his case to the I.G. We also see the first mention of the "post-hypnotic suggestion" idea, which later made it into Jim's article, and on this subject he makes a direct reference to Gerry finding and destroying evidence "supporting the reality of the original story." Mr. Lorenzen is clearly alarmed at the implications of Gerry's testimony, and concerned that Gerry could suffer more harm if similar tactics were applied in the future.

Then there's the line with the revealing quote, "They also advised him that he should 'learn to control his urges,'" which is perhaps illuminating of the Army's general attitude toward Gerry and his difficulties. And even though it's indirect, it's the only quote we've seen anywhere in which an Army official refers to a detail specific to Gerry's return-trip to Utah—in this case Gerry's "urges."

A Scared Kid in Real Trouble

In these letters by Jim and Coral Lorenzen, we see a poignant emotional truth emerge that was only hinted at previously; namely, Gerry's vulnerability. We have certainly seen his anger and frustration, as reported by his doctors and psychologists, but here we catch sight of a young man caught in a very frightening situation—struggling to recover from a debilitating neurological condition while having to face the cold and unforgiving calculus of the Army command structure.

It's probably not surprising that the Army had little patience for him—after all, it's an institution whose primary purpose involves transforming humans into reliable components of war machinery. Any machine part that reverts back to human unpredictability (and thus jeopardizing the smooth functioning of the system) must be either repaired or discarded. Gerry's repair process was not going at all according to the manual, and thus he was skating close to the edge of the discard bin. The Lorenzen letters reveal a scared and confused young man who really had nowhere else to turn except Jim and Coral, and his access to them seems to have been highly restricted due to intense pressure from his CO. In short, Gerry was caught in a tight spot.

As far as Coral and Jim were concerned, it's obvious they saw his plight quite clearly, and felt compelled to do whatever they could to help him. You can sense their frustration in the face of the Army's relentless rigidity, but they did what they could. They were paying for psychiatric services (that were never utilized) out of their own pockets, and it seems likely they were springing for legal advice as well. On that score, they finally did get some feedback from the attorney they consulted. Here's his response dated June 15, 1959:

While I sympathize very much with your position in this matter yet since the Subject is an enlisted man in the U.S. Army he is completely under the jurisdiction of the military authorities, subject only to such privileges as are granted to him or to which he is entitled by virtue of the pertinent provisions of the U.S. Army regulations and laws.

However, in reply to your questions, may I advise as follows:

1. An enlisted man cannot be penalized for seeking civilian medical help, according to my best information.
2. Apparently he does not have recourse against Army medicos for malpractice but he might well have a claim against the U.S. Government since the medicos are acting on its behalf.
3. The enlisted man can legally refuse sodium amytal unless the injection thereof is indicated in the treatment for a condition from which the enlisted man is suffering, in the opinion of the doctors. This is usually a question for medical interpretation giving due consideration to all of the facts and the case history of the subject. I am sure that without the support of the medical authority any layman's opinion in this matter would be of no force or effect.
4. While I am not familiar with the Army regulations relating to this question, yet it would seem to me, based on preliminary and cursory investigation, that the patient has a right to insist on having an unbiased witness present at any examination involving the application or injection of a drug about which there is some question. It should be borne in mind that an enlisted man is governed solely and completely by the laws and regulations of the U.S. Army and is subject to the disciplines thereof.

The questions asked would seem to indicate that the problems involved are as much a medical problem as a legal one. In case of apparent abuse of authority or violation of the Army laws, rules and regulations, a complaint by parents or other interested parties to the proper authority as outlined in the rules of procedure applicable thereto, might have some effect. There have been cases of complaints made to the U.S. Senator or Congressman of the enlisted man's own State which have expedited or brought about a review of a particular situation.

In so many words, it appears the attorney was saying there wasn't much he could do for Gerry under the circumstances. As we've touched upon elsewhere, Gerry's rights were fairly restricted as a soldier, as the lawyer states quite succinctly. However, one notable exception is pointed out in his recommendation number 1: "An enlisted man cannot be penalized for seeking civilian medical help..." On this count at least, it would seem that Gerry actually did have some rights; and it appears they were violated.

Regardless of his conclusions, however, the attorney's advice evidently came to naught—because after that weekend when Gerry came to visit the Lorenzens at their home (May 30), they never saw or heard from him again. Therefore, the Lorenzens didn't know that on July 5, Gerry went to the El Paso police in a state of confusion, reporting that "he did not know who he was or anything about himself. He allegedly bought a newspaper to find out what city he was in."[10] In short, Gerry's troubles were far from over, but he was truly on his own now. Why didn't Gerry ever talk to the Lorenzens again? Was it his problem with memory lapses, or his fear of getting into more trouble, or both perhaps? We'll never know at this point, and Gerry certainly doesn't remember.

It's quite sad to consider, though—the thought of a frightened and bewildered young man who had friends who were willing to go to great lengths to help him, if only he could get to them. It is sad as well that the Gerry of today does not even remember meeting the Lorenzens. In other words, the very problems that the Lorenzens were trying to help Gerry overcome, resulted in the Lorenzens themselves disappearing from Gerry's memory. Given the fact that this was happening even while they were in contact with him (as Jim reported in his article, "...he did not recall our previous conversations due to the memory lapse previously mentioned..."[11]), perhaps this should come as no surprise. But again, we must ask, *what caused the amnesia?*

Chilling New Clues Emerge
Among the documents I received in the package from the APRO archives was an intriguing batch of papers we have not yet fully explored. This

---

10 Hospital records. See Chapter 5.
11 Lorenzen, L.J., 24.

is the small collection of handwritten notes— presumably written by Coral or Jim Lorenzen—during their investigation of Gerry's case in the spring of 1959. We previously saw some of the still legible information from the portion of the notes that is badly faded. Reproduced below is the remaining, clearly legible material. Some of this material sent a bit of a chill up my spine when I first read it.

Friday, March 13th, 1959: Went to Bldg. 1002 as per apt. (3:30) by phone 11 Mar 1959. Waited until 4:15. Orderly said Irwin not at duty phone— not in room.[12] Seemed to get run-around. Contacted him again at 9:30 by phone. He had been called into hospital for "check-up"—due to go in again on Monday.

Subsequent calls (S to S) thru Ft. Bliss op. revealed Irwin kept in hospital. Dr. B. later informed he had been released on 17 April. [no new date entered here, simply a continuation in the log, but clearly we have skipped ahead in time here—D.B.]

During one call Orderly at Bldg. 1002 said "book says A.W.O.L.—chart says he's still in hospital."

1 May 1959: Went to E.P. [El Paso], made contact with Irwin at Bldg. 1002—as per prior arrangement by phone. D. Holbert went into bldg., got Irwin, we took him to drive-in for a cold drink—then to Dr. T. office. Afterward, went to dinner at Martino's in Juarez. Irwin seemed grateful for our interest. We took him back to Ft. Bliss, then proceeded to L.C. [assuming this is Las Cruces, between El Paso and Alamogordo] to let H. off, then home to A. [Alamogordo]

8 May: Dr. B's sec. called, relayed message that Irwin had not kept appt. on 6 May at 3:30 as planned.

13 May: Did not show up for appt.

20 May: Called H.—asked him to investigate.

---

12 In Army talk as noted previously, "orderly" refers to clerical staff in the company level of Army administration.

25 May: Called Dr. T.—who is leaving on vacation. He is very disappointed—agrees that I. may be under post-hypnotic suggestion to forget anyone who contacts him, etc.

Also called H.—who wasn't in. He was supposed to call in any results, neg. or otherwise, but hadn't.

The first entry that really calls out for attention here is "book says A.W.O.L.—chart says he's still in hospital." I get a very uncomfortable feeling when I read this. The exact date of this entry is not recorded, but we can determine from its order of appearance in the log that it was sometime between April 17 and May 8. It *could* be merely a filing or clerical error, but what if it's not?

If not, then just what on earth was going on at that moment for Gerry? According to Jim's 1962 article, Gerry went AWOL on April 18, but as we saw previously (in Chapter 8), the handwritten notes claim he didn't leave until two days later, in accord with Army records. However, these same notes *do* say that Gerry developed his *urge* on the 18th, so on that point there is complete agreement. If we can't be sure what else happened on the 18th, at the very least we know Gerry felt the "urge."

One detail that could be important comes from a report we've already discussed from Dr. Valentine dated April 28. As we recall, he prepared this report in response to a request from Gerry's C.O., to help him determine if Gerry was mentally fit and therefore responsible for his recent actions (i.e. his AWOL return trip to Utah). Dr. Valentine recounts Gerry's clinical history as previously recorded, adding only one detail. He states, "The only other significant piece of information is that the patient reported in to the Ft. Bliss dispensary about a week ago, complaining of blackout spells." When he says "about a week ago" technically that would be around April 21. Given that Gerry went AWOL on the 20th, it must have occurred just before that. Furthermore, the Lorenzens' notes, as we've seen, said Gerry developed his "urge" to return to Utah on the 18th.[13]

In other words, sometime between developing his "urge" and then abandoning Ft. Bliss, Gerry complained to the dispensary about having

---

13 See Chapter 8.

blackouts—so, probably on the 19th (to keep as close as possible to Valentine's timeline). Meanwhile, we see from the handwritten notes that evidently, between the time Gerry was released from the hospital and the time he actually went AWOL, he was listed as being *both AWOL and in the hospital at the same time*. This is a very troubling convergence of events to say the least. A mysterious urge followed by blackouts, and all the while the Army can't decide whether Gerry is AWOL or still present on their own psych ward! *Was Gerry being subjected to secret procedures in the hospital, with the AWOL story as a cover-up?* Or only slightly less disturbing, was it the other way around? *Were they trying to cover up his AWOL for some reason?*

Whatever it was, the very next day (April 20) Gerry entered a trance and boarded a bus to Utah, thereby initiating that whole bizarre sequence of events. And to add yet one more small but intriguing wrinkle, recall for a moment our earlier discussion regarding repeated dates. It's an interesting coincidence that Gerry's entranced return to Utah occurred *exactly* two months after the original incident (i.e., February 20 and April 20). Could this be an indication of a timetable under someone else's control?

There is one other entry of concern from the notes we saw above, which is a reference to something "Dr. T." had said: "He is very disappointed— agrees that I. [Irwin] may be under post-hypnotic suggestion to forget anyone who contacts him, etc." "Dr. T." is undoubtedly the civilian doctor with a specialty in hypnosis, whom Coral referred to in her letter to Jung (and whom Jim spoke of in his 1962 article as well). So a *medical hypnotist* suspected that *post-hypnotic suggestion* was being utilized to isolate Gerry. If this is what was going on, then the barely concealed rage we see in Jim's letter to the attorney seems all the more understandable.

Disconcerting Dates

As I considered these two entries together (i.e. the note placing Gerry in two places at one time, and the note about "Dr. T"'s suspicion) they seemed to take on a greater significance. Then suddenly, a new piece clicked into place, as a previously disregarded detail sprang to mind. *The dates! There are differing dates given for the sodium amytal interview!* This discrepancy, which until now had seemed little more than a nitpicking distraction, was taking on a whole new meaning. Let's take a look.

The notes above state that according to "Dr. B.," Gerry was released from the hospital psych ward on April 17, a Friday.[14] This agrees with Gerry's testimony as recorded by the Lorenzens as well as with hospital records. All well and good so far, right?

Now Coral's letter states that the sodium amytal interview took place on the Thursday before his release, i.e. April 16. In Jim's letter to the attorney, he observes that "Abruptly after the 'truth serum' session he was released from the hospital." (So, basically the same time frame.) In Jim's 1962 article, he notes that the amytal session occurred "after about 30 days" on the ward",[15] which would be roughly April 15. Since it's a rough estimate, it could easily be the 16th. So the Lorenzen sources basically agree the amytal interview happened on April 16th. So to recap: Amytal on the 16th, release on the 17th, and the "urge"—on the 18th.

Not Adding Up

Now we're about to get way out of kilter, because according to *hospital* records, "On 27 March 59 he was given an intravenous Sodium Amytal interview."[16] This date is *19 or 20 days earlier* than the time frame given by the Lorenzens. So, what can this mean? Were there *two rounds* of sodium amytal? Or even *more,* perhaps? Was Gerry made to forget the previous amytal session (or sessions)? These are serious questions to say the least!

Now, as if the confusion over the amytal dates wasn't enough, we also have a discrepancy over the AWOL dates. The three Lorenzen sources quoted here all agree that Gerry returned to Utah the day following his release, i.e. April 18. But as we've seen, this disagrees with the handwritten notes which state that Gerry "returned to scene" on April 20—a date corroborated by Army AWOL records.[17] What's going on here? It's hard to know what to make of this, but we can say that one of two things

14 Incidentally, the logical identity for "Dr. B." would be the anonymous doctor in charge of Ward 30, whom we first met in Chapter 5.
15 Lorenzen, L.J., 21-22.
16 See Chapter 11.
17 See timeline in Chapter 8.

happened on April 18: either Gerry simply developed his "urge" to return to Utah, or, he not only developed his "urge," but he also went into a trance and boarded the bus to Utah that day. If the latter is true, that would mean the Army records are incorrect.

But either way, something very significant happened on the day following Gerry's release. Maybe he eventually conflated his "urge" with his follow-through (two days later) in his memory. Whatever the case, it appears Gerry was clear about two critical details here: 1) that he had the amytal interview right at the end of his confinement at WBAH, and 2) that his urge (at least) to return to Utah happened the day after being released.

His (relative) clarity on this timeline makes sense, considering that these are events you would think one would not easily forget—the "truth serum" session, followed by his release from the psych ward, and then developing a powerful urge and going to Utah in a trance (whether that same day, or two days later)—all in quick succession. Considered in this light, the 20-day amytal session discrepancy seems all the more disturbing. It would be quite bizarre to mistake a *nearly three-week gap* (between the amytal session and his return to Utah) for a one-or-two-day gap, especially if you were recalling these events shortly after they happened, as was the case here.

It seems reasonable then to propose that Gerry had an amytal interview on March 27 as stated in the hospital records—which disappeared from his memory (perhaps with a little "help")—and that he *then* had a *second amytal session* on April 15 or 16, which was not recorded in the hospital records. And one can't help but wonder if—on this latter date—someone besides the regular medical staff was involved! Of course, these new details alone don't prove anything. But added to everything else we've uncovered in our investigation, the proposition that there was a secret program in place to alter Gerry's mind and memories is getting harder and harder to dismiss.

Hypnotic Suggestion—It's All in the Timing

Before we move on, there's another very important point to consider. To recap for a moment, the records mention an amytal date that Gerry didn't seem to remember. Furthermore, Gerry recalled a *later* amytal date that doesn't appear in the records. This begins to make more sense if you think in terms of a secret operation.

If you wanted to give someone a post-hypnotic suggestion in order to send them on a secret mission, would you do it a day or two before the mission, or would you do it three weeks beforehand? Common sense would dictate that the smaller the time interval the better, right? In other words, the *later* amytal session—the one Gerry remembered, only a couple of days before his trance-induced AWOL—was probably the one in in which he was secretly programmed, in this scenario.

While that idea seems to make *intuitive* sense, is there any science to back it up? Well in fact, there is. According to the published abstract for a study dating all the way back to 1929, "The power of post-hypnotic suggestion steadily *decreases during the first three weeks after it is given.*"[18] (emphasis added) Note that the study was published 30 years before these events, which means—presumably—this information would have long since been known to hypnosis specialists, at least. So in this light, hypnotizing Gerry three weeks before his hypothetical secret mission to Utah would seem ill-advised to say the least! Thus it seems reasonable to guess that the only amytal session he was able to remember—i.e. the later one—was the one in which he was given his fateful post-hypnotic suggestion. That would also explain why this second session doesn't show up on the record!

Not only does this scenario begin to make sense out the otherwise bewildering discrepancies; but importantly, it would also serve to validate Gerry's beleaguered memory of these events.

Ultimately it all points to a larger question: If the scenario just outlined is accurate, why did they do it? Was it simply because Gerry fulfilled the criteria for a good mind-control research subject? Or was it because they were afraid of something that Gerry *might* remember, i.e. something about what he saw on that fateful night in Utah? These are questions that cannot be easily laid to rest.

The bottom line is that it looks like somebody wanted Gerry to destroy the only physical evidence of his encounter. If this is true, it would point

---

18 Kellogg, E. R. "Duration and Effects of Post-hypnotic Suggestions." *Journal of Experimental Psychology* 12.6 (1929): 502-14. *ResearchGate.* Web.

to a cruel irony in the quote we saw from Jim's letter to the attorney, "he should learn to control his urges"—that is, the Army may have been punishing Gerry for doing the very thing they had programmed him for![19]

But hold on...there's more.

Nazis in Bliss

There is one crucial aspect of Gerry's story that we have thus far skipped over, which is the unsettling history of Gerry's duty station—Ft. Bliss. Immediately after the defeat of Germany in World War 2, a desperate race ensued between the U.S., the U.K., and the Soviet Union to capture Nazi scientists and intelligence officers and...*to secure their professional services!*

This high-stakes game between the recent wartime Allies could be summed up as, *He who ends up with the most Nazis wins,* because at that time the Third Reich boasted many of the best scientists in the world, in fields ranging from rocketry, engineering, and aerospace technology to military intelligence and counter-intelligence, medicine, and mind control. The Army's slogan "WE WANT YOU" could have been the motto of this secret Nazi recruitment program, which on the U.S. side was dubbed *Operation Paperclip* (aka *Project* Paperclip).

Under Paperclip, approximately 1,500 Nazi scientists, doctors, and engineers were essentially smuggled into the U.S. and put to work developing American military technology, military intelligence, and mind control. (It was later revealed that a large proportion of them were actually *ardent* Nazis, which explains why they had to be essentially smuggled in!) By 1946, Ft. Bliss had received 104 Nazi rocket scientists under Paperclip, many of whom, including Wernher von Braun, had worked at Peenemünde, Germany, developing the V-2 rocket—which was employed to devastating effect against England during the war. (Von Braun later went on to head NASA's Marshall Space Flight Center, where he oversaw the development of the Saturn V—the rocket which powered the Apollo

---

19 Of course, in such a large organization, oftentimes the right hand doesn't know what the left hand is doing, especially where black-ops are concerned!

Program's moon expeditions.)[20]

Bluebirds Beget Artichokes

As always, one good black project begets another, and Paperclip was no exception. According to author Annie Jacobsen's book on the subject, "Eventually, physicians and chemists from Operation Paperclip would work on jointly operated classified programs, code-named Chatter, Bluebird, Artichoke, MKUltra and others."[21] So, basically, MKUltra (chartered in 1953) emerged from Artichoke (1951), which came from Bluebird (1950), which in turn was born (at least in part) from Project Paperclip.

As we saw previously, MKUltra was a CIA program for developing mind control techniques. As one government report stated, "According to Sidney Gottlieb, a medical doctor and former CIA agent [and crucially, head of MKUltra], MKULTRA was established to investigate whether and how an individual's behavior could be modified by covert means."[22]

And where did the subjects for those investigations come from? In answer, it would appear that the program followed in the footsteps of its Nazi precursors (not to mention—undoubtedly—its Nazi *participants!*). Author John Marks observed:

> Wherever their extreme experiments went, the CIA sponsors picked for subjects their own equivalents of the Nazis' Jews and gypsies: mental patients, prostitutes, foreigners, drug addicts, and prisoners, often from

---

20 Von Braun was no Nazi lightweight, either. He admitted he was a member of "Hitler's elite SS" in a letter to Major General Julius Klein dated August 2, 1969. After making this startling admission, Von Braun continued, "I would appreciate it if you would keep the information to yourself, as any publicity would harm my work with NASA." See: Ross, Colin A., M.D. *The CIA Doctors: Human Rights Violations by American Psychiatrists* (Richardson, TX: Manitou Communications, 2006), Ch.1.

21 Jacobsen, Annie. *Operation Paperclip: The Secret Intelligence Program that Brought Nazi Scientists to America* (Boston, MA: Little, Brown and Company, 2014), 302.

22 United States Senate, 103rd Congress, 2nd Session, Committee on Veterans' Affairs. *Is Military Research Hazardous to Veterans' Health?* John D. Rockefeller, West Virginia, Chairman (Washington, DC: U.S. General Accounting Office, 1994), Print, Web. 10.

minority ethnic groups.[23]

To further illustrate this point, an article from the *New York Times* quotes a CIA official—who aptly described the program's victims as "'people who could not fight back.'"[24]

Soldiers were among the preferred subjects as well. Witness the following excerpt from an official report of the U.S. Senate's Committee on Veteran's Affairs:

> Working with the CIA, the Department of Defense gave hallucinogenic drugs to *thousands of "volunteer" soldiers* in the *1950's* and 1960's. In addition to LSD, the Army also tested quinuclidinyl benzilate, a hallucinogen code-named BZ. (cit.) Many of these tests were conducted under the so-called MKULTRA program, established to counter perceived Soviet and Chinese advances in brainwashing techniques. Between *1953 and 1964*, the program consisted of 149 projects involving drug testing and other studies on *unwitting human subjects*.[25] [emphasis added]

There's a LOT More Where That Came From

Note that the word "volunteer" appears in quotation marks in the original. When you're already enlisted in the Army, I guess volunteering is a relative term. (The quotes probably also refer to claims of soldiers who said they were coerced into participating—as noted in a previous chapter.) But regardless, we need to bear in mind that the official facts and figures are only the proverbial tip of the iceberg.

As we've seen, the vast majority of the program's documents were ordered destroyed by then CIA Director Richard Helms in 1973. The trifling portion that survived was due to a serendipitously overlooked archive of financial records; otherwise there would be virtually nothing

---

23 Marks, John. *The Search for the "Manchurian Candidate": The CIA and Mind Control* (New York: Times, 1979), 9-10.

24 Weiner, Tim. "Sidney Gottlieb, 80, Dies; Took LSD to C.I.A." *New York Times* 10 Mar. 1999.

25 United States Senate, 103rd Congress, 2nd Session, Committee on Veterans' Affairs. *Is Military Research Hazardous to Veterans' Health?* John D. Rockefeller, West Virginia, Chairman (Washington, DC: U.S. General Accounting Office, 1994), 9. Regarding BZ, see also footnote in Chapter 12 of present work.

left. Hence, there were 149 MKUltra projects (aka "subprojects") *that we know of.* There were thousands of "volunteer" soldiers being experimented on *that we know of,* and who could guess how many non-volunteers? And "Eighty-six universities or institutions were involved."[26] Again, *that we know of.*

The important point here is that although I have never found an exact match for MKUltra experimentation coinciding with Gerry's dates and locales, this actually tells us very little. Essentially there's a black hole where all the records should be. Be that as it may however, what we have just seen actually amounts to some very compelling circumstantial evidence. To begin with, Gerry fell into *three of the main categories* that were favored for MKUltra research—i.e. mental patients, prisoners, and soldiers. In addition:

- Ft. Bliss was a hub of Operation Paperclip activity.
- Paperclip scientists participated in MKUltra (although we don't know if any of these Nazi mind control experts were actually working at Ft. Bliss).
- Gerry was stationed at Ft. Bliss during the height of the MKUltra program
- MKUltra was run in partnership between the CIA and a branch of the U.S. Army (i.e. Gerry's employer.)

The Academic Angle
Other than this, I did manage to uncover one more interesting tidbit. It turns out that one of the 44 universities that participated in MKUltra research was the University of Texas, which has a campus in El Paso—right next door to Ft. Bliss. An article typical of the newspaper coverage (at the time of these revelations) reported that the CIA informed the University of Texas that there had been CIA funded "research on human behavior" at one of their facilities during the "1950s or 1960s."[27]

---

26 United States Senate, Senate Select Committee on Intelligence. *Project MKULTRA.* 95th Cong., 1st sess. Washington D.C.: U.S. Gov. Printing Office, 1977, 3.

27 "UT Did CIA Work on Human Behavior." *Abilene Reporter-News* [Abilene, Texas] 3 Sept. 1977: 80. Print.

The CIA refrained from specifying which particular school was involved, but according to a UT official, this information was being requested. The CIA said the purpose of the research was to discover "materials and methods" that could be effectively employed to modify human behavior. The CIA representative further commented that, unlike the CIA drug-testing research that had garnered so much media attention, the majority of the research at UT dealt with "far less controversial investigations…" The agency official deigned to toss out one more crumb of information—the project name, i.e. MKUltra. But, true to form, he or she wouldn't provide any specific information about the research or who was engaged in it.[28]

It is certainly difficult to take the reassurances of the CIA at face value, considering the fact that deception is practically the agency's modus operandi; that, and the lack of available records to check its statements against. Furthermore, if the research was so harmless, *why the ongoing and intense secrecy?* And speaking of the missing records, the quoted CIA official actually acknowledged this point (i.e. that most of the MKUltra documents had been purged in 1973), adding that only records of finance remained—which presented only a "fragmentary picture" of what was going on.[29]

The bottom line seems to be: they're not telling, and we'll never find out anyway because they got rid of the files. But strangely, *somehow the feds still seem to know all the facts.* What documents are *they* consulting? And incidentally, I can vouch for the "fragmentary picture" description, having personally spent too many hours poring over what remains of these files online. It's all very Orwellian—document after document, many thousands of them, with mundane details about payments owed or payments made, with all identifying information blacked out. You can't tell who is performing the services, what the services entail, or even where they are taking place. About all that's left are the dates and the bare

---

28 Ibid.
29 Ibid.

accounting details.[30]

But getting back to Gerry, here he was in the middle of what was potentially a real nexus of MKUltra activity; right in the belly of the beast so to speak. Just look at what was available in El Paso: an enormous Army base, an Army hospital psych ward, a university campus, and a beehive of Paperclip/Nazi scientist activity. On top of all that, El Paso is a Mexican border town, which could open up the possibility for international hijinks as well. All told, it certainly looks like fertile ground for the mind-control crowd.

Given all the damning evidence that has emerged, one has to wonder what was going on in the minds of those employed by the project. On that count we actually have a document that may shed some light, at least, on how one agent in particular felt about his work. In a letter from George Hunter White (the head of a particularly lurid MKUltra subproject codenamed "Operation Midnight Climax") to Sydney Gottlieb (MKUltra chief), White looked back on his career with the program:

> "I was a very minor missionary, actually a heretic, but I toiled wholeheartedly in the vineyards because it was fun, fun, fun. Where else could a red-blooded American boy lie, kill, cheat, steal, rape, and pillage with the sanction and blessing of the All-Highest?"[31]

Methods of Madness

A rare surviving MKUltra document from 1955—that is actually both intelligible and intact, provides a telling glimpse into the scope of the program regarding some of its research aims for testing mind-altering drugs and other mind control means (I've added emphasis to the items that could be relevant to Gerry's story):

---

30 Luckily, there actually are some scattered nuggets of revealing data buried in this bureaucratic haystack, and some very dedicated researchers (beginning with John Marks) have sifted through, recovered them and actually succeeded in piecing together a coherent—though necessarily partial—picture of the program. See Bibliography under "MKUltra and Mental Health" for some of the better books that examine this data.

31 Lee and Shlain, 35.

A portion of the Research and Development Program of TSS/Chemical Division is devoted to the discovery of the following materials and methods:

1. Substances which will promote illogical thinking and impulsiveness to the point where the recipient would be discredited in public.
2. Substances which increase the efficiency of mentation and perception.
3. Materials which will cause the victim to age faster/slower in maturity.
4. Materials which will promote the intoxicating effect of alcohol.
5. Materials which will produce the signs and symptoms of recognized diseases in a reversible way so that they may be used for malingering, etc.
6. *Materials which will cause temporary/permanent brain damage and loss of memory.*
7. Substances which will enhance the ability of individuals to withstand privation, torture and coercion during interrogation and so-called "brain-washing".
8. *Materials and physical methods which will produce amnesia for events preceding and during their use.*
9. *Physical methods of producing shock and confusion over extended periods of time and capable of surreptitious use.*
10. Substances which produce physical disablement such as paralysis of the legs, acute anemia, etc.
11. Substances which will produce a chemical that can cause blisters.
12. Substances which alter personality structure in such a way that the tendency of the recipient to become dependent upon another person is enhanced.
13. *A material which will cause mental confusion of such a type that the individual under its influence will find it difficult to maintain a fabrication under questioning.*
14. Substances which will lower the ambition and general working efficiency of men when administered in undetectable amounts.
15. Substances which promote weakness or distortion of the eyesight or hearing faculties, preferably without permanent effects.
16. *A knockout pill which can surreptitiously be administered in drinks, food, cigarettes, as an aerosol, etc., which will be safe to use, provide*

*a maximum of amnesia, and be suitable for use by agent types on an
ad hoc basis.*

*17. A material which can be surreptitiously administered by the above
routes and which in very small amounts will make it impossible for
a person to perform physical activity.* "[32]

Note specifically the repeated term "materials and methods." This is
the exact same term we saw used in the newspaper article regarding the
UT MKUltra experiments, in which the CIA insisted these experiments
were "...far less controversial investigations..." I wonder which of these
"materials and methods" were so non-controversial?

A Scary Proposition

Tying all these threads together served to inflame a suspicion that had
been simmering on the back burner until these new revelations emerged:
*Was Gerry's entire ordeal the result of a mind control experiment, from the
very start?* As I was beginning to take this idea seriously, I stumbled across
one author's appraisal of this very possibility. The author is Jeff Wells,
and his very thought-provoking and hard-to-categorize book, *Rigorous
Intuition*, takes on everything from political intrigue and disinformation
to the occult and the paranormal.[33]

After summarizing Gerry's story, Wells lays out his case. He comments
that all the accounts of Gerry's story he's seen seem to regard the "military
backstory" as being "incidental." He sees this as a serious oversight,
because Gerry was based on an Army installation (Ft. Bliss) that served as
a nexus for Nazi scientists recruited by Project Paperclip. Wells observes
that, besides their prowess in rocket engineering, Paperclip scientists also
brought along their expertise in mind control.[34]

After noting the hypnotic suggestion-like behavior in Gerry's return-

---

32 United States Senate, 95th Congress, 1st Session. Select Committee on Intelligence
   and Committee on Human Resources. *Project MKULTRA, The CIA's Program of
   Research in Behavioral Modification* (Washington D.C.: U.S. Gov. Printing Office,
   1977), Appendix C, 123-124.
33 Wells, Jeff. *Rigorous Intuition: What You Don't Know Can't Hurt Them*
   (Walterville, OR: TrineDay, 2008), Kindle ed., 12-14.
34 Ibid., 13.

trip to Utah, especially his sudden awakening upon burning the note, Wells writes:

> The only tenuous UFO connection is Irwin's claim to have seen a bright object traversing the sky, though it looked to him no stranger than an aircraft in trouble. And given the tricks his mind was playing, or the tricks someone was playing on his mind, perhaps we shouldn't assume there was anything to see at all. There were no other witnesses, and no evidence of a landing.
>
> Was Irwin the unwitting subject of an experiment in mind control? Could be. Even though I'm persuaded of a UFOlogical reality that transcends hoaxes and cover stories, I think the confluence of military research and psychological trauma in the Irwin case are far more suggestive of a fairly sinister and secretive human agency.[35]

It seems to me that Wells has good instincts, especially considering the relatively limited information on this case that's been available until now. The scenario he describes seems plausible, and he certainly could be right. But before we jump to any conclusions, is there anything in Gerry's case—uncovered in our present inquiry—that does *not fit* this scenario?

"Mind Control All the Way" vs "Two Locations"

Potentially, the biggest challenge to this "mind control all the way" hypothesis is the problem of the two locations (the "TLC"). To revisit this conundrum, thinking now in terms of mind control tactics, let's say that Gerry actually *was* "programmed" to believe he saw a strange light in the sky on the night of February 20. Now, the fact that he and his car were found along Highway 20 is well-documented. Here is the tricky part: If Gerry is right, and he went back to Utah in April and found his missing jacket near Highway 14, how on earth did it end up nearly 50 miles away from the place where he saw the UFO? And how did he know where to find it?

This is quite an interesting question from the mind control perspective. Are we looking at a plan so elaborate that the government operatives actually removed his jacket and physically relocated it to its new location,

---

35 Ibid. Reproduced with permission from the author.

only to "program" Gerry with the exact directions on how to find it, somewhere out there in the wide-open desert scrub of southern Utah? Or conversely, did they somehow "implant" the entire memory of his return-trip to Utah, embellishing it with all those fascinating details to make it feel more believable? (In that case, we would have one possible explanation for the fact that Gerry was listed both as AWOL and as an in-patient of the psych ward at the same time.) Either option seems far-fetched, but who knows? As we'll see later on, it appears that we've possessed the technology (hypnosis) to—at least hypothetically—achieve similar results for quite a while.

All things considered then, and unless and until more evidence surfaces, the "mind control all the way" proposal remains a distinct possibility.

The Ring of Truth

At this juncture, let's step back briefly and take a moment to reflect on the role of the Lorenzens in all of this. When I began writing this book, I never would have guessed how deeply they were involved in Gerry's story. The more I've learned about them along the way, the more I've been impressed by them. They demonstrated real integrity, and there is little doubt that they truly cared about Gerry. On that count, it seems they remembered Gerry long after they lost contact with him. According to researcher Loren Gross, "Coral Lorenzen would not forget the Erwin [sic] case. In fact it haunted her."[36]

For me, discovering the Lorenzens' true colors has helped to bring Gerry's story to life, to make it real, knowing that the details of the story they provided can (for the most part) be relied on, even when Gerry's own memory cannot. And one of those details points right back to the heart of the mystery.

An Enigma, Wrapped Around a Pencil...

If there is one particularly compelling sequence of events in Gerry's story, it is the one that begins with Gerry's utterance of the words "jacket on the bush" while he was still unconscious, and ends with Gerry finding

---

36 Gross, Loren E. *The Fifth Horseman of the Apocalypse: January-March, 1959*, (Fremont, CA: ©Loren E. Gross, 2005), 57.

his jacket in the desert, removing a pencil from a buttonhole with a note wrapped around it, and burning the note without reading it. A note, wrapped around a pencil, inserted through a buttonhole... it calls to mind Churchill's famous allusion to Russia as "a riddle wrapped in a mystery inside an enigma." Here is a literary device *par excellence,* akin to Citizen Kane's *Rosebud.* The image of the proverbial "message in a bottle" also springs to mind—it's as if this tantalizing bundle of clues, set adrift on the sea of time, survived independently of Gerry's (mostly absent) memory just so it could be found and puzzled over by a future generation.

And it seems all the more compelling considering Gerry's nature. Knowing Gerry as a person, the notion that he may have somehow invented all this material himself from the get-go would seem nearly as strange as the story itself. It just wouldn't seem to be his cup of tea, from what we've seen; not to mention the lack of any clear motive for attempting such a feat.

It would appear that Gerry was more the actor than the screenwriter in this drama. The stage was set by a forgotten encounter with something unknown, after which Gerry could just vaguely remember that the key to solving his mystery was attached to his missing jacket, hanging on a bush somewhere in the desert. And then, inexplicably, he sought out and destroyed that very key. It all works admirably well from a literary or cinematic standpoint, leaving us with the troubling question of authorship.

For now, we can only gaze in slack-jawed wonder at the strangeness of it all—and there is still more to come. Our investigation is not yet complete, but for the moment at least there is *one* aspect of Gerry's story for which we actually have some real and concrete answers.

Chapter 14: Moving On

A
lthough Gerry had been through a tremendous ordeal, culminating in seven months of hard labor in the U.S. Disciplinary Barracks at Ft. Leavenworth, somewhere along the line he was able to put himself together again and get his life back on track. Like a caterpillar in its cocoon, his transformation took place in the dark; both in the dark of imprisonment and in the black hole of his amnesia. While he would always retain a large blank spot on the map of his past, his memory seems to have re-engaged soon after regaining his freedom, with no further blackouts or spells of unconsciousness—that is, as far as what's on record at least.

Gerry next to his 1950 Desoto. (Photo by David Booher)

A Fresh Start

Gerry was released from confinement on August 23, 1960. Of course, Gerry does not even remember being confined, which could certainly raise questions about what may have happened to him while he was there! As we have seen, the memory he actually retains is that he turned himself in following his AWOL and shortly thereafter was taken to the Ft. Leavenworth Army base—to serve as a soldier, not as a prisoner. Furthermore, he recalls that, at that juncture, he was asked what he wanted to do for the rest of his enlistment, since he still had five and a half years remaining in his contract.

He maintains that he asked for an assignment overseas and that his wish was granted. Since this is at the very beginning of where Gerry's memories seem to pick up again, and because of his recent past in the Army, I can't help but wonder if he was really asked his preference. At the very least, I would guess that he was given a little nudge in that direction (overseas, that is). In any case, shortly after his return to active duty, Gerry was shipped to Bad Kreuznach, Germany, where he was assigned to the Eighth Infantry Division.[1] Bad Kreuznach, which means "the bath by the cross," was a tourist spot known for its healing springs.

As Gerry remembers, this was a very enjoyable period in his life. Whatever the benefits of his new life were, they must have been all the more welcome considering all he'd been through and managed to come out the other side of.

Gerry explained that he was picked to run the Eight Infantry Division's radio school, since he had served for years as a ground radio operator when he was in the Air Force. Among other things in this line of duty, he was responsible for Morse Code training.

Gerry had a second line of duty as well. He was assigned to a Long Range Reconnaissance Patrol or LRRP— pronounced "lurp." The LRRP was tasked with penetrating enemy lines during a conflict (most likely with Russia in those Cold War days) and providing intelligence, primarily via radio communications. Gerry was in command of a big truck— equipped with a radio transmitter—that could be strategically positioned to communicate with the long-range patrols and relay their messages back to headquarters. Drills were performed weekly to maintain readiness.

While in Germany, Gerry advanced rapidly from private to Pfc. to

---

1   Gerry's memory of events beginning at this point in time is well-substantiated by his service records.

corporal to sergeant. Then Gerry received an offer for an intriguing line of duty, which he accepted. He said he was sent to Vienna and assigned to a unit of the Austrian Army in a strictly unofficial capacity. "…We were kind of advisers to them," Gerry recalled. Officially Gerry was just a tourist on vacation in Vienna. He was not allowed to wear a uniform or carry a weapon. When I asked him what he actually did, he said not much. "We were just there to carry the flag," Gerry explained. Actually there was more to it than that, as Gerry explained to me on earlier occasion. He said he was sent there—along with a fellow soldier—to teach classes on operating some new American communications equipment the Austrians had purchased.

Gerry explained that his tourist guise was necessary because of a U.S.-Russia treaty that prohibited either country from sending military personnel into Austria—a neutral country. As Gerry put it, "…they had to be careful not to upset the apple cart." And although the Austrians were officially neutral, Gerry maintained that actually, "…they were pro-American or pro-Western; they hated the Russians with a passion—but they couldn't say that…they had to play their cards *real* careful."

Gerry portrayed it like it was a game with the Russians, who also had a covert/unofficial presence in Austria. According to Gerry, both sides knew of each other's existence in Austria: "…they probably knew we were there. But they couldn't do anything about it…because we weren't wearing a uniform, and there was no record. [We were] just showing the flag and rubbing the Russians the wrong way, but…you *had* to!"

Sergeant Irwin Goes Home

Soon Gerry's enlistment was winding down and it was time for a change. He came back to his post in Germany for a while and rented an apartment off base. He received an honorable discharge from the Army on January 26, 1966. He rather enjoyed his life in Germany and he had a Czech girlfriend who lived with him, so he stayed for almost another year. At that point, he felt compelled to move on in order to take advantage of a helpful Army policy: as long as ex-personnel moved within a year of leaving service, the Army would absorb all the costs of their relocation.

So Gerry said his good-byes to his companion, and he hopped on a ship to New York. The Army shipped all of Gerry's belongings to Boise, except his car, a Karmann Ghia, which went on the ship with him. After disembarking in New York, he made the long drive to Boise. While there, he stayed with a sister and brother-in-law for a while, and then he saw an ad for a job with Kodak. Gerry drove to Portland, Oregon, to apply with them and soon landed a position as a service technician for their Computer Output Microfilm (or "COM") equipment. Basically, this was a system that, just as it sounds, recorded a computer's output on microfilm— a stable storage medium that was guaranteed to last a hundred years.

Gerry was rapidly promoted to teaching other technicians in Kodak's schools in Boise and Portland, and soon he was shipped to teach at their school in Rochester, New York. Eventually, they promoted Gerry to a supervisory position in San Francisco, of which Gerry fondly recalled: "…we used to have our after dinner drink and go play golf, and that was our meeting —everybody would…say couple of words and (claps hands) play golf!"

When I asked Gerry if it was a good job he replied, "Well yeah, I was a supervisor. Good money. Those days are long gone now. Now I'm relegated to fixing a toilet (laughs). But that's the way life goes. Some days it's roses other days it's stones."

Family Life

Gerry had gotten married to his second wife, Nina, in Portland shortly after moving there. They had a daughter together, Gerry's third and last child. Gerry's new family moved with him first to Rochester, New York, and then to San Francisco.

The marriage fell apart while they were in San Francisco, whereupon Gerry's soon to be ex-wife took their daughter with her back to Oregon. Shortly thereafter, Gerry took early retirement from Kodak and moved back to Boise, where he took a job with a microfilm technology firm— servicing their equipment. Around the same time, he met his last wife, Arlene. When Gerry finally retired for good in the 1990s, the two of them enjoyed traveling around the western states together in their RV. Then, sadly, Arlene developed lung cancer and Gerry took care of her at home until she passed away about two years before I met him.

During the times when I was interviewing Gerry, he was staying at home most of the time, working on various home-improvement projects. The first time I went to his house he was remodeling his bathroom, doing all the work himself. The next time I was there, several months later, he had all new flooring installed, which he hired out, but it required him to move everything out of his house and into the garage for a while. He was up to the task.

Gerry at his home in Boise (Photo by David Booher)

When Gerry wasn't fixing up his house or restoring antique radios, he was busy taking care of his small menagerie of creatures. He had his little dog, Fifi, his cat, and a family of feral cats in his back yard that he fed and looked after. All of these pets, wild or tame, were fed on a very regular schedule, a few times each day, and always with special treats on the side. Gerry had a soft spot for the neighborhood squirrels as well. He had constructed three or four sheltered feeding stations that were fastened to the top of his fence. From these extended simple ladders made of thin boards that gave access to overhanging branches of a walnut tree.

My impression of Gerry in his old age is of a man who is satisfied with the life he has lived. In fact, once when I asked Gerry if he was having a good day, he replied, "I haven't had a bad day yet!" He seems to possess a natural buoyancy and good humor that keep him on an even keel. Although he seems to lead a fairly solitary existence, he enjoys keeping in touch with his daughters and grandchildren (tragically his son passed away several years ago), and attending to the everyday details of his life. He seems to regard the whole series of events from 1959 as nothing more than an unaccountable blip, not really worth even thinking about, and certainly not worth being the subject of a book. In a way, this makes his story all the more believable.

Overall, Gerry seems like the proverbial "guy next door" who had a run-in with something truly incomprehensible, and came back to tell the tale—or at least what little he could remember of it. Whatever it was he experienced, it appears that, aside from the gaps in his memory, he has recovered well, and for the most part he has enjoyed a normal, happy and productive life.

Of course—as we know—the term "normal and happy" would hardly have applied to the Gerry Irwin of 1959. In that regard, we still have some very compelling questions left to explore. So let's return now to our discussion of that fateful year—and what was, quite possibly, the true original cause of Gerry's troubles.

Chapter 15: Abduction Revisited

You will not speak wisely about this night.
— Nebraska patrolman Herb Schirmer, repeating the words of a
UFO occupant he encountered in 1967.[1]

After mulling over the Gerry Irwin story for a few of years, Jim Lorenzen considered another scenario—one that would "just about explain everything" that had happened to Gerry.

In his analysis at the end of his 1962 article, Jim proposed that upon reaching the summit during his rescue attempt, Gerry had caught sight of something so frightening that he assumed he'd be gone by the time other rescuers showed up. Jim guessed that this prompted Gerry to write the second note and attach it to his jacket, which he left hanging from a shrub where he hoped others would find it.

Jim believed that Gerry had been subjected to a "bizarre influence" that produced his "hysteria" and planted "memory blocks" in his mind.[2] In his conclusion he wrote:

> Suppose the Influence which I mentioned earlier had placed memory blocks to prevent Gerry's remembering anything of his original experience? (I propose that the note and jacket had already been placed when this happened.) And suppose that every time he began to pry at these blocks a mental mechanism was set in motion to enhance his

1 Clark, Jerome. *The UFO Book: Encyclopedia of the Extraterrestrial* (Detroit: Omnigraphics, 1998), 529.
2 Lorenzen, L.J., 25.

amnesia *or otherwise complicate matters* to prevent solution.
Wouldn't that just about explain everything?[3] [emphasis added]

Jim seems to be implying that this inscrutable "Influence" lies at the root of Gerry's memory and behavior problems. It seems evident that the words "otherwise complicate matters" are meant to account for Gerry's strange behavior in general, which would certainly include the return-trip to Utah, and—you would think—even Gerry's desertion as well. After all, he closes his article by suggesting that this theory could virtually "explain everything." And finally, we recall that for comparison, Jim discussed the Brazilian reports of children who had gone missing amid UFO activity, only to reappear—sometimes after days had elapsed—with amnesia.[4]

Non-Human Intervention?
In in his conclusion, Jim proposes that human interference may have only played a secondary role in Gerry's behavior, i.e. in triggering "mental mechanisms" that had already been installed by the "Influence" associated with the UFO Gerry encountered.

It's a rather ominous image Jim has conjured, this mysterious and inscrutable "Influence," blocking memories and installing subtle triggers that would go off whenever Gerry was getting too close to the truth. Bear in mind that Jim and Coral were, by this time, veteran UFO investigators whose files were bulging with all manner of strange cases. On top of that, they had been directly in contact with Gerry as he was struggling just to keep mind and body together, which allowed them to observe his emotional and psychological state as he went through the after-effects of his encounter.

And with all their experience, knowledge, and first-hand observation to draw upon, they came up with a theory that was ahead of its time. Their ideas about alien abduction—what they would have called "contact with UFO occupants" in those days—put them at the leading edge of a wave that was right on the verge of breaking.

And then, little over two years after the Lorenzens lost contact with

---

3   Ibid.
4   Ibid.

Gerry, a new case came along that would virtually *define* the abduction phenomenon.

The Hill Abduction Case

There has been plenty of media exposure of this amazing case, including at least two books, a TV movie starring James Earl Jones,[5] and a profusion of articles. It's a long and extensively documented story, but for our purposes a brief summary will suffice—which I draw for the most part from John Fuller's account, *The Interrupted Journey*.

The story begins with Betty and Barney Hill, a married couple, driving through rural New Hampshire late on the night of September 19 to September 20, 1961. They were returning home to Portsmouth, N.H. after a vacation to Niagara Falls and Montreal. Around 10:15 they noticed a light in the sky that was behaving strangely. After watching it for a while, Betty thought it might be a flying saucer, based on the description her sister had related to her of her own UFO sighting in 1957. Barney was initially convinced that it was a commercial airliner, and a little later he thought it was a Piper Cub, but after the "plane" broke off from its flight path and descended to within a short distance of them, he was forced to change his mind.

At one point the object approached so closely they felt compelled to stop along the road, at which time Barney got out to investigate. Looking through his binoculars, Barney observed what appeared to be a huge and silent craft of some kind hovering not far above the ground. The craft had a row of windows through which he could see humanoid figures in uniforms, looking down at him and moving around inside. Suddenly Barney was seized by a panic—an intense fear of being captured—prompting him to run back to the car and drive away in great haste.

They heard strange beeping sounds on the drive home and they both experienced a long interval of time for which they had no memory. When they arrived at their house around 5 a.m., they both felt odd sensations and noticed inexplicable details such as the fact that both of their watches had stopped working. The next day, on her sister's advice, Betty called Pease

---

5   Anderson, Hesper, and Jake Justiz. *The UFO Incident*. Dir. Richard A. Colla. NBC. 20 Oct. 1975. Television.

Air Force Base to report their experience. The official report—later sent by the base to Project Blue Book—was probably rather typical of the Air Force's general attitude toward civilian UFO testimony, in that it labeled the sighting first as a misidentification of an "advertising search light," which was later changed to "optical conditions."[6]

Walter Webb's Inquiry

Some days after the encounter, Betty borrowed a UFO book from the local library, and after reading it she sent a letter describing her and Barney's recent encounter to its author, Major Donald Keyhoe. Since Keyhoe was head of NICAP (National Investigation Committee on Aerial Phenomena), he initiated an official investigation into the case. The prominent Boston astronomer and NICAP investigator Walter Webb was tapped for the job, and he interviewed the Hills for six hours at their home on October 21, 1961.

Webb noted in his official report that Barney experienced a "mental block" whenever he spoke about the "leader" who was looking down at Barney through the craft's window. Webb went on to report that Barney was of the belief that there was something he'd seen that he didn't wish to remember. Betty similarly experienced an inability to remember a portion of the night's events. As they were both to discover later, the size and importance of that interval was much greater than they initially realized.[7]

Ten days after the encounter, Betty began having extremely vivid and disturbing dreams of the night of the encounter, which she later wrote down. These dreams contained very detailed images depicting a type of scenario which today we would recognize as an alien abduction event. Barney, who was reluctant to talk about the incident, listened sympathetically to Betty's dreams at first, but then felt it was better to drop the matter. After that, Betty did not speak with Barney again about her dreams. For his part, Barney suffered severe stress (what we'd probably call PTSD in today's terminology) in the following years, driving him to seek treatment from a physician and then a psychiatrist.

---

6   Lorenzen, Coral E. "USAF Report on Hill Case." *APRO Bulletin* (Jan. 1972): 6.
7   Fuller, John G. *The Interrupted Journey: Two Lost Hours "aboard a Flying Saucer"* (New York: Dial, 1966), 35.

On November 25, two science and engineering professionals who took an interest in the Hills' case, Robert Hohman and C.D. Jackson, were interviewing the Hills at their home when one of them asked the Hills why it took them so long to get home on the night of their encounter. Going back over the chronology, the Hills realized there were two full hours they could not account for. They were suddenly faced with an episode of "simultaneous amnesia" that had occurred in the interval between the initial set of beeps and a second set of beeps heard in their car near Ashland, 35 miles further down the road.[8]

This revelation left the Hills feeling shocked. Little did they know that their experience represented a landmark in UFO history—the first clearly documented case of "missing time."[9]

NICAP Plays It Down

The first NICAP report of the Hills' story appeared in the January/February 1962 issue of their newsletter, *The UFO Investigator*.[10] NICAP tended to avoid covering reports that involved claims of humanoids—which they generally regarded as suspect. (APRO, by contrast, "would accept reports of [UFO] occupant sightings if the evidence warranted it..."[11]) Instead NICAP concentrated on reports involving objects, and the attempts made by the Air Force to cover up the UFO phenomenon. Thus, their article on the Hill case was decidedly "underwhelming."

Though Walter Webb had submitted a lengthy and comprehensive report to the NICAP office, this was distilled into just seven rather brief paragraphs and buried in a news roundup column. There is no mention of Betty's dreams, or of Barney's memory blocking "curtain," or of their strange sensations afterward, or of the inexplicable beeping inside their car, either. This brief summary would remain the *only* information published on the Hill case for *nearly four more years!* We'll soon see why this is such an

---

8 Ibid., 46.

9 Ibid., 47.

10 "UFOs Cause Panic, One Death." *The UFO Investigator* Vol. ll, No. 3 (Jan.-Feb. 1962): 2.

11 Jacobs, David Michael. *The UFO Controversy in America* (Bloomington: Indiana University Press, 1975), 183.

important point.

It was not until January 4, 1964, that the Hills finally began their hypnosis sessions, which continued through June of that year. This is when the truly incredible story of their abduction aboard some kind of alien vessel finally began to emerge from the darkness of their "double amnesia." Betty and Barney were hypnotized separately, yet their stories were remarkably similar. Betty's regressed memories were also similar in many respects to the dreams she had recorded shortly after the event.

Big Media Crashes the Scene

The following year the Hills—who had never wanted media attention—were surprised when a sensational version of their story appeared in the October 25, 1965 edition of the newspaper *The Boston Traveler*,[12] which opened the reticent Hills to their first widespread public exposure. The next year Fuller's book, *The Interrupted Journey*, was published and then excerpted in a two-part article for *Look*, a widely read and influential magazine at the time.

NICAP was dubious of the abduction aspect of the story. It was really an entirely new phenomenon at the time, and as we have seen, APRO as well had held off on publishing the abduction story they'd received back in 1958—the Villas Boas case—until after it appeared in 1965 in the *Flying Saucer Review*; that's how controversial the abduction topic was—even in the eyes of APRO.

The chronology is important because we're looking at the extent of the information the Lorenzens would have been privy to. The idea of alien abduction was still quite novel (and not even yet identified as such) when they came upon Gerry's story, having learned about the Villas Boas story less than a year earlier. So to recap, the order in which these cases came to the Lorenzens' attention was: Villas Boas in 1958, Gerry in 1959. Now recall that they did not publish their full story on Gerry's case until November of 1962—more than three years later—but just 10 months after the Hills' story appeared in *The UFO Investigator*.

It's quite likely that within the small world of ufology, the Lorenzens

---

12 Luttrell, John. "UFO Chiller: Did THEY Seize Couple?" *Boston Traveler* 25 Oct. 1965: n. pag.

had heard some of the more intriguing details of the Hill incident that were not published in the newsletter, including the blocked memories. Researcher Loren Gross has asserted that indeed, they were familiar with the case. He comments that, compared to NICAP, the Lorenzens considered themselves more receptive toward "direct contact" cases, but since NICAP was already covering the Hill case, the Lorenzens were in danger of "missing out on what might be a 'watershed' development in UFOlogy." He continues:

> The Lorenzens, however, had their own impressive "amnesia" incident, involving an Army Private they questioned back in 1959. The Lorenzens had been unable to use hypnosis on the soldier because he apparently went AWOL before a session could be conducted.[13] Coral and Jim thought they might be able to locate their man and make another try at filling in the fellow's "missing time."[14]

According to Gross, they hoped to accomplish this by getting their article about Gerry into *Flying Saucers* magazine, which had nationwide distribution. "It was a long shot, but the possible payoff was great."[15] If this is true, it adds an intriguing new wrinkle to the story. It makes sense that the Lorenzens still hoped to utilize hypnosis to get to the bottom of Gerry's mystery. However, it hadn't occurred to me before that their *primary* motivation for publishing the article was their hope of reconnecting with Gerry, in order to finally obtain the complete story. If nothing else though, this scenario fits with the known facts.

It's an interesting picture we see here, emerging from the haze of ufological history; leading researchers were grappling with the implications of a shocking new development in the phenomenon. The Lorenzens were, in a sense, exploring an unknown continent, tentatively drawing a map based on the meager data at hand. That data included the Villas Boas case (which notably, did *not* feature amnesia); the amnesic Brazilian children;

---

13 Although as we've seen, the original problem was interference from Gerry's C.O. (see Chapter 12)

14 Gross, Loren E. *The Fifth Horseman of the Apocalypse: July-December, 1962,* (Fremont, CA: ©Loren E. Gross, 2005), 68.

15 Ibid.

Gerry's case; and now, the Hills.

Off the Radar

There is one important item that was *definitely not* on the Lorenzens' radar: the results of Gerry's March 27 sodium amytal interview. As we've seen, the only thing the Lorenzens knew about the interview—which, as we saw in Chapter 13, was probably not even the *same* interview—was that Gerry had been told, "It didn't work." To recap, here's an excerpt from the report they never saw: "He [Gerry] stated there was a special 'intelligence' that he couldn't explain to me, since it would be incomprehensible to me, which has directed him not to remember or not to tell me about any of the events in Utah."[16]

The similarity here between Jim's *"Influence"* placing *"memory blocks"* and Gerry's special *"intelligence"* that directed him *"not to remember"* is downright uncanny. Since Jim could not have seen this report and Gerry had no recollection of what he'd said to the doctor, there is no way Jim's specific formulation could have originated from Gerry. Of course, it's true that Gerry consciously suspected that the UFO caused his condition, but these suspicions were rather vague and ill-defined. Taken alone and out of context, Jim's conjecture could easily be perceived as a little "out there," but when placed side-by-side with Gerry's "truth-serum" testimony, it suddenly becomes eerily compelling.

Gerry vs the Hills: Side by Side

As I looked more deeply into the Hill case, I began to see a growing number of fascinating parallels with Gerry's case. In both we have "an interrupted journey" that begins with an unidentified light in the sky, involving people who had previously expressed little if any interest in UFOs.[17] In both cases, we have amnesia. Also, in both there is evidence of trauma-induced symptoms.

In regard to the memory lapses, it's worth recalling that until his hypnosis revealed otherwise, Barney Hill did not suspect that the dark

---

16 Hospital records. (See Chapter 11 for the full excerpt.)

17 This was especially true of Barney and Gerry. Betty actually did have some interest in UFOs that was sparked when her sister had a UFO sighting some years earlier.

"curtain" he perceived was placed there by the alien beings, but rather attributed it to his own fear of remembering what was later revealed to be quite a terrifying experience. This all changed, however, when the hypnosis succeeded in bringing forth Barney's hidden memories.

At one point during a hypnosis session Barney talked about how he didn't want to remember the events and that he didn't think that he would. Dr. Simon wanted to know who was influencing him in this way, and Barney said, "I was told in my mind that I would forget that it happened. It was imprinted on my mind."[18] When he was pressed further on the source of these messages, Barney implied they were coming from one of the craft's occupants.[19]

This Never Happened

But it wasn't just persuasion, insistence, and suggestion that was involved in Barney's interaction with them; there was also a threat. As the hypnosis session proceeded, Barney recalled a warning he received. He was informed that it was pointless to try to remember, and that, "…you have to forget it, you will forget it, and it can only cause great harm that can be meted out to you if you do not forget."[20]

Now let's compare this to a longer excerpt from Gerry's amytal interview:

> He stated there was a special "intelligence" that he couldn't explain to me, since it would be incomprehensible to me, which has directed him not to remember or not to tell me about any of the events in Utah. He says that if he tells what was behind the incidents in Utah there will be a 'big investigation' that he does not want to be bothered with and also because it will harm many people and he doesn't want that to happen.[21]

Another threat. When it comes to "leak" proofing, these guys— whoever they may be— aren't taking any chances! They make threats, they utter vague warnings of obscure consequences, they block memories, and

---

18 Fuller, 199.
19 Ibid.
20 Ibid., 240.
21 Hospital records. (See Chapter 11 for the full excerpt.)

they issue directives reminiscent of hypnotic suggestion—in statements like, "you will forget it."

In Gerry's case, it's fascinating to look at the particular way in which the warning is worded, i.e. "there will be a 'big investigation.'" This formulation seems to reflect the orientation of a soldier who is accustomed to the military bureaucracy. Perhaps the message Gerry received was tailored specifically for him in a way that he could understand it; a possibility we're about to see more evidence for in the Hill case.

A More "Humane" Approach?

What about Betty? What was she told? At one point in her experience, Betty had an argument with one of her captors over a book of theirs that had been promised to her, written in a strange, vaguely Japanese-like script. When the promise was broken, she complained bitterly; her captor explained that his crew members objected to letting her take it. She persisted on the grounds that it was going to be her proof of the encounter. He responded that that was exactly the reason she couldn't have it, and that the others wanted her to forget the whole thing. She protested loudly that she would never forget about it, and furthermore that they could never make her forget.

At this point her captor laughed and agreed that perhaps she would recall it, though he wished not. He continued, saying that it wouldn't help her anyway, because Barney wouldn't remember anything. Furthermore, he said that if she managed to remember something, Barney's recollection would be different from hers, and thus, "...all you are going to do is get each other so confused you will not know what to do."[22]

It's interesting how in this instance we see an approach based on reasoning, persuasion, cajoling, and humor, rather than threats and rigid pronouncements. As in Gerry's case, it appears as if "they" understood the personality differences between Betty and Barney and adapted their techniques accordingly, in order to better facilitate the desired effect. The main point communicated is the same however, which is basically: *Don't even try to remember!*

The prohibition against speaking and/or remembering is now a

---

22 Fuller, 176-177.

common theme in the UFO literature. On particularly interesting example occurred in the case of Nebraska highway patrolman Herb Schirmer, who experienced an abduction-type event on December 3, 1967. Among the messages Schirmer received was this strangely worded request/demand against talking:

> "I wish you would not tell that you have been aboard this ship. You are to tell that [gives specific instructions here about what to report]. You will tell this and nothing more. You will not speak wisely about this night."[23]

Here Schirmer explains some of the reasoning behind the absurd and confusing nature of UFO encounters, as he was informed by his captors:

> "They have no pattern for contacting people. It is by pure chance so the government cannot determine any patterns about them. There will be a lot more contacts…to a certain extent they want to puzzle people. They know they are being seen too frequently and they are trying to confuse the public's mind."[24]

Away to Fairyland

Now for the moment, let us examine a passage from Evans-Wentz's classic study of fairy lore, which we saw quoted in part by Jacques Vallee in Chapter 11:

> The mind of a person coming out of Fairyland is usually a blank as to what has been seen and done there. Another idea is that *the person knows well enough all about Fairyland, but is prevented from communicating the knowledge.*[25] [emphasis added]

As Vallee was among the first to observe, UFO-type phenomena are not nearly as recent as we may be tempted to believe. In *Passport*

---

23 Clark, *The UFO Book: Encyclopedia of the Extraterrestrial.* 1998, 529.
24 Good, Timothy. *Above Top Secret: The Worldwide UFO Cover-up* (New York: William Morrow &Co., 1988), 441.
25 Evans-Wentz, W. Y. *The Fairy-Faith in Celtic Countries; Its Psychical Origin and Nature* (London: Oxford, 1911), 39.

to Magonia, Vallee demonstrated the many remarkable parallels between traditions of fairylore, demonology, Marian apparitions, encounters with angels and nature spirits, etc., and the world of UFO encounters.

A common theme of fairylore is the phenomenon of fairy abduction. When the typical features of fairy abduction are compared side-by-side with alien abduction, the similarities are quite striking; they include trance states, amnesia, sexual relations for the purpose of producing hybrids, and of course the prohibition or prevention of speaking about the encounters. Regarding this last item—to paraphrase Evans-Wentz—both Gerry and the Hills knew "well enough" what had happened (in some sense at least), but were prevented from telling it.

What Time Is It *Really*?

Maybe our language lacks the subtleties needed to convey the full meaning of these received messages, and thus we get paradoxical statements like Gerry's: "…which has directed him not to remember or not to tell me about any of the events in Utah." Well, which is it? Did it direct him not to tell or not to remember? Well, maybe it's both somehow, due to a third, larger concept that encompasses these other two possibilities in way that's hard or even impossible to articulate. In that vein, Vallee has observed, "If you strive to convey a truth that lies beyond the semantic level made possible by your audience's language, you must construct apparent contradictions in terms of ordinary meaning."[26]

Vallee correlates this hypothetical communicative strategy with the absurdity so often reported in close encounters, which he refers to as "meta-logical." By way of example, he mentions a 1954 encounter in France in which the UFO occupant asked a witness for the time, and the man informed him it was 2:30. The occupant retorted, "You lie— it is 4 o'clock." Vallee suggests that there is a "symbolic meaning" that transcends the absurd contradiction of the exchange, possibly with the intent of challenging our assumptions about the nature of time itself.[27]

---

26 Vallee, Jacques. *The Invisible College: What a Group of Scientists Has Discovered about UFO Influences on the Human Race* (1975. Reprint. San Antonio, TX: Anomalist Books, 2014), Kindle. loc. 501.
27 Ibid., loc. 488.

Another example Vallee provides is a detail from the Brazilian case of Antonio Villas Boas in 1957. While onboard the alien vessel, Villas Boas saw a device that looked like a clock—with markings at the four quarter-hour positons—but with only one hand. As time went on and the hand remained stationary, Villas Boas decided that it wasn't actually a clock. Vallee comments on the poetic, dream-like quality of the episode, remarking:

> … We are reminded of the fairy tales…of the country where time does not pass, and of that great poet who had in his room a huge white clock without hands, bearing the words "It is later than you think."[28]

It's intriguing that Vallee mentions the dreamlike aspect of the clock detail, because that very year, 1957, Ingmar Bergman released his masterpiece film *Wild Strawberries*, which contains an unforgettable dream sequence in which the main character (a retired doctor) sees a clock with no hands and then checks his pocket watch, which also has no hands. (Not that it would be likely for a Brazilian farmer from the hinterlands to see a newly released Swedish film anyway, but it's worth noting that Bergman's film was not even released in Sweden until more than two months after Villas Boas had his encounter.)

In wrapping up this "timely" discussion, recall as well that interesting detail we saw in the Hills' case, where they both noticed that their watches had stopped working when they arrived home after their close encounter.

Tongue-Tied

We've seen the tradition described of fairyland visitors being blocked in some way from telling what they know of their adventures. We've looked at Gerry's "not to remember or not to tell" message, as well as the various messages of this sort received by the Hills and Herb Schirmer—which seem to underlie their difficulties in remembering and/or talking about what they've experienced. In that same vein, there's a fascinating case from Aveyron, France, that features a particularly clear example of this kind. Beginning in 1966, a farmer there experienced a series of close encounters,

---

28 Vallee, 1969, 115.

and at one point the UFO investigator working the case, Fernand Lagarde, told the farmer to let him know of any new developments. One day the farmer made the lengthy trip to the Lagarde's house to give him an update:

> But when he was in the investigator's house he could not talk. The part of his brain that handled verbal expression and the mechanism of language could not process the data that he knew were there.[29]

What could possibly explain this "mental muteness"? While it's probably impossible to pin down the exact cause in cases like these, it should be noted that *simple hypnosis* could presumably produce a very similar result. What I'm referring to here is the ability of hypnosis to block specific memories. In fact, Dr. Simon himself successfully used hypnotic suggestion to prevent the Hills from remembering the content of their sessions with him (for their own benefit, of course). As Fuller explained, "During hypnosis, the incidents described in the trance can be wiped from conscious memory."[30]

Furthermore (and rather eerily), the Hills remarked on the similarity between the trance-like states they experienced among their captors and their hypnotic trances induced by Dr. Simon. In one example, Simon asked Betty (while under hypnosis) if she thought "they" had put her to sleep, to which she replied "yes." When he asked how, she explained that she couldn't remember all of it, but she recalled a man putting his hand up, after which point she "didn't know anything." Later on, she made a comparison between this experience and that of being hypnotized. [31]

Walking after Midnight
As we've seen, Sheriff Fife wrote in his letter that Gerry remembered walking all the way to the top of the hill where he thought the object had crashed, and that the light given off seemed to grow brighter as he got closer. This vivid image may well be one of the aspects of Gerry's experience that later vanished from his memory. In all the later accounts

---

29 Vallee, 1975, 2014, loc. 614.
30 Fuller, 62.
31 Ibid., 271.

Gerry gave, he maintained that he could remember nothing starting from shortly after he left his car. Indeed, when I personally questioned Gerry on this point, this was the way he still recalled it. So we need to be careful here and bear in mind that Gerry quite possibly did remain conscious all the way up the hill, or alternatively that his mind was in an in-between "twilight" state of consciousness at that point.

However, if all of his later recollections are in fact accurate, then a very intriguing question arises: How was it that Gerry managed to walk anywhere from a quarter-mile to a mile, uphill through foot-deep snow— before collapsing—if he was unconscious? It raises the startling possibility that he was walking in some kind of mysteriously induced trance-state, what we could call "trance-walking" for the sake of convenience.

Initially this might sound strange, but in thinking this through a little we can readily observe that people can do all sorts of things while they are unconscious. Sleep-walking is but one common example.

A walking trance-like state also appears in the Hills' story. Betty explained that as she and Barney were walking, there were two "men" walking behind her, while Barney had a "man" on each side of him. She said that her eyes were open, but Barney was still asleep even though he was walking. She turned to Barney and implored him repeatedly to awaken. Barney remained asleep however, and kept walking.

It seems plausible to suggest then that perhaps Gerry was trance-walking as well, which is something that could conceivably be produced by hypnosis. Evidently, not only can hypnosis be used to block out memories recalled in a trance, but in the "somnambulistic stage," it can also generate a wide assortment of other effects and behaviors, as Dr. Simon—the Hills' hypnotist—observed:

> ...almost any phenomenon can be produced, and the patient will be amnesic unless he is definitely told to recall the trance state. Positive or negative hallucinations may be induced, and post-hypnotic suggestions given in this somnambulistic stage will be very effective.[32]

---

32 Simon, Benjamin. "Hypnosis—Fact and Fancy." New York Academy of Medicine (Lecture), in: Fuller, 63.

Therefore, if "someone" wanted to prevent Gerry's memories from leaking out, the simplest way would be to put him in a deep trance from the very beginning, i.e., just after he began walking, or somewhere along the way. And given the pervasiveness of trance states reported by abductees, it looks fairly clear that whoever "they" are, they're quite adept at producing these states in their subjects.

Absence of Evidence

Apparently—as a rule—no evidence can be brought back from these encounters. UFO abductees often try to bring home 'proof' of their encounters; the unsuccessful attempts of both Betty Hill (to bring the alien book home), and Antonio Villas Boas (to steal a "clock" from his captors) being prime examples. Similarly, visitors (or those abducted) to fairyland often attempt to bring precious objects—frequently gold—back home with them, only to find that their treasure has turned into something essentially worthless, like dried leaves or an ordinary lump of coal when they arrive back home.

Was this rule at work in some way in Gerry's compulsion to destroy his only evidence?

A Site to Behold (Again and Again)

The veteran ufologist Richard Hall noticed a parallel between the Hills' and Gerry's cases I had failed to consider:

> Irwin changed from a reliable soldier into an erratic individual, compelled to return to the site and troubled by some unknown experience there…in retrospect, his loss of memory, site compulsion, and emotional turmoil over an experience he could not recall parallel the behavior of the Hills and many subsequent abductees.[33]

Site compulsion, indeed. The Hills repeatedly returned to the area where their encounter took place, searching for the exact spot where the abduction occurred.[34] Although Gerry only returned once to the scene

---

33 Hall, Richard. *The UFO Evidence: A Thirty-Year Report* (Lanham, MD: Scarecrow, 2001), 511.

34 Fuller, 50.

of his encounter, it was certainly dramatic. As Gerry later recalled: "I experienced an urge to return to the location of my original experience and I proceeded to follow this urge..."[35] What could explain this compulsion of Gerry's?

There are a few possibilities that spring to mind, one of which we've already explored, i.e. post-hypnotic suggestion.[36] Another option is that perhaps it was simply an attempt on Gerry's part to try to understand what had happened to him. There's a third option as well, which is quite intriguing. In light of the similarities between the Hill case and Gerry's case—and the fact that the Hill case seems strongly suggestive of a genuine UFO contact—what if Gerry's site compulsion was a delayed effect of this same sort of contact? As we've seen, Jim Lorenzen himself—after considering the possibility of post-amytal suggestion—ultimately seemed to favor this explanation, i.e. that some mysterious force or influence associated with the UFO caused Gerry's compulsion.

An Impressive List

The Hill case can serve as a kind of Rosetta stone as we try to piece together the relatively fragmentary evidence in Gerry's case. Like an archaeologist attempting to recreate events in the distant past with only a handful of scattered artifacts, we need a database in order to cross-reference our findings. The Hill case works quite well in this regard for two important reasons: (1) Its wealth of documentation, and (2) Its early occurrence (only 2 ½ years after Gerry's incident, the full story of which was not published until over a year after the Hills' encounter)—virtually ruling out the possibility of mimicry or influence from other cases. In terms of our archaeological metaphor, the Hill case would be the equivalent of an undisturbed or pristine site, and thus exceptionally valuable for research.

To summarize the results of our study, let's take a look at the compelling list of parallels we've seen between the two cases:

1. Both had amnesia.
2. Both saw a bright light in the sky that behaved strangely.

---

35 Lorenzen, L.J., 22.
36 See Chapter 13.

3. Both commented on the absence of sound associated with the object.
4. Both suffered emotional turmoil over the inability to recall events.
5. Both demonstrated "site compulsion."
6. Both received messages directing them to forget their experiences.
7. Both received threats of reprisal for remembering and/or talking about their experiences.
8. Both experienced trancelike states.
9. Both suffered symptoms typical of psychological trauma.
10. Both parties were returning from vacation.
11. Both had their close encounters in remote areas.
12. Neither of the parties wanted media attention.

While it's true that this list is far from conclusive, it's hard not to be struck by a suspicion that we are looking at two examples of *one and the same very bizarre phenomenon.*

The Way Things Might Have Been
Finally, it's worth mentioning the difference in treatment outcomes for Gerry and the Hills. Gerry's symptoms did not seem to improve at all from his brief, one-off treatment by Capt. Valentine, and as we know, there was no attempt made to help him reintegrate the content he recalled in his trance state. The Hills on the other hand, received an extensive, six-month long series of treatments by Dr. Simon that culminated with their retrieved memories being skillfully reintegrated into their conscious minds. Their treatments were declared successful, with both of the Hills, especially Barney, experiencing dramatic recoveries.

In view of the successful treatment received by the Hills and how it turned things around for them, it's hard not to wonder how different things might have been if Gerry had been able to keep his appointments with the civilian doctor. All the necessary ingredients were in place for Gerry: his own desire and willingness; a competent doctor whose office was within easy reach in neighboring El Paso; and even a means to pay for treatment—the Lorenzens were footing the bill. All the ingredients were there, that is, save one—a commanding officer who would allow him to go through with it.

Looking back now, it stands out as a pivotal moment in determining Gerry's future. At this point, we can only wonder about the true motivations of Gerry's C.O., or for that matter, whether the officer himself was merely taking orders from someone behind the scenes.

Aliens vs. Spies: Some Words in Closing

We've covered a lot of ground in our inquiry. We've seen the details of Gerry's encounter from multiple perspectives, pondered the two locations problem, examined the amytal date discrepancy, and sought out explanations that could account for Gerry's blackouts, amnesia, and bizarre behavior. We've also seen an intriguing convergence of circumstances and possible clues hinting at covert government involvement. Ultimately, do we even really know if Gerry's story is a UFO case?

The answer to this question has eluded us for a number of reasons, not least of which is that there are so many parallels between mind control cases and UFO close encounters. "UFO abductees" describe trance states that are virtually indistinguishable from those produced by very human hypnotists, and it is well within the means of the latter to implant very convincing false memories in subjects, as well as to "wipe clean" any unwanted memories.

On the other hand, if Gerry's case is a mind-control/PSYOP case, then isn't it possible that the Hills' is also? We have just seen a compelling list of similarities between these two cases, and it seems logical to suspect that we are looking at two examples of the same phenomenon. And yet, I see no definitive evidence that can completely rule out the "mind control all the way" hypothesis in *either* instance. I realize this is a controversial statement, especially regarding the Hill case—considering the consistency of testimony involved, elicited by a highly respected and rather skeptical

M.D., along with the internal corroboration of many compelling details.[37] Nonetheless, taking into account the lessons of history—combined with the extravagant funds lavished upon black ops in general—it's a possibility we can't ignore.[38]

But on the flip side of the coin, either case could very well represent a genuine close encounter/alien abduction event. They certainly *look* like close encounters, so if they're really not, then they were cleverly designed to appear that way.

If Gerry's story really is a mind control case designed to look like an alien abduction, then these G-men had some impressive science-fiction writing chops! Because whoever did this had no one to copy, *and* they were setting the stage for thousands, or even hundreds of thousands more cases to follow.[39] Are they *all* mind control cases? This seems doubtful. If one considers the sheer volume of credible testimony and evidence contained in the burgeoning alien abduction literature (not to mention the *worldwide distribution* of the phenomenon), it would require a rather extreme leap of faith to believe it could *all* be chalked up to fantasy or government intrigue.

In the end, it seems that we're faced with an unresolvable question. The UFO phenomenon has been so hopelessly intertwined with government intrigue for so long, it's probably a safe bet that we'll never know what really happened. But whatever it was, suffice it to say that once, long ago, the answer was tied to a young soldier's jacket, twisting in the sage-scented wind of southern Utah.

---

37 External corroboration is another matter. One piece of evidence often cited in the Hill case is the positive radar return received by Pease AFB during the timeframe of the UFO encounter. When examined closely, however, this evidence appears quite weak. For more details see: [Sheaffer, Robert. "There were no Extraterrestrials" in Karl Pflock and Peter Brookesmith (editors), *Encounters at Indian Head: The Betty and Barney Hill UFO Abduction Revisited* (San Antonio, TX: Anomalist Books, 2007), 193-194.]

38 As of 2014, the proposed U.S. black budget was nearly $60 billion, which did not even include the funds for the "war on terror." See: Zadrozny, Brandy. "Read the Pentagon's $59 Billion 'Black Budget.'" *The Daily Beast*. The Daily Beast Company, 06 March 2014. Web. 19 May 2017.

39 Whitley Strieber and Jacques Vallee have both published compelling data in this regard—See notes, Chapter 11.

Epilogue

*We see what we believe, and not just the contrary: and to change what
we see, it is sometimes necessary to change what we believe.*
— Jeremy Narby[1]

*I understand why the ancient Irish saw wisdom as a salmon…Who is
wiser than the one who knows the way home?*
— Patricia Monaghan[2]

It's good to know that for Gerry at least the story seems to have a happy ending. As of this writing, Gerry has passed his 81st birthday, and by his own reckoning he has lived a long and satisfying life. And yet there must be something about those gaping holes in his memory that, at least on some level, have troubled him. Because otherwise, I cannot account for the way he so generously allowed me into his life to poke around and investigate his lost year (or year and a half) that had slipped through the cracks of his mind—which outwardly he maintained was not even worth talking about.

There are so many kinds of hardship a human can endure. It is true that Gerry never had to suffer the terrible privations of war, which—although he was willing—he narrowly missed by accident of his age. Yet he experienced an ordeal that was quite devastating in its own right.

---

1   Narby, Jeremy. *The Cosmic Serpent: DNA and the Origins of Knowledge* (New York: J.P. Tarcher/Putnam, 1998), 139.

2   Monaghan, Patricia. *The Red-Haired Girl from the Bog: The Landscape of Celtic Myth and Spirit* (Novato, CA: New World Library, 2003), 190.

With a mind broken by an encounter with something that officially didn't exist, his recurring problems in the aftermath were met with punishment, threats, and accusations, and quite possibly a form of "treatment" that was actually harming him. He had become a de facto outcast, with no help in sight. But in a situation where many might have simply imploded in a downward spiral of alcoholism or insanity, what did Gerry do?

He lit out for the high country, alone and on foot, with an instinctive understanding that the domain of humanity and its institutions could be of no help to him, and that indeed, they could only worsen his affliction. Braving the inevitable consequences of deserting the Army, he went to meet wild nature on her own terms, to let his healing unfold as it would. And perhaps most amazingly of all, to a large degree it seems to have worked. While it's true that much of his memory from that time seems to have simply vanished, at the very least his self-applied cure worked well enough for him to return to society and move forward to meet his fate.

First, he had to face a court martial and imprisonment. When he emerged back into the light of day, he embraced his new life with gusto and enjoyed success both in the Army and in civilian life. Apart from everything else, this tale of personal triumph makes Gerry's story well worth remembering. Indeed, the very act of remembering itself would perhaps be the best way of all to honor this man, whose own memory of these events has never returned.

Of Rivers and Forgetting

And so, like our totem salmon, we come full circle now, back to where we started. Our odyssey is complete. We commenced our journey in mystery, followed the trail of clues, investigated the evidence, formulated possible solutions, and in the end, we return to the mystery. It looks different than the one we started with, and we know a lot more about the events and details surrounding it, but ultimately this has only served to deepen the questions.

Although the title of the book is *No Return*, in a deeper sense, as we know, everything returns. The River of No Return is full of water returning to its source in the ocean, and during spawning season, it's full of salmon returning in the opposite direction to their place of origin as well. The ones who don't make it return to their ultimate source, as do we all in the "ashes to ashes" sense, if nothing more. It would seem, however, that Gerry's memories did not return to his awareness, leaving us to return to the mystery. Where did those memories go? What do they contain? And what was written on that note, wrapped around a pencil, inserted through a buttonhole?

It seems to me that besides whatever else Gerry's story is about, it's also a journey through perhaps one of the strangest places of all: the human mind, steering an uncertain course through the vast archipelagos of memory. Each time a memory appears along the way, another fades into the mist—perhaps never to be seen again. Somtimes, of course, entire archipelagos can sink beneath the waves. What is it like to forget over a year of one's life? How would it feel to suddenly be faced with a troubling past of which one had known only scattered fragments?

And furthermore, why do questions like these seem to exert such an irresistible pull? Is it because, in the end, we're all suffering from amnesia? Aren't we all, in our own way, trying to recall something we forgot once upon a time, and long, long ago? It hearkens back to fairy tales of the hero/heroine who can't remember his or her true identity due to a powerful spell. Are we all spellbound? Is that what it's really about? If so, how do we break the spell? Can we help each other with that?

I think so. Buckminster Fuller once famously wrote, "Man is the great antientropy of the universe."[3] And since amnesia strikes me as a kind of entropy of the mind, a corollary of sorts seems in order. I think that—in our better moments at least—we can, and do, serve as a great force of "anti-amnesia" in the world.

Gerry grew up on a fork of the River of No Return; a name we've called upon to evoke a figurative "flood of experience" that washed away his memories. The ancient Greeks—who gave us the very word "amnesia"—had their own flowing source of aquatic oblivion, known as Lethe, the River of Forgetfulness. They believed that in order to be born into this world, we must first drink from its waters. However, some hapless souls—like Gerry—seem destined for a double draught of this

---

3 Fuller, R. Buckminster. *Utopia or Oblivion: The Prospects for Humanity* (New York: Overlook, 1972), 41.

mind-emptying brew.

For what it's worth, I've made an effort in these pages to restore some of what the river swept away. It's a flawed attempt to be sure; since one can never see the entire river, but only that part which falls within one's limited view. But I hope I've helped at least to set the boat aright and sailing back upstream, like some quicksilver salmon slipping headlong toward home.

Acknowledgements

I wish to extend my heartfelt thanks to the many people who made this book possible:

To those who kindly gave their time to be interviewed: The family and friends of the illustrious Otto Fife—Lee Fife, Boyd Fife, Stephen Carlos Fife, Ira Schoppmann, and Alva Leon Matheson; Casey Kuenzli for his memorable stories about Del Davis; Michael Broadbent, for telling me a little about his remarkable father, L.Verl Broadbent (the doctor who treated Gerry in Cedar City); and special thanks to John and Shirley Irwin, who told many a good story—I wish I could have included more of them.

To all those who helped with my research and documentation: The dedicated staff at the Idaho Historical Society; Mark Rodeghier and Mary Castner at CUFOS for their marvelous assistance; Tina Choate for her crucial help in providing the vital APRO documents—which brought a stalled investigation back to life; Larry Lorenzen for kindly allowing the use of the Bulletin material; Anders Liljegren and Leif Åstrand at Archives For the Unexplained, for their generous help in providing the Rehn-Lorenzen correspondence; Jeff Fereday for some excellent background on the South Fork area as well as on salmon ecology; Paula Mitchell, archivist at Southern Utah University's library, for her friendly and unstinting assistance; Rich Heiden, for patiently fielding my many questions about APRO; Loren Gross, for taking time out of his much-deserved ufological retirement to speak with me; and George Filer of Filer's Files, for good information on the way UFO radar data tends to be handled—or more often, apparently, not handled—i.e. dropped like a hot potato!

To those who offered their knowledge and expertise: Marshall Cook for his good research and writing tips; Katherine Seibold, whose professorial feedback (and diverting tales) couldn't have come at a better moment; Myron Eshowsky for his singular insights that opened new possibilities; James Campbell, for some solid writerly advice; and Melissa Nobert, for shining a light in a very unexpected direction.

Much gratitude to friends who listened and offered their valuable ideas and support: Mary Bowman; Earlene and Charles Ginter; Roan Kaufman; Mike Melee (from day 1); Chris Robertson; Joanna Fanney; and a special bow to Barbara and Micha Namenwirth.

A big, whole-hearted thanks to Jacques Vallee, whose writings inspired me to attempt this investigation in the first place. Thus, it was a real and unexpected blessing when Dr. Vallee offered both his good counsel and at times, his pivotal assistance, along what often seemed an obscure and circuitous trail.

A very special thanks to my editor, Patrick Huyghe, whose encyclopedic knowledge, wit, and expert guidance were truly indispensable.

And of course a huge thanks to Gerry Irwin himself, who patiently spent so many hours speaking with me; and who helped out in any way he could—with characteristic grace, humor, and a generous spirit.

Most of all I wish to thank my mother, my brother, and especially Schuhchen Guo and Fred Kolyszko—who were there through thick and thin.

Bibliography

UFOs etc.

- Birnes, William J. *Aliens in America: A UFO Hunter's Guide to Extraterrestrial Hotspots across the US*. Avon, MA: Adams Media, 2010. Print.
- Chalker, Bill. "Australian 'Interrupted Journeys'". (©Bill Chalker, 1979). Published in *MUFON UFO Journal* No. 150, Aug. 1980.
- Clark, Jerome. *The UFO Book: Encyclopedia of the Extraterrestrial*. Detroit: Omnigraphics, 1998. Print.
- Clark, Jerome. *The UFO Encyclopedia*, 2nd ed. 2 vols. Detroit: Omnigraphics, 1998. Print.
- Coppens, Philip. "Doctoring Villas Boas and Aliens on Ice." *Philipcoppens.com*. N.p., n.d. Web. 30 Dec. 2016.
- Creighton, Gordon. "Even More Amazing: Part I." *Flying Saucer Review* July-Aug. 1966.
- Creighton, Gordon. "The Most Amazing Case of All." *Flying Saucer Review* Jan.-Feb. 1965.
- Doore, Kathy. "Integratron's George Van Tassel and the Giant Rock Spaceship Conventions with George Hunt Williamson 1950s." *Labyrinthina*. kathydoore.com, n.d. Web.
- Fort, Charles. *The Book of the Damned*. New York: Boni and Liveright, 1919. Print.
- Fuller, John G. *The Interrupted Journey: Two Lost Hours "aboard a Flying Saucer"* New York: Dial, 1966. Print.
- Good, Timothy. *Above Top Secret: The Worldwide UFO Cover-up*. New York: William Morrow &Co., 1988. Print.
- Gross, Loren E. *The Fifth Horseman of the Apocalypse: UFOs: A History*. Fremont, CA: Loren E. Gross, 1974-2005. Print, Web.
- Hall, Richard. "Congressional Interest in UFOs." *Journal of UFO History* 1.5 (2004): 2. NICAP. Web.

- Hall, Richard. "Radar-Visual Sightings Establish UFOs As a Serious Mystery." *The 1952 Sighting Wave*. NICAP, 15 Dec. 2005. Web.
- Hall, Richard. *The UFO Evidence*: *A Thirty-Year Report*. Lanham, MD: Scarecrow, 2001. Print.
- Harpur, Patrick. *Daimonic Reality: A Field Guide to the Otherworld*. 1996. Reprint. Enumclaw, WA: Pine Winds, 2003. Print.
- Jacobs, David Michael. *The UFO Controversy in America*. Bloomington, IN: Indiana University Press, 1975. Print.
- Jung, C. G. *Flying Saucers: A Modern Myth of Things Seen in the Sky*. Princeton, NJ: Princeton University Press, 1978. Print.
- Keel, John A. *The Mothman Prophecies*. 1975. Reprint. New York: Tom Doherty Associates, 2002. Print.
- Keel, John A. *Operation Trojan Horse: The Classic Breakthrough Study of UFOs*. 1970. Reprint. San Antonio, TX: Anomalist Books, 2013. Print.
- Lorenzen, Coral E. "Soldier Sees Flash: Unconscious 24 Hours." *APRO Bulletin* Mar. 1959. 1, 10.
- Lorenzen, Coral E., and Jim Lorenzen. *Encounters with UFO Occupants*. New York: Berkley, 1976. Print.
- Lorenzen, L. J. "Where Is Private Irwin." *Flying Saucers* Nov. 1962: 17-26. Print.
- Mack, John E. *Passport to the Cosmos: Human Transformation and Alien Encounters*. New York: Crown, 1999. Print.
- *Mirage Men: How the U.S. Government Created a Myth That Took Over the World*. Dir. John Lundberg and Roland Denning. By Mark Pilkington. Perception Management Productions, 2013. DVD.
- Pilkington, Mark. *Mirage Men: An Adventure into Paranoia, Espionage, Psychological Warfare, and UFOs*. NY, NY: Skyhorse, 2010. Print.
- Ridge, Francis, and Joel Carpenter. "1948 UFO Chronology." *Nicap.org*. NICAP, 15 Dec. 2005. Web.

- Ruhl, Dick. "A History of APRO." *Official UFO* Vol. 1, No. 5, January 1976, 24. Republished on: Internet Archive Wayback Machine, 02 Feb. 2005. Web. 11 May 2017.
- Ruppelt, Edward J. *The Report on Unidentified Flying Objects.* Garden City, NY: Doubleday, 1956. Print, Kindle.
- Strieber, Whitley. *Breakthrough: The Next Step.* New York: HarperCollins, 1995. Print.
- Strieber, Whitley. *Communion: A True Story.* New York: Avon, 1987. Print.
- Strieber, Whitley. *Solving the Communion Enigma: What Is to Come.* New York: J.P. Tarcher/Penguin, 2012. Print.
- Vallee, Jacques. *Passport to Magonia: From Folklore to Flying Saucers.* 1969. Reprint. Brisbane, Australia: Daily Grail Pub., 2014. Print.
- Vallee, Jacques. *Confrontations: A Scientist's Search for Alien Contact.* New York: Ballantine, 1990. Print.
- Vallee, Jacques. *Dimensions: A Casebook of Alien Contact.* 1988. Reprint. San Antonio, TX: Anomalist Books, 2007. Print.
- Vallee, Jacques. *Forbidden Science: Journals, 1957-1969.* Berkeley, CA: North Atlantic, 1992. Print.
- Vallee, Jacques. *Messengers of Deception: UFO Contacts and Cults.* 1979. Reprint. Brisbane, Australia: Daily Grail Pub., 2008. Print.
- Vallee, Jacques. *Revelations: Alien Contact and Human Deception.* 1991. Reprint. San Antonio, TX: Anomalist Books, 2014. Kindle.
- Vallee, Jacques. *The Invisible College: What a Group of Scientists Has Discovered about UFO Influences on the Human Race.* 1975. Reprint. San Antonio, TX: Anomalist Books, 2014. Kindle.
- Villarubia Mauso, Pablo. "Antonio Villas Boas: Total Abduction." *Inexplicata- Journal of Hispanic UFOlogy* 05 Nov. 2007: n. pag. Web.
- Wells, Jeff. *Rigorous Intuition: What You Don't Know Can't Hurt Them.* Walterville, OR: TrineDay, 2008. Kindle.

South Fork, Central Idaho History and Natural History, etc., and Otto Fife

- Brock, C. Eugene, "Homesteads" in Woods, Shelton. *Valley County Idaho: Prehistory to 1920*. Donnelly, ID: Action Pub., 2002. Print.
- Carson, Rachel, *Silent Spring*. Boston: Houghton Mifflin, 1962. Print.
- Craig, Wes, "Indians in the Later Valley County Area" in Woods, Shelton. *Valley County Idaho: Prehistory to 1920*. Donnelly, ID: Action Pub., 2002. Print.
- Dixon, Jerry S. *South Fork of the Salmon River, Wild and Free*. McCall, ID: Dixon, 1979. On-line book—Pocatello, ID: Idaho State Univ. Outdoor Program, 2001. Web.
- Edmunson, Cletus R. *A History of Warren, Idaho: Mining, Race & Environment*. Boise, ID: Boise State University, 2012. Print.
- Elsensohn, M. Alfreda, and Eugene F. Hoy. *Pioneer Days in Idaho County*. Caldwell, ID: Caxton Printers, 1947. Print.
- Fife, Steven Carlos, *"The Original 'Otto Biography'"*: Original Interviews, Speeches, and Articles of Otto Root Fife. Cedar City, UT: Southern Utah Univ. Library, Special Collections. [no date]
- Hawley, Steven. *Recovering a Lost River: Removing Dams, Rewilding Salmon, Revitalizing Communities*. Boston: Beacon, 2011. Print.
- Helmers, Cheryl. *Warren Times: A Collection of News about Warren, Idaho*. Odessa, TX: C. Helmers, 1988. Print.
- Hockaday, James. *History of Payette National Forest* (USDA Forest Service, 1968), 81. Payette National Forest History and Culture, USDA. Web.
- Hull, Valerie. "The History of the South Fork Ranch." *Judy's Idaho Backcountry Cookbook*. Idaho-backcountry-cookbook.com, 2017. Web.
- Lewis, David. "Yellowstone's Sheep Eater Indians." *Montana Pioneer* Feb. 2014. Web.

- Loendorf, Lawrence L., Nancy Medaris Stone, and David Joaquín. *Mountain Spirit: The Sheep Eater Indians of Yellowstone.* Salt Lake City: U of Utah, 2006. Print.
- Mann, John W. W. *Sacajawea's People: The Lemhi Shoshones and the Salmon River Country.* Lincoln: U of Nebraska, 2004. Print.
- Peterson, Harold. *The Last of the Mountain Men.* New York: Scribner, 1969. Print.
- Reddy, Sheila D. "The Story of Sylvester S. 'Three-Fingered' Smith." USDA Forest Service, July 2002. Web. Condensed from Reddy's book *Wilderness Pioneer.*
- Wilson, Greg. "Del Davis: A Life in the Saddle." *Sun Valley Magazine* Summer 2004: 107-09.
- Woods, Shelton. *Valley County Idaho: Prehistory to 1920.* Donnelly, ID: Action Pub., 2002. Print

MKUltra, Project Paperclip, Mental Health, etc.

- Hacking, Ian. "Automatisme Ambulatoire: Fugue, Hysteria, and Gender at the Turn of the Century." *Modernism/modernity* 3.2 (1996): 31-43. *Project Muse.* John Hopkins University, Apr. 1996. Web.
- Jacobsen, Annie. *Operation Paperclip: The Secret Intelligence Program that Brought Nazi Scientists to America.* Boston, MA: Little, Brown and Company, 2014. Print.
- Klein, Naomi. *The Shock Doctrine: The Rise of Disaster Capitalism.* New York: Metropolitan /Henry Holt, 2007. Print.
- Lee, Martin A., and Bruce Shlain. *Acid Dreams: The Complete Social History of LSD: The CIA, the Sixties, and beyond.* New York: Grove/Atlantic, 1992. Print.
- *Magic Trip: Ken Kesey's Search for a Kool Place.* Dir. Alex Gibney and Alison Ellwood. Perf. Ken Kesey, Neal Cassady. Magnolia Pictures, 2011. DVD.
- Marks, John. *The Search for the "Manchurian Candidate": The CIA and Mind Control.* New York: Times, 1979. Print.

- Martin, David S. "Vets Feel Abandoned after Secret Drug Experiments." *CNN*. Cable News Network, 01 Mar. 2012. Web.
- Ross, Colin A., M.D. *The CIA Doctors: Human Rights Violations by American Psychiatrists*. Richardson, TX: Manitou Communications, 2006.
- Stevens, Jay. *Storming Heaven: LSD and the American Dream*. NY: Grove, 1987. Print.
- Turbide, Diane. "Television: DR. CAMERON'S CASUALTIES: A series revisits Canada's 1950s brainwashing scandal." *Maclean's*, [magazine] 04-21-1997.
- United States Senate, 103rd Congress, 2nd Session, Committee on Veterans' Affairs. *Is Military Research Hazardous to Veterans' Health?* John D. Rockefeller, West Virginia, Chairman (Washington, DC: U.S. General Accounting Office, 1994), Print.
- United States Senate, Church Committee. *Church Committee Reports*. Washington D.C.: U.S. Gov. Printing Office, 1975. Assassination Archives and Research Center. Print.
- United States Senate, Senate Select Committee on Intelligence. *Project MKULTRA*. 95th Cong., 1st sess. Washington D.C.: U.S. Gov. Printing Office, 1977. New York Times. Print.
- Zadrozny, Brandy. "Read the Pentagon's $59 Billion 'Black Budget'." *The Daily Beast*. The Daily Beast Company, 06 March 2014. Web.

Perspectives on Unexplained Phenomena, Folklore, etc.

- Evans-Wentz, W. Y. *The Fairy-Faith in Celtic Countries; Its Psychical Origin and Nature*. London: Oxford, 1911. Print.
- Fort, Charles. *The Book of the Damned*. New York: Boni and Liveright, 1919. Print.
- Harpur, Patrick. *Daimonic Reality: A Field Guide to the Otherworld*. 1996. Reprint. Enumclaw, WA: Pine Winds, 2003. Print.
- Narby, Jeremy. *The Cosmic Serpent: DNA and the Origins of Knowledge*. New York: J.P. Tarcher/Putnam, 1998.

- Narváez, Peter, ed. *The Good People: New Fairylore Essays*. New York: Garland Pub., 1991. Print.
- Sheldrake, Rupert. *The Sense of Being Stared At: And Other Aspects of the Extended Mind*. New York: Crown, 2003. Print.
- Wells, Jeff. *Rigorous Intuition: What You Don't Know Can't Hurt Them*. Walterville, OR: TrineDay, 2008. Kindle edition.

Index

abductee(s), 66, 125, 203, 206

abduction (alien/UFO), 26, 35, 65-71, 125, 128, 141, 188-191, 193, 198-199, 203, 207

abduction (fairy), 199

Acid Tests, 46

Adamski, George, 62

Aerial Phenomena Research Organization (APRO), 6, 12, 42, 64, 67, 69, 73, 82, 88, 96, 144, 149-150, 157, 164, 192-193

AFI 10-206 (Air Force Instruction 10-206), 136n2

Alamogordo, New Mexico, 42, 69, 96, 165

Alaska, 30, 32, 58, 99, 135

alien abduction. See abduction, alien/UFO

alien(s), 59, 62, 91, 140-142, 144, 193, 196, 200, 203

Allan Memorial Institute, 47, 50

amytal interview, 43, 45, 73, 87, 124, 128-129, 138, 154, 160, 167-169, 195-196

amytal, sodium, 13, 43, 45, 48, 73, 124, 128-129, 148, 154, 161, 163, 168, 204, 206

anonymous doctor (aka unnamed doctor, supervisor of Ward 30), 53-55, 121n7, 130-131, 157, 168n14

Apollo Program, 171-172

APRO Bulletin (newsletter), 9n2, 68, 70, 86, 150, 191n6

Army Chemical Corps, 45, 49, 146

Army Inspector General (I.G.), 5, 96, 121, 161

Army, Austrian, 184

Arnold, Kenneth, 60

Article 15 (non-judicial punishment), 86, 155, 161

attorney (letters to and from), 150, 160, 162-164, 167-168, 171

Australia, 92, 151

Austria, 8, 12, 136, 184

Austrian Army, 184

automatisme ambulatoire (aka ambulatory automatism), 151, 152, 153, 156. *See* also fugue

Aveyron, France, 200

AWOL (Absent Without Official Leave), 4, 26, 83, 85-86, 88, 101, 106-107, 110, 114-115, 121-122, 130, 132-133, 166, 166-168, 170, 180, 183, 194

Bad Kreuznach, Germany, 183

Big Creek (river), 32-33, 98

Big Creek, Idaho, 32

Birnes, William, 61

black ops, 139, 171n19, 207

Black Vault, The, 136n2

blackout(s), 2, 11-12, 51, 53, 72, 90, 93, 118, 120-121, 124, 130, 132, 154, 157-159, 166-167, 182, 206

blocked appointments (for civilian doctor), 54, 135, 138, 146

blocked memories, 72-73, 125, 128, 188-189, 191-192, 194-196, 200-202
Bluebird, Project, 172
Boise, Idaho, 29, 107, 185
Brazilian children (possibly abducted), 73, 189, 194
Brazilian Naval Intelligence officers, 144, 145
Brewer Creek, 26
Brewer Ranch, 21, 26
Brewer, Curly, 21
Broadbent, Dr., 88, 152
Buckskin Bill (aka Sylvan Hart), 101
BZ (hallucinogen), 146n23, 173

Cameron, Dr. Ewan, 47-50
Canada, 30
Cape Prince of Wales, 30
Cascade, Idaho, 28, 103, 106-107, 115-116, 133
Cedar City, Utah, 2-4, 10-12, 35-36, 41, 52, 70, 74-76, 80-85, 88, 90, 148, 152, 154-155, 159
Center for UFO Studies (CUFOS), 75
Central Idaho Wilderness Act, 99
Chalker, Bill, 92
Chief Joseph, 98
Chinook salmon (aka king salmon), 23, 25
Church Committee, 45
Church, Frank, 45, 98-99
CIA, 45-49, 58, 139-141, 156, 172-175, 178
CIRVIS, 136
Civil Aeronautics Administration (CAA), 36
Clark, Jerome, 68

Clark, Saunders, 36
Clark, William (Corps of Discovery), 19
close encounter(s) 35, 66, 69, 92, 126, 199-200, 205-207
Close Encounters of the Third Kind (movie), 11-12
Cold War, 47, 183
Columbia River, 24
contactee(s), 62-63, 66
Coppens, Philip, 144
Corps of Discovery, 19
counter-intelligence, 171
court-martial, 105-107, 116, 118, 120, 122, 132-134, 209
cover-up, 82, 137-138, 140, 145, 167, 192
crash site, 36, 38, 77, 137
crashed saucers, UFOS, 60, 140, 144, 145

Davis, Buzz, 102-103, 106
Davis, Del, 101-102, 115n2,
DDT, 33
deserter, 5, 12, 88, 96, 99, 107, 131
desertion, 107-108, 110-113, 121, 189
disinformation, 138-140, 143-144, 178
dissociative amnesia, 51,
dissociative fugue, 51-52, 151
Distant Early Warning (DEW) Line, 30-32, 57
Donnelly, Idaho, 28

ECT (Electro-Convulsive Therapy), 46, 48, 51, 146-147. *See* also electro-shock
Edgewood Arsenal, 146n23

Eighth Infantry Division, 183
El Paso General Hospital, 3, 41, 154, 159
El Paso, Texas, 3, 12, 39, 41-42, 53-54, 69, 87, 97, 124, 148, 148, 153-155, 157, 159, 164-165, 176, 205
electro-shock, 43-44, 46. *See* also ECT
Elk Creek Ranch, 20
Elk Creek, 20
Emmet, Idaho, 125-126
Encounters with UFO Occupants (Lorenzen & Lorenzen), 79
epilepsy, 153, 157-158
Espionage Act, 137
Evans-Wentz, W.Y., 198-199
extraterrestrial, 63, 145

fairy abduction, 199
Fairyland, 198, 200, 203
fairylore, 199
Feres Doctrine, 147
Fife, Sheriff Otto, 36-37, 75-78, 82, 85-86, 91, 126, 153, 158, 201. *See* also sheriff
Flying Saucer Occupants (Lorenzen & Lorenzen), 69
Flying Saucer Review (FSR), 69, 193
flying saucer(s), 42, 59-62, 143, 145, 190
Flying Saucers (magazine), 60, 79, 194
Flying Saucers Are Real, The (Keyhoe), 63
Flying Saucers-Serious Business (Edwards), 89
Fontes, Dr. Olavo, 68-69, 73, 142-145
Frank Church-River of No Return

Wilderness, 18, 45, 98-99
Freedom of Information Act (FOIA), 7
Ft. Bliss, Texas, 1, 3-4, 8-10, 34, 39, 57, 75-76, 82, 86, 97, 106-107, 120-121, 129, 132-133, 148, 154, 155, 165-166, 171, 174, 178
Ft. Leavenworth, Kansas, 9, 12, 104, 106, 118, 133, 146, 182-183
Ft. Lewis, Washington, 104, 107, 118, 120, 131, 133
Ft. Ord, California, 4, 86, 148, 155
fugue, fugue state, 51-52, 151
Fuller, John, 190, 193, 201

Garcia, Gerry, 46
General Court Martial, 105, 118, 132
General Court Martial Order (GCMO), 105
Germany, 8-9, 12, 106, 135-136, 171, 183-184
Giant Rock Interplanetary Spacecraft Convention, 62
gold dredges, 20
gold mining, 22
gold rush, 20, 27
Gottlieb, Sydney (head of MKUltra), 172, 176
Grateful Dead, 46
Greenwald, John (*theblackvault.com*), 136
Gross, Loren E., 75, 77-79, 180, 194

Hall, Richard, 66, 203
handwritten notes (from the APRO files), 85-86, 149, 165-168
Harpur, Patrick, 65

Helms, Richard (CIA Director), 46-47, 173
Highway #14, 4, 52, 74, 78, 80-81, 83-85, 90-91, 179
Highway #20, 74, 77-78, 80-83, 85, 90-91, 179
Hill Air Force Base, 32
Hill case, 192, 194-195, 197, 204, 206-207
Hill, Barney, 66, 190-193, 195-197, 202, 205
Hill, Betty and Barney, 66, 190, 193, 197
Hill, Betty, 66, 190-193, 195n17, 197, 201-203
hoax(es), hoaxing, 7, 65-66, 92-93, 120-121, 126-127, 130-131, 139, 179
Howe, Linda Moulton, 140
humanoid, 66-67, 190, 192
hypnosis, 46, 54, 138, 146-147, 152, 155, 167, 170, 180, 193-196, 201-202
Hypnosis—Fact and Fancy (Simon), 202n32
hypnotic regression, 135, 138, 146. *See* also post-hypnotic suggestion
hysteria, 72, 152, 188

Idaho Primitive Area, 33, 98-99
intercontinental ballistic missile (ICBM), 58
International Center for UFO Research (ICUFOR), 149
Interrupted Journey: Two Lost Hours "Aboard a Flying Saucer," The (Fuller), 190, 191n7, 193
Iron County Hospital, 76, 88

Iron County, Utah, 35, 75
Iron Police Puzzled by Unconscious Man (Deseret News and Telegram), 35
Irwin, Catherine (Gerry's mother), 17, 21, 28
Irwin, John (Gerry's brother), 22, 24-28, 102, 115n2
Irwin, Patrick (Gerry's father), 18, 20-23, 28,
Irwin, Shirley (John's wife), 24-25
islands of memory, 128, 133

jacket, "jacket on bush," 1, 3-4, 11-13, 52, 70-72, 74, 83-85, 89-91, 93, 131, 133, 154, 159, 179-181, 188, 207
James, William, 65
Joint Army Navy Air Force Publication 146 (JANAP), 136
Jung, Carl, 150-153, 156-157, 167

Kastner, Gail, 50-51
Keel, John, 62-63, 125-126
Kesey, Ken, 43, 46-47, 94
Keyhoe, Major Donald, 63, 191
king salmon, 23. *See* also Chinook salmon
Klein, Naomi, 48-51
Kodak, 185
Korea, 29-30, 61
Korean War, 29
Kuenzli, Casey, 102

Lagarde, Fernande, 201
Lemhi River, 19
Lemhi Shoshone, 19
Lewis, (Meriwether), 19

Long Range Reconnaissance Patrol (LRRP), 183
Look (magazine), 193
Lorenzen, Coral, 9, 11-12, 42, 64, 68, 70-71, 82, 86, 89, 91, 122, 132, 149-150, 152-160, 162, 165, 167-168, 180, 189, 191, 194
Lorenzen, James (Jim), 6-7, 12-13, 34, 41-42, 44, 52-53, 60, 64, 70-73, 78-79, 81, 85-90, 96, 129, 138, 149-150, 152, 155-156, 158-162, 164-168, 171, 188-189, 194-195, 204
Lorenzens, Coral and James (Jim), 14-15, 42, 53-54, 64, 68-69, 74, 78-79, 82, 85-86, 88-90, 93, 96, 133, 144, 154, 157, 160, 164, 166, 168, 180, 189, 193-195, 206
LSD, 46, 48, 95, 146-147, 173

Marck, C.H., 75
Marks, John, 172, 176
Martins, Joao, 68, 144
Maury Island Incident, 60
McCall, Idaho, 17, 97, 103, 108, 110, 112
McDonald, Dr. James, 126
McGill University, 47
memory blocks/memories blocked, 72-73, 125, 128, 188-189, 191-192, 194-196, 200-202
Mental Hygiene Clinic, 121
mental muteness, 201
MERINT (Merchant ship Intelligence), 136
Merry Pranksters, 46-47
Microfilm, 185
Middle Fork (of the Salmon), 32, 99, 102

mind control, 45, 139, 146-147, 170-172, 174, 176, 178-180, 206-207
missing time, 66, 192, 194
MKUltra, 45-47, 49-51, 143, 145-147, 172, 174-176, 178
Montreal, Quebec, 47, 50, 190
Monumental Creek, 32-34, 100
Morse code, 30, 183
Mountain Home Air Force Base, 107, 133
Mt. Rainier, 60

Nampa, Idaho, 9, 29, 35, 37, 75, 81-82, 109, 153, 157
NASA, 58, 143, 145, 171, 172n20
National Archives and Records Association (NARA), 7
National Investigations Committee on Aerial Phenomena (NICAP), 63-64, 66, 125, 191-194
National Personnel Records Center (NPRC), 40, 105
Nazi, 49, 171-172, 174, 176, 178
Nez Perce, 98
Nidelcovic, Bosco, 141, 144
Nike Missile Training Program, 34
Nike Missile, 34, 41, 56-58, 88
Nome, Alaska, 31
Nuremburg Code, 49
Nuremburg tribunal, 49

Ogden, Utah, 32
One Flew over the Cuckoo's Nest (Kesey), 43
Operation Midnight Climax, 176
Operation Mirage, 141
Operation Paperclip (aka Project Paperclip), 171-172, 174, 176, 178

Pacific Northwest, 24
Page-Russell device (for ECT), 48
Palmer, Ray, 60, 61n8
Passport to Magonia (Vallee), 61n8
Payette National Forest, 33
Pease Air Force Base, 190, 207
Peenemünde, Germany (rocket
    factory), 171
Pilkington, Mark, 139
placer mining, 28
plane crash, 1-2, 9-10, 35-38, 41-
    42,72, 76-77, 93, 127, 132, 135, 159
Portland, Oregon, 185
post-amytal suggestion, 72-73, 204
post-hypnotic suggestion, 72, 145,
    161, 166-167, 170, 178, 197, 201-
    202, 204
Post-Traumatic Stress Disorder
    (PTSD), 54-55, 191
power plant, 20, 22, 26-28
Powers, Gary, 30
Project Blue Book, 56n1, 126, 191
Project Bluebird, 172
Project MKUltra, 45-47, 49-51, 143,
    145-147, 172, 174-176, 178
Project Paperclip. (aka Operation
    Paperclip), 171-172, 174, 176, 178
psychiatric ward (psych ward), 3-4,
    13, 41, 43-44, 51, 87, 94, 121, 133,
    146, 160, 167-169, 176, 180
psychochemicals, 147
PSYOPs (psychological operations),
    139-141

Queensland, Australia (UFO case), 92

radar, 30, 39, 61, 137, 207n37
radio school, 30, 183

Rehn, K. Gösta, 91, 150
return trip (to Utah), 3-4, 13, 72, 74,
    83, 85-87, 89-90, 93, 133, 148, 154,
    155n6, 158-160, 162, 166-169, 178,
    180, 189, 203-204
Rigorous Intuition (Wells), 178
Rio de Janeiro, 144
River of No Return, 18-19, 24, 32, 96,
    209-210. *See* also Salmon River
Rockefeller Commission, 45
Roswell Crash, 60
Ruppelt, Captain Edward, 56n1
Russia, 30, 181, 183-184. *See* also
    Soviet Union

Sacajawea, 19n7
Salmon River Mountains, 18, 20
Salmon River, 17-19, 24, 26, 32-33,
    98-99, 101, 132. *See* also River of
    No Return
salmon, 19, 22-26, 33-34, 98-99, 208-
    209, 211
Samford, General John, 61
sarin nerve gas, 146n23
Saturn V rocket, 171
Schirmer, Herb, 188, 198, 200
schizophrenia, 51, 130, 152
searchers, 3, 71-72, 91
Secesh River, 25
Section 8, 122
security clearance, 32, 34, 41, 138,
    155
seizure, 157-158
sensory deprivation, 46, 48
Serling, Rod, 60
Sheep Eater Indians, 20, 98

sheriff, 2, 4, 35-37, 65, 75-78, 81, 85-86, 91, 101, 103, 106-107, 115-116, 126, 138, 148, 153-155, 201
Shoshone, 19
Siberian mainland, 30
silent contactee(s), 62-63
Simon, Dr. Benjamin, 196, 201-202, 205
site compulsion, 203-205
Sleep Room, 48
Smith, Walter Bedell (CIA Director), 139-140
Snake River, 23-24
sodium amytal interview, 43, 45, 73, 87, 124, 128-129, 138, 154, 160, 167-169, 195-196
sodium amytal, 13, 43, 45, 48, 73, 124, 128-129, 148, 154, 161, 163, 168, 204, 206
Soldier Sees Flash; Unconscious 24 Hours (Lorenzen, Coral), 9
South Fork (of the Salmon), 17, 20-23, 25-29, 33, 98, 101
Soviet Union, 56-58, 135, 171, 173. *See* also Russia
Soviets, 58, 61
space brothers, 62
Sputnik, 58
Stevens, Jay, 94
Strieber, Whitley, 128n9, 207n39
Surface to Air Missile (SAM), 34, 36
Symposium on Unidentified Flying Objects, 126

Three-Fingered Smith, 20
timeline, 52n24, 85-86, 167, 169
Tin City Air Force Station, Alaska, 30
trance, trance state, 3-4, 32, 66, 83, 93, 121, 128, 148, 153, 167, 169-170, 199, 201-203, 205-206
trance-walking, 202
Truffaut, Francois, 12
truth serum, 9, 13, 129. 160-161, 168-169, 195. *See* also sodium amytal
Twilight Zone, The (TV series), 60
Two Locations Conundrum (TLC), 74, 78-79, 83, 85, 158, 179, 206

U.S. Army Board of Review, 118
U.S. Army Chemical Corps, 45, 49, 146
U.S. Disciplinary Barracks (USDB), 118, 133, 146-147, 182
U.S. Forest Service, 18, 25, 27, 32-34, 98
U.S. Senate Select Committee on Intelligence, 45, 47
U.S. Senate's Committee on Veteran's Affairs, 173
U2 spy plane (and "rocket planes"), 30, 35-36, 58
UFO abductees. *See* abductee(s)
UFO abduction. *See* abduction (alien/UFO)
UFO Investigator, The (NICAP newsletter), 192-193
UFO occupant(s), 66-67, 189, 192, 196, 199
ultraterrestrials, 63
United States v. Bernard G. Irwin, 107
United States v. Stanley, 147n26
Unity Gold Mines, 20
University of Texas (UT), 174-175, 178

V-2 rocket, 171

Valentine, Captain (aka Dr. Valentine), 41-42, 52-54, 87-88, 124, 128-130, 138, 166-167, 205

Vallee, Jacques, 6-7, 12-13, 94, 128n9, 139-140, 198-200, 207n39

Valley County, Idaho, 107, 115

Van Tassel, George, 62

Vets Feel Abandoned after Secret Drug Experiments (Martin), 146n23

Vienna, Austria, 184

Villarubia Mauso, Pablo, 143, 145

Villas Boas, Antonio, 66-69, 73, 141-145, 193-194, 200, 203

Von Braun, Wernher, 171, 172n20

War of the Worlds, The (book, radio play, film), 59

Ward 30 (at WBAH), 41, 43, 52-54, 121, 157, 168. *See* also psychiatric ward

Warren, Idaho, 17, 20, 23, 25, 27-28, 98

Washington Flap (of 1952), 61

Webb, Walter, 191-192

Wells, Jeff, 178-179

Where is Private Irwin (Lorenzen, L.J.), 13, 60

White, George Hunter, 176

Wild and Scenic Rivers Act, 99

Wild Strawberries (film), 200

Wilderness Act, 98-99

William Beaumont Army Hospital (WBAH), 3, 5, 11, 13, 41, 43, 53, 55, 85-87, 114, 121n7, 124, 131, 133, 147-148, 157, 169

World War 2 (WW II), 27, 49, 58, 102, 171

Yellowstone National Park, 18

Zamora, Lonnie, 89

Zurich, Switzerland, 151-152

CPSIA information can be obtained
at www.ICGtesting.com
Printed in the USA
BVHW051916090421
604365BV00002B/40